Bob Burton is a freelance journalist and the editor of Source-Watch <www.sourcewatch.org>, an online wiki-based database on the global PR and lobbying industry for the US-based media non-profit group, the Center for Media and Democracy (CMD). Since 1996 he has been a regular contributor to CMD's flagship publication, *PR Watch*. He also writes for the *British Medical Journal* and the Bangkok office of Inter-Press Service. Between 1996 and early 2003 he edited a quarterly news magazine on the mining industry, *Mining Monitor*, for the Mineral Policy Institute, a Sydney-based non-government organisation. After completing an Arts degree at Sydney University in 1979 he worked until the early 1990s as a researcher and campaigner on energy, mining and forestry issues for The Wilderness Society. He was a member of the council of the Australian Conservation Foundation (1981–91) and vice president from 1985–91. In 1992 he was entered on the United Nations Environment Program Global 500 Roll of Honour for an outstanding contribution to the protection of the environment.

Disclosure: A small part of the costs of the author's lawyers for the 1998 hearings before the Victorian Administrative Appeals Tribunal over Victoria Police's Coode Island documents was covered by grants from the Tasmanian Conservation Trust and Greenpeace Australia.

inside SPIN

The dark underbelly of the PR industry

BOB BURTON

ALLEN&UNWIN

FOR WRITING ON PUBLIC ISSUES

First published in 2007

Allen & Unwin
83 Alexander Street
Crows Nest NSW 2065
Australia
Phone: (61 2) 8425 0100
Fax: (61 2) 9906 2218
Email: info@allenandunwin.com
Web: www.allenandunwin.com

National Library of Australia
Cataloguing-in-Publication entry:

Burton, Bob, 1959– .
    Inside spin: The dark underbelly of the PR industry.

    Includes index.
    ISBN: 978 1 74175 217 5 (pbk.).

    1. Public relations. 2. Mass media - Influence. I. Title.

659.2

Set in 11/14 pt Minion by Bookhouse, Sydney
Printed by McPherson's Printing Group, Maryborough

10 9 8 7 6 5 4 3 2 1

CONTENTS

The book is dedicated to the memory of Charlie Pahlman (1960–2005), a much-loved advocate for social justice and the environment who is greatly missed.

INTRODUCTION

Just two days ahead of the 1993 federal election, a 'bomb' was found on a railway line near a log yard in north-west Tasmania with a banner implying it was the handiwork of environmentalists. The 'bomb' was breathlessly reported in the media at face value as 'eco-terrorism', coverage that undoubtedly helped defeat the Green's bid to win their first-ever Senate seat in what was a knife-edge election result (*see* chapter 6 for more details). To me, it just felt wrong, but gut instinct that it wasn't environmentalists didn't constitute hard evidence. Whoever was behind it, it seemed obvious that it was something worth investigating. Discussions with a handful of the journalists soon revealed there was widespread disinterest in investigating further. 'Why bother', 'too hard', 'old news' was the gist of the responses. If journalists weren't going to investigate further, then I decided I would.

It became apparent to me that I would need to understand how PR campaigns were developed and implemented to understand this story. The mainstream media was of little use, as the PR industry went largely unreported. PR textbooks were bland, focused on the basics of harmless publicity campaigns, and they often relied on uncritical case studies. The global PR trade industry press had little Australian content and was generally uncritical. Internal PR industry documents were very difficult to obtain, and even then usually just provided a fleeting snapshot. The cumulative effect was that the PR industry remained invisible and was left to do what it liked.

Eventually, I started attending PR conferences in the hope I would gain some insight. At one, run by a UK crisis-management consultant, we broke into workshops. Our hypothetical scenario was to help a mining company overcome opposition from environmentalists. In the course of the discussion, one of the participants proffered some advice: 'Get the police to allege that they were involved in sabotaging equipment.' While I was stunned at the suggestion as there was nothing in the scenario suggesting this was the case, none of the others in the workshop raised an objection. It was at that point I knew I was onto something: a new corporate activism.

In the last decade, I have collected internal PR documents wherever I could find them. Some were leaked to activists in community groups, some to journalists willing to pass them on, others emerged in various court proceedings or were tabled in parliament. Others were gained by attending conferences, filing freedom of information searches or digging them out of various archives. My initial case studies collection was skewed towards environmental issues, partly because this is where I had an extensive network of contacts, and partly because this was where leaked internal documents were most plentiful. Sometimes, PR people in one industry would accidentally provide useful leads by citing the success of strategies used by another industry. Sometimes PR campaigns run in Australia were derived from a global template. With the benefit of a network of international colleagues at the Center for Media and Democracy in the United States and Spinwatch in the United Kingdom, it was possible to track down documents and leads from overseas. The campaigns documented in this book, though, are just the tip of the iceberg.

Within the PR industry, there is widespread resentment of the term 'spin doctors'. Many of those who work within the industry—perhaps even a majority—are in federal, state and local government agencies and non-profit groups working on everything from producing annual reports through developing websites to handling media inquiries. Much of what they do is intended to be visible and is rarely the source of controversy. Some PR practitioners can indisputedly lay claim to the profession's stated aspiration of serving the public interest. When natural disasters occur, we need government agencies to be skilled at crisis communications. We want public health agencies to effectively communicate measures aimed at changing the behaviour of individuals to prevent the spread of HIV/AIDS or the prevalence of skin cancer, or to reduce the incidence of smoking. Even much of what is undertaken within the lower levels of specialist PR companies for corporate clients is the mostly harmless hustling of products via media releases and stunts aimed at garnering sympathetic media coverage. In this guise, PR is seeking to capture our attention as consumers, which is part of the reason for the conflation of PR with advertising. But there is an important distinction between the two. Advertising is designed to be visible, memorable, and to motivate us to buy products. PR is at its most powerful when it is invisible.

The premise behind this book is simple: that the proliferation of invisible forces increasingly shaping public debate is incompatible with a healthy democracy. Perhaps optimistically, I believe that shining a light on the PR industry can help citizens, journalists and activists understand how spin really works, and help curtail its seemingly never-ending spread. We like to think of Australia as having a long tradition of being a fully fledged democracy, where all adults can vote. But it was only in 1978, when New South Wales became the last state to abolish the requirement of voters in its upper house elections to be property owners—known as the property franchise—that we could accurately claim every citizen over 18 in Australia was entitled to determine who sat in all state and federal parliaments.

The rise of PR—overwhelmingly the preserve of deep-pocketed corporations and governments—threatens to effectively reinstate the property franchise by stealth. Everyone might still be able to vote, but the ability of citizens to shape public debate between elections seems to be narrowing. If the only voices we hear in public debates belong to those with enough wealth to fund PR campaigns, and clandestine PR campaigns at that, our democracy will be all the poorer for it.

ONE
INVISIBLE PR

Just after Joseph Goebbels was appointed Minister for Popular Enlightenment and Propaganda in Hitler's first government in March 1933, he lamented that the word 'propaganda' had got bad press. 'Propaganda', the one-time journalist turned Nazi activist complained, 'is a much maligned and often misunderstood word. The layman uses it to mean something inferior or even despicable. The word propaganda always has a bitter aftertaste.'[1] In 1917, in the midst of the First World War, the British government had created the Ministry of Information and two other agencies to launch a concerted campaign in support of its war objectives. With a mixture of censorship and propaganda, the British government propped up flagging domestic support for the war and demonised their enemies. After the war, the realisation by many in the British public that they had been comprehensively lied to about the conditions at the front caused a political backlash. For the British public, propaganda was synonymous with deception.

But in the inter-war years the word 'propaganda had only been sullied in some circles. In 1925, Adolf Hitler wrote in *Mein Kampf* that Germany 'had failed to recognise propaganda as a weapon of the first order whereas the British had employed it with great skill and ingenious deliberation'.[2] A few years later, Edward Bernays, a pioneer of the PR industry in the United States, titled his 1928 landmark book *Propaganda*, and in it he wrote approvingly that:

> the conscious and intelligent manipulation of the organised habits and opinions of the masses is an important element in democratic society. Those who manipulate this unseen mechanism of society constitute an invisible government which is the true ruling power of our country.[3]

The techniques of propaganda, which had been honed in wartime were subsequently applied for the benefit of corporations in peacetime. Goebbels' propaganda successes, however, underpinned post-war uneasiness about the implications for democracy that could flow from the abuse of these powerful new techniques for manipulating public opinion. By 1947, there were just two individual 'Public Relations Counsellors' listed in the Sydney Pink Pages, as the phone directory was then called. One was George Fitzpatrick, who candidly described himself as a 'registered practitioner in public persuasion, propaganda, publicity'.[4] A few blocks away from Fitzpatrick's Bridge Street office was the office of Asher Joel. Joel, who had started out as a copy boy on the *Daily Telegraph*, established his PR consultancy after cutting his teeth as a war-time propagandist with the Royal Australian Navy. When General Douglas MacArthur established his headquarters as Supreme Commander of the Allied Forces in the Southwest Pacific Area in Brisbane in July 1942, he brought with him a PR team of 35, headed by Brigadier General LeGrande Diller. Joel worked under Diller and observed

US propaganda techniques at work.[5] In the years after the Second World War, Joel and Fitzpatrick became the founders of the Australian PR industry. Within a few years, there were enough PR practitioners to warrant a separate category in the Pink Pages. By the early 1960s, there were an estimated 500 practitioners employed across the country.[6]

Today, the Sydney phone book alone lists 395 PR consultancies, accounting for just over one-third of the more than 1150 public relations companies listed across Australia. The best estimates are that the Australian PR industry turns over more than $1 billion a year and employs in the order of 10 000 people. Globally, the PR industry is estimated to employ more than 120 000 people in the United States and another 48 000 in the United Kingdom.[7] One PR practitioner has rather optimistically estimated that three million people are employed in PR globally,[8] while another estimate puts its worth at approximately US$5 billion, with a growth rate of 20 per cent in the last five years.[9] Exactly who falls within the PR profession is something of a moot point, as the boundary lines between PR, marketing and lobbying are often blurred.

Most major PR consultancies gravitate towards corporate work, which is where the real money is, with a little government work on the side. While those employed in these firms account for a small percentage of those in the profession, it is here and with the increasing number of government agency PR managers that the tension between participating in public debate and preventing it is greatest. Their role can span from advising on everything from behind-the-scenes lobbying and covert advocacy campaigns to strategic targeted sponsorship and philanthropic programs designed to build bridges and enhance a client's image with key 'influencers'. Many others included in the profession under a broad definition of PR are far removed from shaping corporate or government strategy, and more involved in the less controversial aspects of events management, product promotion, and publicity and information provision.

The modern PR industry is keen to distance itself from the old-style propaganda of which Bernays and Goebbels would have approved. The reincarnation of PR saw the propaganda model of PR jettisoned to be replaced by what US PR academic James Grunig clumsily dubbed the 'two-way symmetric' model of communication.[10] In this model, the theoretical role of PR practitioners is to fearlessly hold up a mirror to their client's face, not to simply put a spin on indefensible practices and policies. Out went the militaristic jargon of bombarding 'target' groups with messages, and in came commitments to 'listen' and 'respond' to the views of citizens. Accompanying this approach were pledges of loyalty to 'transparency' and 'corporate social responsibility'; 'We're from PR, we're here to help you', could well be their motto. It sounds good, but even its ardent enthusiasts accept that it is rarely achieved, except perhaps at the least controversial end of the industry.

For a public sceptical of PR, this theoretical rebirthing is meant to be a reassuring distancing of twenty-first century PR from its twentieth century origins in Goebbels-style manipulative propaganda. But the techniques the Nazis used to devastating effect aren't that far removed from the emphasis on 'issues management' by many of the high-level corporate and government consultants in today's PR industry. In January 1942, Goebbels wrote:

> ...propaganda must always be essentially simple and repetitive. In the long run, basic results in influencing public opinion will be achieved only by the man who is able to reduce problems to the simplest terms and who has the courage to keep forever repeating them in this simplified form, despite the objections of the intellectuals.[11]

If Goebbels were alive today and landed a job as a corporate or government spin doctor, he would easily grasp the current industry emphasis on focus groups, 'staying on message', 'talking points', 'sound bites' and disparaging the 'café latte set'. It's all twentieth century-propaganda techniques dressed up in twenty-first century language.

These days, PR industry leaders avoid using the 'p' word, though some lament its demise. 'There was a time when the word propaganda was a perfectly good word…It's been coloured by its misuse by famous people like Mr Goebbels', said Peter Lazar, a senior practitioner and the former chair of the Public Relations Institute of Australia's inner sanctum that oversees ethical issues.[12] Even 'public relations' has lost is lustre, with many in the industry eschewing the term in preference to blander job titles such as 'public affairs manager' or 'communication consultant'.

Limiting your rivals' conversations

Paul Taaffe, an Australian who is the London-based Chairman and Chief Executive of Hill & Knowlton, one of the world's biggest PR firms, argues that a critical role for PR is in 'limiting your rivals' conversations and accelerating yours. And whoever gets the most attention wins the commercial battle.' Of course, not all groups in society have equal access to the media, and some cases are more meritorious than others. And not all PR campaigns are marketplace battles between corporations pushing products. Taafe argues that demand for the services of the PR industry is greatest 'where you have free media, which governments listen to, capitalism, democracy and where there is an educated citizenry and lots of controversy'.[13] But Hill & Knowlton are just as happy to work for clients embroiled in 'lots of controversy' and not renowned for their commitment to democratic rights. For example, in recent times Hill & Knowlton's London office has counted among its clients the government of the Maldives, which has been heavily criticised by human rights groups for the brutal treatment and imprisonment of journalists, opposition politicians and democracy activists.[14]

Many of those in the PR profession resent, sometimes with justification, being tarred with the exploits of others in the industry. While the peak body of the Australian profession, the Public Relations Institute of Australia (PRIA), has a membership that accounts of approximately only one-quarter of those employed in the industry, it boasts that members are obliged to comply with what is often described as a 'strict' code of conduct. A central provision of the code is that 'members shall be prepared to identify the source of funding of any public communication they initiate or for which they act as a conduit'. But it is a provision that provides plenty of wiggle room, as members are only required to disclose details if they are requested to. While asking who is funding an activity seems like a basic first question journalists should pose, all too often they don't.

Some senior practitioners in the industry don't believe they need disclose who the sponsors of a group are, even when they are asked. In March 2006, Tony Harrison, the CEO of the Hobart-based Corporate Communications, authorised a major television and newspaper advertising campaign on behalf of 'Tasmanians for a Better Future', a previously unknown group, in the last weeks of the 2006 Tasmanian election campaign. This shadowy group—which was not incorporated, was not a political party, a business or a charity—blitzed television programs and newspapers with a saturation advertising campaign designed to ensure the Tasmanian Greens did not win the balance of power.[15] They succeeded.

While the bulk of the clients of Corporate Communications are befittingly corporate, it also undertakes work for the Tasmanian

Department of Economic Development and the Department of Tourism, Parks, Heritage and the Arts. In a later submission to PRIA for its annual Golden Target Awards, Harrison revealed that he 'gained access to government research' which showed that the most likely outcome was that the Greens would win the balance of power. While the funders of the campaign, Harrison wrote, had wanted to:

> mount a campaign critical of, and attacking the Greens, the consultancy's research revealed a clear public view that the party was viewed as a legitimate segment of the Tasmanian political landscape and little would be gained by an all-out assault on its policies or personalities.[16]

Instead Harrison opted to run a campaign promoting a vote for whichever political party had the best chance of forming a majority government. Concluding his pitch, Harrison boasted that the 'effect of the campaign was to assist the incumbent Labor Government'.[17]

In the ranks of the PR industry and the PRIA itself, Harrison is one of the heavy hitters. He was the National President of PRIA in 2000 and is a member of the College of Fellows, the inner sanctum of members which assists the board by 'clarifying policy on such matters as ethics'. In 2003, Harrison was awarded the 'prestigious national President's award by the Public Relations Institute of Australia for his contribution to the profession at a national level'.[18] Repeatedly before the election, journalists asked Harrison who was funding the group and the advertisements. Repeatedly he refused to disclose the names of specific contributors.[19]

The funders, he told Hobart's *Mercury* journalist Sue Neales, were a 'group of concerned Tasmanian business and community people'.[20] 'No one in Tasmania has a problem with these ads and I have complied with the Electoral Act', he told the *Australian Financial Review* journalist Julie Macken.[21] He was right that Tasmanian electoral legislation did not require disclosure of who was funding the group, but his optimism that no one in Tasmania objected was misplaced.

The week before the March election, Australian Greens Senator from Tasmania, Christine Milne, lodged a detailed complaint with the PRIA National Secretary, Jim Mahoney. PRIA's 'code of conduct', she later told the Senate, 'requires members to reveal who has funded any PR campaign. Tony Harrison, on behalf of Corporate Communications, utterly refused to do so.'[22] Two months after lodging her complaint, Jim Mahoney sent a one-sentence response to Milne, stating that PRIA's National Board accepted a recommendation from the College of Fellows that Harrison 'did not have a case to answer'.[23] Milne pressed PRIA for a statement of reasons. Once more Mahoney declined, though he added that PRIA was not a 'partisan political organisation', and that he 'was disappointed that its investigation may have been used as part of the election campaign'.[24]

It was a bizarre response, as PRIA's consideration of the complaint began only *after* the election was over and the complaint was concerned with a secretive partisan political advertising campaign initiated by a PR company and PRIA member. Milne was stunned. In a speech in the Senate on changes to provisions governing federal electoral funding disclosure she said that PRIA's decision:

> makes a complete mockery of any kind of code of conduct for the public relations industry and confirms what people in the general community think of them... The result is that a group of unknown, unnamed shadowy figures can emerge from somewhere and call themselves anything, such as Tasmanians for a Better Future—and, interestingly, that is a

similar slogan to the one that the government ran with—and get away with it.

In her opinion the consequences extended far beyond Tasmania:

If you do not rein this in now it will mean that there will be a blank cheque for public relations agencies going into the federal election, with the full blessing of the Public Relations Institute of Australia, which will be saying: 'Forget about our code of conduct. It doesn't operate. It doesn't matter. We're completely self-regulated. We'll just do as we like and you just go right ahead'[25]

Unknown to Milne was that the panel appointed by PRIA determined that the obligation to disclose sources of funding was trumped by another provision in the code of ethics requiring members to 'safeguard the confidences' of clients. A few months later, the judges for PRIA's annual Golden Target Awards were so impressed by Harrison's campaign that they gave it a commendation in the public affairs category.[26]

Harrison, a former press adviser in the 1980s to Tasmanian Liberal Premier Robin Gray, has long advised the Tasmanian mining and forest industries on how to handle its opponents. In the aftermath of the rescue of two trapped miners at the Beaconsfield gold mine in Tasmania in May 2006, Harrison, who advises the Tasmanian Chamber of Mines, took a swipe at the mine's PR consultant, Michael Lester from CPR communications. In a column in *Tasmanian Business Reporter*—a free monthly newspaper co-published by Corporate Communications and the Tasmanian Chamber of Commerce and Industry—Harrison complained that a consequence of regularly briefing Australian Workers Union boss Bill Shorten was to allow the union to dominate media coverage.[27]

Fronting a domestic political campaign is one thing, but Australian PR companies have also been called in to defend companies embroiled in human rights controversies in distant countries. The day after a band of rebels took over the town of Kilwa in the Democratic Republic of Congo (DRC), the President of the Perth-based Anvil Mining, Bill Turner, felt compelled to issue a media release to reassure investors about events near the company's Dikulushi copper and silver mine, which had opened a few years earlier. Turner explained that the government of the DRC were 'moving quickly to return the situation to normal' and that he expected the disturbance to be 'resolved within the next 72 hours'.[28] Turner's information was so good that he even explained that the leader of the estimated 50 to 100 rebels was 'not dressed in uniform and wears sandals'. A little over three months later, in its next quarterly report to the Australian Stock Exchange, Anvil was in a congratulatory mood, noting that 'the government and military response on both provincial and national levels was rapid and supportive of the prompt resumption of operations'.[29] Certainly the military response had been rapid, but not reported was that it had been ruthless and indiscriminate.

What Anvil blandly referred to as the 'Kilwa Event' was found by local human rights groups and United Nations peacekeepers to involve the military arbitrarily executing many of the rebels, their suspected sympathisers and civilians. UN peacekeepers, who were in Kilwa a little over a week after the massacre had no difficulty piecing together much of the story, despite getting little cooperation from the military. They identified who the military commander at the time had been, and confirmed the deaths of at least 73 people, of which 28 were summary executions. The preliminary UN report noted that the troops had been flown into Kilwa on an aircraft under charter to Anvil, and were then driven around in Anvil trucks with the assistance of three Anvil employees. The trucks, the United Nations stated, were also used to transport prisoners to a spot where they were executed. The UN investigation confirmed that the soldiers had been provided with food rations by Anvil and that the company admitted 'it contributed to the payment of a certain number of soldiers'. Just as Anvil had initially appreciated the military's support, the commander of the military unit told the United Nations that the Kilwa operation had been possible due to the logistical support provided by the company.

If Turner had sought the advice of a PR company, the odds are that he would have been warned off agreeing to an interview for ABC TV's investigative 'Four Corners' program. But agree he did. Turner confirmed that the company 'provided' the trucks and planes the military had 'requested' from them, and expressed little concern about the military's response to the rebels: 'Look, a rebel group came in and took over the military establishment and took over the police—the police station in Kilwa... You don't do those things if you don't want to get shot at.' In the wake of the massacre, Anvil funded the costs of building a new school and upgrading the local hospital. 'We are doing some damn good stuff and it would be kind of pleasant if people were to focus a little bit on some of the good things instead of picking some tiny little aspect that someone thinks they've got some hold on to blow up into something that is totally irrelevant to what we're doing,' Turner told 'Four Corners'. As for questions about the massacre of civilians, Turner just wished people would 'focus on some of the good things instead of picking some tiny little aspect that someone thinks they've got some hold on to blow up into something that is totally irrelevant to what we're doing'.[30]

The day after the damning current affairs program, the company issued a media release restating that it had provided the military with the trucks and air services they had 'requested', before going on to highlight a school the company had built and a trust fund established for community development projects.[31] Not surprisingly, the story of the company's role in assisting the military echoed around the world. Human rights groups in the Congo and the United Kingdom demanded the perpetrators be brought to justice. Lawyers in Australia, acting for the victims and their families, signaled possible legal action and pressed the Australian Federal Police to investigate Anvil. An arm of the World Bank, which had provided financial guarantees for the development of the mine, was investigating the matter too.

As the crisis unfolded, Turner turned for advice to Caroline de Mori, the director of Perth-based PR company Purple Communications. De Mori boasts that, as a result of her 25 years experience in public relations, she has an ability to get a 'quick and effective grasp of complicated and/or controversial issues'. Within weeks of the 'Four Corners' program being screened in June 2005, Anvil began shifting ground. Earlier references to Anvil willingly supplying trucks and air transport to the military were replaced with a claim that they had been 'commandeered at gunpoint'. Out went the expression of gratitude to the military for their 'supportive' response, and in came concern that, eight months after the massacre, the company was only 'now learning it was a terrible event'.[32] Even though Turner could describe what the leader of the rebels was wearing within a day of their wandering into Kilwa, Anvil now explained how difficult it was to get information about the events that had occurred in the DRC. It was a claim that also sat incongruously with Anvil's boast that it had a close relationship with the local community. Anvil pledged to cooperate with UN investigations, and also pointed to a supportive statement from some local community leaders, denying that Anvil had any role in the massacre.

By August 2005, Anvil announced that following a 'comprehensive' internal investigation undertaken by a lawyer from

Clayton Utz, Gary Berson, the allegations against the company of providing support to the military were 'unfounded'.[33] Berson, spent two weeks in the area of the mine, and his report was reviewed by Perth Queens Counsel, Wayne Martin.[34] But if the mining company were so confident that the 100-page report exonerated them entirely, why wouldn't they release it for public scrutiny?

'Up to whose scrutiny? Up to your scrutiny?', de Mori said, laughing. 'I'm sorry to be a bit funny about this but we are not obliged to provide the full 100-page report publicly and we are not doing so', she said.[35] Nor did Anvil's willingness to 'cooperate with the UN' extend to sharing the results of its internal investigation with them. The company also claimed that they had a letter from the military commandeering the vehicles, but this, too, was not for public release.[36] Anvil even went so far as to ominously warn that it was considering defamation actions against a range of groups in the DRC, Australia and the United Kingdom.

Anvil's effort to extricate itself from controversy is just one small example of what happens in the world of spin. But it has many of the elements that are found in the PR toolbox: trying to reposition the company as the victim rather than the culprit; approvingly pointing to support from seemingly independent local leaders while ominously warning critics about possible defamation actions; an unhealthily close relationship with government agencies; seeking to emphasise the company's community-oriented philanthropic works; touting an internal review as providing a ringing exoneration of the company, but not disclosing it; and publicly promising full cooperation with authorities, but then the company withholding information from the investigators. Of course, we would expect a mining company accused of complicity in human rights abuses to call in the spin doctors. Few PR campaigns are for clients like Anvil Mining, but on most issues that are the subject of public debate there are usually PR companies and professionals lurking in the background. The sustained growth in the PR industry is being driven by big and small companies, government agencies and a smattering of non-profit groups in what is the PR equivalent of the nuclear arms race. Once a rival gets the upper hand because it hired well-connected spin doctors and lobbyists, others think they have to have them too.

Anvil called in spin doctors after a crisis erupted, but the former asbestos manufacturer, James Hardie Industries (JHI), turned to Gavin Anderson & Company (GA) ahead of an announcement of a major corporate restructuring. JHI aimed to quarantine its asbestos liabilities to two small companies with assets limited to approximately $300 million. JHI planned that once the 'separation' was completed and announced, the value of the main company would increase significantly as a result of possible takeover interest. But limiting the company's asbestos liabilities would be bad news for the unknown number of future asbestos claimants, with the prospect that funds would be exhausted well before the incidence of asbestos-related diseases had passed. The 'central communications conundrum', GA wrote, was that the company could not guarantee 'with any certainty that the funds set aside to compensate victims of asbestos diseases will be sufficient to meet all future claims'.

In February 2001, GA, with assistance from Hawker Britton, a PR and lobbying company with close connections to the Labor Party, crafted a 36-page communication strategy for the company's senior executives and members of the board. With the benefit of behind-the-scenes meetings with key New South Wales government figures, the company felt confident that it could limit any public backlash to its plan. Central to its strategy was pitching the story to the business media, where it expected an easier run and hoped to bypass the more general news reporters, where it anticipated a more sceptical hearing. GA was particularly concerned that general reporters would be more receptive to the views of unions, the victims of asbestos diseases and their lawyers. If media coverage focused too heavily on the suggestion that JHI were cutting and running, it could result in government action, though the strategy paper assessed the risk of this as low. In particular, GA identified three key journalists with the *Australian Financial Review*, one from *The Age*, and three from Rupert Murdoch's News Limited as critical to their hopes of confining the story to the business pages. 'We, and our advisors, have very sound relationships with the journalists which routinely cover JH. We will provide them with deep background if necessary', the strategy paper stated.[37] But timing would be everything.

A date was selected when key state parliaments were not sitting to eliminate the chance of ministers being pressed to make commitments unfavourable to the company. Instead, the company planned on making the announcement at the time of its normal quarterly financial results. Instead of the normal two-and-a-half hours between the announcement to the market and a briefing for investment analysts, they proposed reducing it to just one hour. 'By limiting the time between the announcement and the presentation we would aim to minimise the risk that non-business media and perhaps other stakeholders would attend and "hijack" the briefing', the strategy stated.

To sweeten what could be seen as a bitter pill for asbestos victims, the company planned on announcing the establishment of a new research centre as a part of the Medical Research and Compensation Foundation, which compensated claimants. 'This will enable the Foundation to step forward and talk about the good works it proposes to carry out in the future. We will aim to divert general media attention to the Foundation's aim of ensuring that genuine claimants are properly compensated', the strategy stated. A media release issued by Hardie's Executive Vice-

President of Corporate Affairs, Greg Baxter, reassured the public that the compensation scheme would be a 'fully funded Foundation for both claimants and shareholders'.[38] Hardie's strategy largely went according to plan. There were a couple of upbeat reports by business reporters, and a couple of more critical ones. But within days, the issue had largely sunk without trace.

Eight months after the foundation was established, Hardie moved its head office to the Netherlands to reduce tax. But no sooner had the 'separation' been announced than the directors of the foundation were advised that liabilities had been massively underestimated. JHI refused their pleas for additional funding and, in an act of desperation, the foundation launched legal action in late 2003. Once court documents started to tumble out, the story of JHI's corporate manoeuvres started to emerge. The New South Wales Government, fearing that many of the 24 000 people forecast to contract asbestos-induced diseases over the next 50 years would be left without access to compensation, established a special commission of inquiry into the adequacy of the reserves of the foundation. With the powers of a royal commission, JHI documents—including the GA strategy—were made public. The final report by Commissioner David Jackson, tabled in mid-2004, was scathing about the actions of the company and its PR advisers. The reassuring media release, Jackson wrote, was 'a public relations construct bereft of substantial truth... Public relations played a larger than healthy part in the activities of the James Hardie Group'.[39]

As a result of the drawn-out public controversy, the company's share price collapsed and there was a parade of departing executives and directors. In December 2004, JHI finally agreed to provide additional funds and guarantees for compensation to all future victims, potentially amounting to $1.9 billion. Baxter may have got a bollocking from Jackson, but he was the pinup boy of the investor-relations community, a subsection of public relations that deals with the financial community. Baxter was the winner of the 'Best investor relations officer' award by *IR* magazine in 2001, 2002 and 2003 for his work with Hardie,[40] and in 2004 landed the plum job as the Director of Corporate Affairs for News Limited, the Australian operating arm of Rupert Murdoch's News Corporation.

Not long after GA helped JHI out of a fix, the rather dour peak body for the universities, the Australian Vice-Chancellors' Committee (AVCC), called on the company. In 2002, when the federal government was reviewing higher education funding directions, the AVCC allocated $175 000 for GA to shape the debate towards its preferred policy positions. In its strategy, GA stressed the need for the campaign to 'neutralize the media's negative focus on the issue of fees by shifting their attention to the "softer" more appealing options' in its policy. 'Critics needed [*sic*] to be countered with advocates', GA wrote.[41] GA had in mind that the 'key third party advocates' would be identified and courted precisely because they didn't appear to be too closely aligned to the AVCC, to create the impression of 'momentum of support and endorsement for the AVCC's aims and objectives'. As with most PR plans, ensuring 'consistency of message' was seen as critical to the success of their AVCC's campaign.

To help dominate public debate, GA proposed to identify 'pro-AVCC education writers and commentators' and use a 'media leak strategy ... for all major announcements', a strategy that would involve playing favourites with their preferred journalists. Central to this would be a 'select previewing of key announcements, policy papers and milestones to a key media outlet'. The media were also to be provided with 'a range of positive "human case studies" type-stories' that highlighted core campaign themes such as a 'regional community leader who benefited from his post grad studies, brain drain reverse, examples of clever country'. The incongruity of this body of academics—seemingly dedicated to the pursuit of knowledge, enquiry and the free exchange of ideas—employing spin doctors to smother dissenting points of view seems to have escaped them.

The price of invisibility

Despite the many pages of listings for PR companies in the Australian Yellow Pages, there is a dearth of reporting on the PR industry. In part, this can be attributed to the culture of secrecy, with many PR companies operating on the basis that they are most successful when they are nowhere to be seen. In a chapter on ethics in Australian public relations for a 1961 book, Ron Cameron, one of the leaders of PRIA at the time, advised that 'a practitioner's part in the campaign should always be unobtrusive'.[42] It was a view echoed in 1996 by Ian Robertson from the Perth affiliate of the global PR behemoth, Hill & Knowlton Australia. 'Any PR person who is speaking to an audience of greater than two should resign', he said in a presentation to mining industry executives.[43] Keeping a low profile, avoiding reliance on PR spokespeople, press conferences and public meetings, he said, were critical to running a winning campaign. In short, remain invisible.

There are a few PR or lobbying companies that voluntarily reveal the names of their current clients with an outline of the nature of the work they do on each account. Others, such as Hill & Knowlton, opt for the halfway house of disclosing a sample of some of their clients and some anonymous case studies. Other clients are kept well hidden. For example, Hill & Knowlton don't disclose that they worked for the federal government in a failed attempt to win support for a nuclear waste dump in South Australia, a campaign that ended in tears for both the government and the PR company. For many companies, disclosing the names of clients is a balancing act between wanting to impress potential clients with their PR prowess while avoiding debate over some of their less savoury clients and controversial campaigns.

The culture of secrecy pervades the highest echelons of the PR industry. Speaking via a webcast to a PR conference in Sydney in September 2005, the US-based crisis management guru and member of the peak US PR industry ethics body, James Lukaszewski, was asked by a fellow PR practitioner to identify his clients. 'My particular client list is confidential', he said. Peter Lazar, who is a member of the College of Fellows for the Public Relations Institute of Australia, thinks that one of the reasons behind the secrecy over client lists is that 'they don't want their colleagues to try and rip them off'.[44] Which begs the question: If they don't trust each other, why should we trust them?

If industry leaders, especially those involved with oversight responsibilities of the industry's self-regulatory codes of ethics, don't disclose their clients, it is hardly surprising that others follow suit. In the PR industry secrecy is often seen as an asset. If hired to keep another company *out* of the media, any mention of their role is likely to only invite scrutiny. For a PR company, visibility carries risks of the message being discounted as spin or, worst of all, losing one or more clients if an agency's conflict of interest becomes apparent. For example, at the time of the International Whaling Commission meeting in Adelaide in July 2000, it was revealed that the Japanese Whaling Association had hired Shandwick (now Weber Shandwick) to help campaign for the resumption of commercial whaling. One of the international environmental groups campaigning against whaling in Adelaide, the International Fund for Animal Welfare (IFAW), was stunned to discover from Australian news reports that Shandwick were working for their adversary. Having hired Shandwick to help it run a PR campaign in the United Kingdom against fox hunting, IFAW saw the company's work for the whalers as a fundamental conflict of interest, and terminated the account.[45]

Often secrecy flows from clients requiring PR advisers to sign confidentiality agreements. When AWB, Australia's leading wheat marketer, formerly known as the Australian Wheat Board, hired US-crisis management guru Peter Sandman to advise it on how to handle the Iraq kickbacks scandal, at cost of US$650 an hour, Sandman signed a confidentiality agreement providing for AWB to sue him for breach of contract if he disclosed any confidential information.[46] Why do clients request confidentiality? Often government agencies, Sandman says, fear public criticism over what would likely be portrayed as:

> spending a lot of money bringing in an American spin doctor to advise them on how to pull the wool over people's eyes more effectively... They say 'we'll pay that much but we just want to split it amongst a bunch of people so that your hourly rate isn't embarrassing.[47]

Others extol the virtues of secrecy.

Beth Herskovitz, a journalist with the global PR industry trade publication *PR Week*, suggested ways in which a PR company's clients could be obscured from pesky journalists and noted that sometimes 'slip-ups' were caused by an agency's phone number on a press release or someone disclosing too much information.[48] Ironically, only two months after her column, an editorial in the same publication lambasted companies that 'won't even admit to having a PR firm', and complained that secrecy over clients was at the heart of the PR industry's credibility problem. 'With all the questions today about the effectiveness of advertising, PR people should be shouting from the rooftops the benefits of what they do, not skulking in the background like someone who just bought a dirty magazine but doesn't want his neighbours to know', wrote John Frank, a *PR Week* journalist.[49]

Invisibility may help keep the PR industry away from the gaze of a sceptical public, but it comes with a potentially hefty price tag. If senior management don't understand what PR staff or consultants really do, they are left very vulnerable if newly appointed CEOs embark on a round of cost-cutting. 'Instead of looking at the function as a profit enhancement centre they see it as a cost centre and it is one of the first things to go', observed Geoff Allen from the Melbourne-based Allen Consulting Group.[50]

One of the ways PR companies achieve invisibility is by what industry insiders refer to as the 'third-party technique'. In 1995 Amanda Little, who worked for PR firm Burson-Marsteller in Australia at the time, told a conference that:

> for the media and the public, the corporation will be one of the least credible sources of information, on its own product, environmental and safety risks. Both these audiences will turn to other experts (medical officials, academics, local authori-ties and visible spokespeople from activist groups) to get an objective viewpoint. Developing third party support and validation for the basic risk messages of the corporation is essential. This support should ideally come from medical authorities, political leaders, union officials, relevant academics, fire and police officials, environmentalists, regulators.[51]

The power of the 'third-party technique' relies on invisibly courting what appear to the public as independent players, and incorporating them as part of a PR strategy for a client's benefit. At its worst, this technique cannibalises the independence of professions, agencies, non-profit groups and individuals that the public expects to act as watchdogs. Sometimes the third parties are willing collaborators. Other times the 'third-parties' are rather naive in not realising that they are setting off down a PR slippery slope. Sometimes, if a requisite 'third-party' group doesn't exist, a PR company can create one.

The tobacco industry was one of the early large-scale pioneers of the 'third-party technique' that attempted to quarantine controversy over the health impact of its deadly products. From the 1950s on, it also had the advantage of fat enough profit margins to wage big-budget global PR campaigns to defend the indefensible. It became adept at courting and covertly funding a network of think tanks and scientists that could be deployed when necessary. They were also willing to sue their critics, use political contributions to gain favours, court and threaten the media, and play the divide-and-conquer game with advocacy groups. They became adept at the creation of front groups designed to put a community veneer on a corporate message. Even though many of their campaigns were ultimately unsuccessful, or at best only delayed regulatory action, major PR companies such as Burson-Marsteller, Hill & Knowlton, Shandwick and Edelman grew rich and honed their skills defending Big Tobacco.

The third-party technique assumed greater importance with the emphasis on citizen participation that emerged from the 1960s. Strategies that once aimed at quietly delivering carefully crafted messages to key business, media and political elites were failing in the face of the rapidly changing political landscape. New grassroots movements mushroomed and, by the mid-1970s, the credibility of corporations had crumbled.[52] From the vantage point of the boardroom, it was all a little bewildering. Geoff Allen, the founder of the Allen Consulting Group and one of the best-connected PR advisers in Australia, singles out the rise of environmentalism, the indigenous rights movement and the anti-apartheid movements in the 1960s and 1970s as forcing a major rethink about corporate PR strategies, especially among global corporations. Strategies developed and refined for Big Tobacco were on-sold by PR companies to their clients in other sectors. Sometimes their covert strategies worked and sometimes they backfired badly.

The collapse of corporate credibility that occurred in the 1960s and 1970s has shown little sign of recovering. The Australian Survey of Social Attitudes in 2003 revealed that 62 per cent of those surveyed wanted big business to either have less power or a lot less power, a figure that has remained consistently high for the last two decades.[53] The survey also revealed that almost half of the survey respondents stated that in the previous two years they had bought or boycotted products for ethical, political or environmental reasons.[54] Another Australian survey in 2005 reported that 55 per cent of respondents thought that big corporations have no morals or ethics.[55] For CEOs, there are similarly dispiriting results globally, with a survey by the PR firm Edelman concluding that non-government organisations are now the most credible group of organisations.[56]

Research into the attitudes of CEOs of major Australian companies towards both in-house PR professionals and external consultants should dispel any notion that PR practitioners are likely to make their fortune as a corporate social conscience. In 1999, two Melbourne academics surveyed 64 CEOs across a range of major Australian companies on their expectations of both their own PR staff and external consultants. The proposition that 'I expect our public relations professionals to manipulate stakeholders scientifically' was scored as highly desirable among those surveyed.[57] The results, the authors noted, 'suggested the surveyed CEOs are willing to admit that they are ethically comfortable with persuasion and even manipulation, but they are less confident about being successful'.

For all the talk that PR has moved beyond manipulating public consent, Australia's corporate CEOs are clear in what they want for their money. And one thing that PR consultants know is that those who pay the piper get to call the tune.

PR's reality problem

Barely a year goes by without one or more PR companies or consultants being engulfed in a high-profile controversy. Australian PR companies and their clients have also been sued for organising bogus community groups to block commercial rivals' proposals to build new shopping centres and, in another instance, run regional radio stations. PR professionals have covertly funded think tanks, spread disinformation, aided and abetted companies and governments implicated in human rights abuses, and overseen the infiltration of community groups. And that is just some of the cases that have been revealed. Inspired by the success of the corporate sector in 'managing' debates, federal, state and local governments are now employing spin doctors in trying to shape media coverage and what the public thinks of them.

Speaking at a PR industry conference, Lelde McCoy, a former national president of PRIA, worried about the PR industry's own reputation problem:

> The media's opinion of us is unfair but can we really blame them when their impression of us has been formed by our relentless flogging of manufactured stories, pseudo events, skewed survey statistics, an overuse of celebrities, non-disclosure of information in issues-rich situations and through numerous encounters from over-enthusiastic PR consultants?[58]

But McCoy, who founded The Reputation Group, was primarily concerned that the PR industry's poor reputation is hampering the industry's growth prospects. Perhaps she worries unnecessarily. Since the Australian PR industry emerged from the Second World War propaganda machine, it has grown phenomenally, in spite of its persistent poor reputation.

Instead of worrying about the growth prospects of the PR industry, the more important debate is the extent to which the growth of PR is compatible with the maintenance of a healthy democracy. Our concern as citizens should be about how the quality of our democracy is being degraded by corporate and government adherence to the propaganda techniques pioneered by the military and subsequently refined by the likes of the tobacco industry. In the eyes of too many PR professionals, organised citizens are viewed as a threat to be 'managed'. Instead of celebrating vigorous public debate, disclosure of important information is increasingly restricted, and high-level PR professionals view their role as 'limiting' the 'conversations' of those critical of their clients. Goebbels himself remarked that 'propaganda becomes ineffective the moment we are aware of it'.[59] For this reason, it's time the PR and lobbying industries were brought out from the shadows of public life.

TWO
FOOD FIGHTS

I was making my way to the supermarket checkout with my two-year-old daughter after collecting some milk, when she stopped suddenly. She was transfixed by the image of Nemo, the brightly coloured clownfish from the animated Hollywood film, on a six-pack of Nestlé's flavoured and sweetened yoghurt stacked at her eye-level. Thankfully, she didn't protest when I explained that we didn't need it, but I was amazed that after having seen part of the movie just once at childcare the image was etched in her memory. I might have been surprised but the marketers of the food industry, which use extensive market research to guide their decisions, obviously aren't. The food industry in Australia is mammoth, accounting for nearly half of all retail sales in Australia, with much of that driven by advertising/ marketing. The sheer scale of the industry means they are both vulnerable to tiny shifts in sales and politically powerful.

A few weeks after my trip to the supermarket, against a backdrop of kids playing in the school grounds of Hoxton Park Primary School in the south-western suburbs of Sydney, the federal Minister for Health Tony Abbott extolled the benefits of the government's $6 million *Healthy For Life* advertising program to the assembled media. Obesity, he warned, was so serious that the current generation could become the first to have a shorter life expectancy than their parents. The point of the ads, he said, was to remind children 'just how much fun exercise can be.'[1] But the rising obesity rates were not so serious that he considered government regulatory action was necessary to curb food industry advertising aimed at children; rather, parents should just turn the television off. 'The last thing I want to do is start dictating the menu in every Australian home, dictating what appears on every Australian television program...' he said. A $6 million advertising campaign may sound impressive, but it is no match for the corporate food heavyweights, which are estimated to spend approximately $100 million annually on television food and drink advertising to children.

The ads Abbott unveiled were a response to the mid-2004 commitment by the then opposition leader Mark Latham to ban all food and drink advertising during children's television programming.[2] Latham's support for a ban on television advertising directed at children spooked the Australian Association of National Advertisers (AANA), whose members include McDonald's, Nestlé, Cadbury Schweppes and Coca-Cola, to the extent that they dispatched a submission to Prime Minister John Howard outlining their objections, lest the government conceded ground. In part of their submission, AANA flagged the possibility that they would run a PR campaign and mobilise media proprietors against a ban. 'The current state of what has become known as "the obesity debate" extends beyond a threat to freedom of commercial speech to represent a risk to most large corporations and many small to medium enterprises', they complained.[3] The advertisers' threat had the desired effect. Asked later about whether the government would restrict advertising on television directed at children, Abbott timidly stated: 'I would ask advertisers to be responsible.'

Like many of the rather blandly-named trade associations, AANA counts issues management as a core part of its operations. How it manages issues, though, is not intended for public view: 'The Issues Management section of the AANA website is for members only', it states.[4] 'Issues management' was coined in the mid-1970s and popularised by Howard Chase, a US PR corporate practitioner who had worked for food companies General Foods and General Mills and then, after a stint working for government, turned to academia. As Chase saw it, embracing his issues management approach would mean shifting PR away from simply reacting to each crisis as it reared its ugly head to anticipating emerging issues and focusing the available resources to achieving 'meaningful participation in creation of public policy...' It was an idea born of its time, when the public standing of US corporations had collapsed and was under challenge from new social movements, and when Richard Nixon's presidency was mired in controversy over Vietnam and the Watergate break-in.

There were numerous attractions of the issues management concept for PR professionals: it would shift the PR role to be more closely integrated with senior management, and necessitate the expansion of resources to pre-empt problems, on the promise that there would be fewer high-profile crises that, inevitably, would be more damaging. An untended issue, they argue, could escalate within a year or two to a full-scale crisis from which it would be far harder to recover. Good issues management, its proponents argue, requires an emphasis on substance, not image; performance, not spin. A necessity of issues management, they claim, is having a detailed understanding of the concerns of 'stakeholders' and a willingness to acknowledge and fix problems. In this persona, they insist that the PR function should be welcomed by everyone as a valuable ally and problem solver.

The rise of issue and crisis management, though, has generated a lot of bad PR for the PR industry, with exposés revealing the extent to which some will go to 'manage' an issue. Some have sought to gain information on stakeholder views by infiltrating activist groups. Others have created front groups or, as they have been dubbed in the US, 'astroturf' groups—fake grassroots groups designed to put a community face on a corporate message. In PR parlance, Latham's proposed ban on junk-food advertising to children on television was an issues management problem. If Howard had agreed with Latham's proposal and implemented the change, it would have been a crisis for the advertising industry, the commercial media companies, and particularly the fast-food companies. A common misconception of PR is that it is all about advertising, but PR companies and consultants aren't generally directly involved in product advertising campaigns at all, with the exception of advocacy advertising in support of policy goals. But it does fall to PR and lobbyists to ensure government regulations don't frustrate their clients' advertising and marketing plans.

When Latham backed a ban on fast-food advertising in children's television hours, he also created an issues management problem for the Howard Government. Its *Healthy For Life* advertising campaign seems to be more about *appearing* to do something than actually having any sustained impact. Government advertising campaigns come and go, with little long-term impact, while food industry campaigns go on forever. Among government advertising campaigns, *Healthy for Life* is a minnow—the advertising campaign attempting to sell the Work Choices industrial relations changes cost approximately nine times as much. The message in the government's *Healthy for Life* campaign and their refusal to take action on junk-food advertising aimed at kids sits uncomfortably with the thrust of their own Family Law System advertisements, which proclaim: 'It's not time to focus on who's right. It's time to focus on what's right for our kids'. Of course, the commercial media companies win all-round, with both government and corporate advertising heading their way.

McPR

The companies with most to lose from concern about rising obesity rates are drink manufacturers and fast-food companies, such as McDonald's, which spends big bucks advertising to children. With approximately one million customers going through the doors of McDonald's outlets in Australia every day, the company is vulnerable to the slightest downturn in sales. At a forum on obesity organised by Liberal Senator Guy Barnett in December 2005, the CEO of McDonald's Australia, Peter Bush, explained that media analysis revealed the company had been averaging 60 stories a week, linking its name with obesity.[5] Bush reeled off an impressive-sounding list of changes the company has adopted in the last couple of years—a new range of salads, cutting the sugar content of buns from the parent company's standard of more than 14 per cent to almost 4 per cent, 'reengineering' foods to cut the total calorie count, and shifting to canola oil. Perhaps most significantly of all, it has trumpeted its kids-friendly credentials by cutting the amount of television advertising in children's viewing hours by 60 per cent, and has also launched a series of television commercials dubbed 'never stop playing'. 'They aren't about anything other than Ronald [McDonald] encouraging kids to get up and run and hop and skip', Bush said. However, McDonald's declined repeated requests from the author to clarify whether they had cut their *total* advertising in children's television hours by 60 per cent or had just changed the mix between product promotion and the brand-enhancing exercise ads. While these exercise-promotion campaigns may appear public-spirited, as does their sponsorship deals with

Little Athletics, they simply substitute pushing a brand for selling a product. It is familiar territory for McDonald's.

A decade earlier, the company became alarmed about its association with the 'junk food' tag, debate about advertising to children, and controversy over the nutritional quality of its food. McDonald's Australia turned to the Sydney-headquartered Professional Public Relations (PPR), which it has used as its PR agency since 1980, to rework a campaign run by its US parent company, promoting the message that eating at a fast-food giant was compatible with good nutrition. The 'What's On Your Plate' community service campaign was launched in late 1993 and featured a clay animation character, Willie Munchright, who delivered the message on good nutrition during Saturday morning children's television programming. The campaign created the appearance that McDonald's were promoting the need for a balanced diet, but an internal PPR document revealed they were primarily concerned with reinforcing 'an image of McDonald's as an organisation providing a good quality food service'.[6] The company had also set as a secondary goal to 'establish an active dialogue' with dieticians, many of whom were critical of McDonald's food. Despite spending $200 000 on the short-term advertising campaign, it had little effect—the waistlines of Australian children continued to grow.

A little over a decade later, Bush conceded there were real issues with the nutritional value of its products.

> McDonald's was a business that was slow and lethargic, very much like an elephant meandering through the bush, not listening to customers and being seen as the same very big and very easy target to be blamed for all kinds of things.

One thing that has changed after its Willie Munchright campaign was that McDonald's has been on the receiving end of class-action lawsuits. In the US, it reached multi-million dollar out-of-court settlements, including over its broken promise to phase out trans fats, an additive that increases the risk of heart disease. The most prominent suit, though, was filed in late 2002 in New York, alleging McDonald's breached consumer protection legislation by claiming its food was nutritious and healthy. The two teenage plaintiffs argued that their obesity, and the potential adverse health impacts that flowed from it, was attributable to McDonald's misleading advertising. The case was ultimately dismissed, but it spurred the company to diversify its menu options, redouble efforts to soften its image and—as the tobacco industry has also done—emphasise 'personal responsibility'. In PR terms, success in selling the notion that consumers are solely responsible for their food choices and how much they consume is designed to absolve corporations and governments from accepting any significant responsibility for their role or inaction.

Another catalyst for change was the 2004 documentary by US filmmaker Morgan Spurlock, *Super Size Me*, which chronicled the impact that a McDonald's-only diet had over 30 days. One of Spurlock's ground rules for the film was that, every time McDonald's counter staff asked if he wanted a super-size option on a meal, he accepted. As the film gained more profile, McDonald's felt compelled to act. Three months after the film was first screened, but ahead of its commercial release, McDonald's United States announced it would phase out its super-size menu option. McDonald's also unveiled a new range of meals that included a salad, bottled water and pedometer. In the world of PR crisis management, though, McDonald's overall response was seen as a losing strategy, having allowed Spurlock to gain a dominant voice in the media coverage of the film.[7]

When the film was released in Australia in June 2004, it broke box office records for the opening weekend of a documentary. McDonald's initial preference had been to ignore the film. But McDonald's Australia Chief Executive Officer Guy Russo later revealed to a US PR company publication that market research on the potential impact of the film revealed customers 'took it that our silence basically meant guilt'.[8] McDonald's launched a series of advertisements that emphasised moderation, balance and personal responsibility. Another strand of their campaign was to launch a counterattack, with Russo accusing Spurlock of being 'stupid' and personally 'irresponsible'.[9] Of course, it was obvious to anyone who watched Spurlock's documentary that his regimen was an exaggeration on a normal diet. But it wasn't until after his film was released and gained a significant audience, threatening to become a crisis, that the fast-food company ditched its super-size option. In a world of corporate intransigence, no challenge equals no change.

Kids' play

I sat in the foyer of PPR's Rozelle headquarters, waiting for Peter Lazar, the founder of the company and a member of Public Relations Institute of Australia (PRIA). I was looking at the single-lane lap pool crammed into the rear courtyard when Lazar arrived.

'It looks deeper than it really is', he quipped. It seemed appropriate that those waiting in reception at an illusion factory were greeted with an illusion. 'Not many people ever actually use it though', he added, before proudly showing me around what had once been a pub in the inner-city suburb.

Lazar is one of the grand old men of the Australian PR industry. After working in sports marketing, he moved into PR, where he spent five-and-a-half years in the 1960s working for the Dental Health Foundation, defending and promoting the fluoridation of water supplies. After a brief stint with Eric White Associates, Lazar cut loose, and in 1970 founded PPR. These days, it is among Australia's largest PR companies and a subsidiary of the global advertising and PR conglomerate, WPP. One of PPR's longstanding clients is the fast-food giant McDonald's.

For most of its modern marketing history, McDonald's has made its pitch to children with the red, white and yellow-coloured clown, Ronald McDonald. A McDonald's *Operations Manual* from the early 1990s emphasised that, while Ronald had a lovable, laughable persona, there was a marketing motivation underneath the clown suit:

> Ronald loves McDonald's and McDonald's food. And so do children, because they love Ronald. Remember, children exert a phenomenal influence over restaurant selection. This means you should do everything you can to appeal to children's love for Ronald and McDonald's.[10]

But if Ronald started out as a savvy marketing ploy, he has been rebadged as the epitome of McDonald's corporate philanthropy. Visit a children's hospital just about anywhere in Australia and the odds are that there will be a Ronald McDonald House within cooee. Ronald McDonald House Charities (RMHC) was founded to provide much-needed accommodation for families with children being treated for serious diseases, such as cancer and leukaemia.

As with many PR programs by multinational companies, the project had its origins with the parent company. In the United States, the project coordinator for the program resided in McDonald's PR company Golin/Harris Communications. One McDonald's document refers to the project as not only giving something back to the community but also suggests having the PR objectives of helping 'differentiate by positive action McDonald's from its competitors' and to be 'a source of positive events difficult to ignore by local and national media'.[11] In Australia, the charity now runs a dozen houses across the country.

It also provides family rooms in hospitals, access to beach houses, an education program and a grants program. At face value, all these projects are beyond reproach, but Lazar refers to these as a company making an investment in a 'trust bank'. When a controversy erupts, a company makes an involuntary withdrawal from the 'trust bank'. If the process of making 'deposits' has been sufficiently public and sustained, it is hoped that a short-term crisis will soon be forgiven.

As its contribution to RMHC, which is run as a separate entity, McDonald's covers all the organisation's administrative and management costs. In 1990, McDonald's hired Lazar's PPR to introduce 'McHappy Day' to Australians, an annual event when $1 from the purchase price of a Big Mac is given to RMHC. In the eyes of PPR, 'it was crucial that McHappy Day was not positioned as a commercial McDonald's promotion but as an independent charity event'.[12] To add credibility to the event, and assist in getting media coverage, McDonald's teamed up with the children's charity, Variety. The concept was that Variety could tap into its network of supportive celebrities and encourage them to work in a McDonald's outlet on McHappy Day. McDonald's primary target was to raise $250 000, but it had other goals too. To reach its target, it wanted national publicity to drive sales of Big Mac and 'enhance McDonald's general image as a good corporate citizen'. Variety mobilised 420 celebrities to 197 McDonald's outlets around the country. PPR even gained Variety's permission to use its letterhead to draft a 'live-read kit for on-air announcers'. As part of the project, Variety organised celebrities to deliver a McDonald's breakfast live on television on the day.

All up, PPR was delighted with the results. 'Every McDonald's restaurant in the country broke its highest trading record for a single day as well as for hourly trading', they boasted. Even though the day was publicly sold as a charitable event, PPR revealed that the benefits were measured against marketing yardsticks.

McDonald's needed to be able to judge whether the $100 000 budget, of which PPR's fees accounted for almost two-thirds, was justified. PPR calculated the same amount of air time and newspaper space would have cost in excess of $300 000 on normal advertising rates. However, as most of the coverage was soft-focus human-interest news coverage of celebrities, PPR asserted that editorial coverage was four times more credible than adver-tising. Accordingly, PPR claimed that the advertising value equivalent of the coverage was more than $1.2 million on an investment of a little over $100 000.[13] Not surprisingly, it has become a part of its annual marketing calendar.

Building McDonald's profile as a caring community-focused company is a comparatively easy task in the world of PR. The real character of a company, though, is tested when customers are hurt and the company is at fault.

McDeaths

Brian Page, a 42-year-old railway worker, had been busy before Easter 1992 buying furniture for a house he had just moved into at Mt Pritchard, a south-western Sydney suburb. On their way home, his daughter Melissa wanted to stop at McDonald's in Fairfield for lunch. Shortly after returning home, Brian Page began vomiting and had diarrhoea. As Page's symptoms were initially indistinguishable from a bout of the flu, his doctor gave him a medical certificate and sent him home. Page took to bed for the next three days but on the fourth day went back to work, even though he wasn't feeling well. His boss noticed that Page was unable to write properly and seemed disoriented and confused by his work. He was so concerned about Page that he called a taxi and sent him home, but by then Page recognised something was seriously wrong and went straight to Liverpool Hospital. What was unknown to Page and his doctor was that he had been exposed to Legionella bacteria. If detected early, Legionnaires disease can be treated with antibiotics. Untreated, it can be a killer. Two days after being admitted to the intensive care unit of Liverpool Hospital, Page died. On what would have been his 43rd birthday, more than 100 family and friends attended his funeral.[14]

Brian Page wasn't the only one who reported to hospital with these symptoms. In a short period, 22 people reported to hospitals at Fairfield, Liverpool, Camden, Bankstown and Lidcombe in south-western Sydney. Six, including Brian Page, died. Most Legionella outbreaks originate from poorly maintained water-cooled air-conditioning systems, which are meant to be inspected monthly, tested for concentrations of the Legionella and the small reservoir of biocide used to kill bacteria topped up. Identifying the origin of an outbreak of Legionnaires disease is no easy task as the disease has an incubation period of up to two weeks. Health Department investigators had to collate a list of all possible cases from hospital records and then identify the overlapping paths of those affected. Eventually they narrowed down the origin of the outbreak to a block in the central shopping strip in Fairfield. Within the suspected area sat an unremarkable McDonald's outlet.

In mid-July, McDonald's Engineering Development Manager, Peter Meadows, sent a reassuring memo to all the McDonald's outlets that had water-cooled air-conditioning systems:

> Fortunately for us the restaurant had in place a maintenance system on its cooling tower which was in excess of the Australian standard. Fortunately for us our tower was not the source of the outbreak. Heaven only knows what the result would have been had the store not had good housekeeping practices in place.[15]

According to an internal PPR document, the following month McDonald's got a tip-off from someone in the Fairfield City

Council, stating that it had been specifically named in the Health Department's draft report on the outbreak. With the benefit of advance notice, the company scrambled its crisis management team, comprising senior executives, PPR staff including Peter Lazar, its advertising agency and company lawyers. It is rare for crisis managers to publicly talk about their campaigns, but a few years later Lazar appeared in a food poisoning scare 'hypothetical' at a PRIA conference. Lazar, representing a hypothetical food company, stated that:

> getting community sympathy for the possibility of the company as a victim is much better said by a third party... it would be better for the Health Department or the Minister or the Police Department to suggest that this is a situation where the company might be a victim.[16]

McDonald's Fairfield crisis management team feared that in the worst-case scenario they would be specifically blamed for four of the six deaths, which could trigger lawsuits, 'falling national sales and a long term lack of confidence in the company and its products'.[17] The aim of the crisis plan, PPR noted, was to 'control damage to McDonald's reputation, avoid direct blame for the cause of the epidemic, to position McDonald's as concerned for the health of its customers and staff, to allay public concern and remove the issue from public focus'. Consistent with the desire to be positioned as the victim and not the culprit, McDonald's team developed a strategy, including testing 'the concept of "being downwind of the source"'. The team identified some of their primary objectives as being to 'present the truth—while under no circumstances accepting liability... avoid blame for the epidemic'. The team were also nervous about how the media would cover the department's report. To minimise surprise, PPR noted, 'indirectly, these journalists were approached and the issue, including their key leads were discussed'. How this was done was not revealed.

Anticipating that pressure from the victims' families may force the Health Department to make the report public, McDonald's team identified influencing the report's content as a key strategic goal. Subsequently, McDonald's Managing Director, Peter Ritchie, was informed by the department that the minister wanted the report to be made public. McDonald's crisis team, PPR later wrote, worked with the department to 'approve wording pertaining to McDonald's in the official report'. (The extent of the changes is unclear, but they claim that they were provided with an advance copy of the report 'for review' and that they 'influenced' the final wording.) Given the prospect that McDonald's would be adversely mentioned in the report, the crisis team decided their one hope would be to 'deflect media interest by timing public announcements with other major news events'. PPR claim that 'negotiation between McDonald's executives' and Health Department officers 'resulted in the report being made public on the same day as the NSW State Budget was to be released'. The Health Department provided McDonald's with a copy of its media release ahead of the media conference, and PPR claimed that they organised an 'on side' journalist to introduce a McDonald's-friendly question at the Health Minister's media conference.

In a media statement issued on the same day, McDonald's announced that it would 'put safety first for its customers and staff' and turn off all 19 water-cooled systems at its operations around the country. However, it refused to release information about the location of the 18 other systems in order to 'forestall a crisis of confidence' from customers. That night, McDonald's placed a newspaper advertisement in all national and metropolitan dailies, announcing its policy on the removal of water-cooled air-conditioning towers.[18] The big test, though, would be the potential impact on sales.

Morning radio commentators, PPR later gleefully reported, urged people to 'go out a buy a big Mac'. The crisis team were pleased to note that many did and that for the next four days there was a significant boost in sales, with the only dip in sales being at the Fairfield outlet. At the suggestion of their advertising agency, McDonald's also switched the mix of their television advertisements away from product-specific promotion to those extolling the company's philanthropic works. As Lazar explained a few years later, this was so that if McDonald's role was blown 'out of proportion people are reminded that you are putting a lot of money into tenants, the eisteddfod and Ronald McDonald House. It is a very good ploy... it worked its socks off'.[19] Not surprisingly, PPR and McDonald's turned down requests from journalists to explain how they handled the crisis. PPR thought it sufficiently safe, however, to submit their campaign to be considered for a PRIA's Golden Target Award for crisis management. PRIA, which claims to be the guardian of ethics in the PR industry, were sufficiently impressed with PPR's handiwork to give it a commendation.

Senior Vice-President of McDonald's Communications in the United States, Dick Starmann, wrote a personal letter to Peter Lazar, complimenting him on his assistance: 'I think it is safe to say that "the mission" was a success from everyone's standpoint... I'd like to buy you a beer and chat a little bit about some of my observations from the "legionnaire's week that was"'. Not everyone was a winner, though.

While McDonald's banked their proceeds from their sales boost, the victims and their families struggled with their loss. Several launched legal actions, which eventually turned up documents revealing McDonald's had covered up the extent of the problem with the cooling towers at Fairfield. The maintenance schedule prior to the outbreak contained alarming details. 'Tower was sprayed with hose only due to deteriorating

[sic] condition of tower basin... Tower is badly corroded', one report stated. One month before the outbreak of the deadly disease, another noted that 'both dosing pumps turned off'. Another, from a week before the outbreak, was equally disturbing: 'Inhibitor level is low due to water losses from cooling tower... Refilled dosing tanks with inhibitor/biocide... inhibitor empty, biocide empty'. Despite having previously claimed that it exceeded the Australian standard, another record noted that, after an inspection with a Fairfield Council officer, it was decided that the tower needed further cleaning and that 'monthly Legionella testing be *instituted* to ensure the cleanliness of the tower'[20] [emphasis added].

When Channel Nine's 'A Current Affair' (ACA) ran a story in 2001 about the ongoing legal actions by victims of the Legionella outbreak, McDonald's refused to be interviewed.[21] Instead, they insisted that ACA screen an earnest pre-prepared video news release featuring McDonald's Chief Executive Guy Russo. For more than a minute Russo had a free run to spin McDonald's side of the story:

> Any suggestion that McDonald's tried to diminish its respon-
> sibility at the time or since is wrong. On the contrary we have
> made all the facts available to the Health Department and the
> public in what was a highly emotional and complex situation.[22]

The main concession he did make was that settling the legal claims for compensation had taken too long. But it was cold comfort for Melissa Page and her two sisters who, after years of trying to resolve a compensation claim, gave up in frustration and accepted an offer they weren't satisfied with. Melissa Page told ACA.

> Someone should have been held accountable, someone should
> have been charged. He [Brian Page] didn't see us walk down

the aisle, he hasn't seen his grandchildren, he didn't look at
me and say your...daughter is beautiful. I missed all of that.

McLibel

Perhaps the biggest mistake of McDonald's corporate history
was taking offence at a small fact sheet, 'What's wrong with
McDonalds?—Everything they don't want you to know', distributed by a small group of activists in London. The leaflet outlined
concerns about McDonald's, including the employment conditions
for staff, animal welfare standards of suppliers, nutritional status
of McDonald's food and impact on rainforests from beef suppliers.
As the leafleting campaign built momentum, McDonald's reacted
by hiring private investigators to infiltrate the group.

In September 1990, McDonald's decided to try a legal sledge-
hammer. They served libel writs on five individuals connected
to the group and demanded an apology. Faced with the prospect
that they couldn't get legal aid funding and that their chances
of winning the case under the UK's archaic libel laws were
negligible, three of the five reluctantly apologised. The remaining
two, Dave Morris and Helen Steel, decided to fight the case and
represent themselves. The case was portrayed in the media as a
battle between David and Goliath—a global behemoth with a
dazzling legal team ranged against Morris, an unemployed single
parent, and Steel, a part-time bar worker. McDonald's were so
confident that, on the eve of the trial in 1994, they issued a
media release and distributed 300 000 brochures calling their
critics 'liars'. This opened the door for Steel and Morris to counter-
sue McDonald's, forcing the company to prove that everything
in London Greenpeace's—a group unrelated to the global environmental group Greenpeace—original leaflet was untrue.

The McLibel trial became the longest trial in British history,
involving 180 witnesses. Finally, in mid-1997, the judge delivered

his 800-page verdict, finding in favour of McDonald's on some counts, and awarded damages of £60 000 against the two defendants. However, McDonald's suffered a humiliating defeat on several key points, as the judge found as fact that the company does 'exploit children' through their advertising, and that they were 'culpably responsible' for cruelty to animals. He also found that McDonald's claims on the nutrition content of its food were not matched to reality, and that the company was anti-union and paid low wages.

As the McLibel story gained international profile, McDonald's Australia became aware that '60 Minutes' in Australia had been filming interviews with Steel and Morris. Once more McDonald's called on PPR for damage control advice. Central to PPR's strategy was to refuse to comment in an attempt to 'contain it as a UK issue'. 'We want to keep it at arm's length—not become guilty by association', they advised.[23]

As all crisis managers know, 'no comment' is interpreted by the public as a confession of guilt. Despite wanting to adopt a 'no comment' strategy, McDonald's needed to package non-cooperation a little more palatably and ensure consistency across all its spokespeople in the United States, the United Kingdom and Australia. Having recommended that Peter Ritchie, head of McDonald's in Australia, refuse to be interviewed, the PR team crafted a script for how he could plausibly decline. 'As you know, the UK have chosen not to be interviewed therefore I don't think its [sic] right that I should become the only McDonald's person that speaks on the issue', Ritchie's script stated. To deflect the possibility that other Australian media outlets might follow up on the '60 Minutes' story, the crisis team suggested all callers be referred to McDonald's in the United Kingdom. From Australia, the time zone difference alone would deter all but the most determined journalists. Lazar later explained that PPR told McDonald's they could see no benefit in being interviewed: 'What is the point? All you could possibly be saying is that your colleague in Britain made a bad decision.'[24]

To hose down the possibility that radio talk-show hosts Alan Jones, John Laws and Brian Bury would criticise the company, the team decided Peter Ritchie should speak to them 'because of his relationship with the presenters'.[25] The PPR team decided that ABC Radio and TV should get the cold shoulder 'because they have given significant coverage to the case in a positive [to Morris and Steel] perspective'. Neil Mitchell from Melbourne radio station 3AW was also on the blacklist. Print journalists, on the other hand, were provided with a written statement, but requests for interviews were refused. Radio news journalists were to be referred to McDonald's United Kingdom, while TV news and current affairs would be given only a written statement. It was a disciplined control of the flow of information, designed to ensure that journalists had only one choice when including 'balance' into the story, and avoided any opportunity for executives making unguarded comments or squirming on screen.

One scenario that the crisis team was not ready for was that the crisis management strategy would be leaked to '60 Minutes' for airing on their program. To their surprise, it did. However, several years later, Lazar said that the one thing McDonald's and some other corporations learnt from the court case was the futility of legal action against activists: 'We know how stupid it would be to do that.' Suing activists, he said, was always going to be a PR disaster. Even if McDonald's won the legal case, 'journalists weren't going to let David suffer the weight of Goliath'.[26]

MOP—All washed up

If some PR campaigns are directed at deterring inquisitive journalists or muzzling the voices of dissenting activists, others are designed to undermine corporate rivals. When Mothers Opposing

Pollution (MOP) emerged in late 1993, describing itself as 'Australia's largest women's environment group', many in the environment movement were puzzled.[27] MOP *appeared* to be a community group, but aroused suspicion simply because it seemed to have become too big, too fast to be a real community group. MOP claimed that its newsletter, *Women's Environment News*, was distributed to more than 10 000 women's groups, community centres, schools and others. MOP's primary concerns were with plastic milk bottles being wasteful, the supposed carcinogenic risks of milk in plastic, and purported impact on milk quality as a result of exposure to light. Suspicions grew when MOP's spokeswoman, Alana Maloney, organised a petition directed at Queensco-Unity Dairyfoods, who distribute milk in Toowoomba, 'to make milk available for sale in two litre cartons'.[28]

In no time at all, Maloney claimed 10 000 people had signed the petition.[29] Maloney even succeeded in persuading retail giants Woolworths and Franklins into collecting signatures on the petition and distributing an accompanying leaflet.[30] Soon afterwards, Maloney popped up in South Australia, where she claimed she had 5000 signatures on a petition pushing for a ban on plastic milk containers.[31]

Bruce Atkinson, a member of the Victorian Legislative Council who had received material from MOP, was also sceptical. Atkinson told parliament that there was no existing record of a person by the name of Alana Maloney, and that the dairy industry wondered if MOP 'has been set up as a front by the liquid paper board manufacturers to campaign against plastic milk bottles'.[32] When South Australian Minister of Environment and Land Management, Kim Mayes, raised questions about MOP's funding and real interests, Maloney played the underdog card and claimed that the reason MOP were unincorporated was 'we have had difficulty with the plastic industry hassling members ... so that is why you know we're now under attack, mainly because we are a women's group'.[33]

MOP also campaigned in New Zealand where they issued a 'Worldwide Warning' urging consumers to stop 'buying milk in plastic bottles because we believe there is a very real and deadly risk of innocent consumers contracting cancer'.[34] When MOP urged health authorities to investigate the issue further and act to protect consumers, NZ dairy authorities were dismissive.[35] However, publicity for MOP was a double-edged sword. When word reached Australia of Maloney's trans-Tasman foray, doubts about the group grew. Maloney refused to answer journalists' questions about the organisation's funding, legal status and activities.[36] MOP's push for an inquiry in New Zealand stalled.

MOP's luck ran out in February 1995. *The Courier Mail* in Brisbane revealed 'Alana Maloney' was really Janet Rundle, who ran her own public relations company, J.R. and Associates. Rundle was also a co-director of a Brisbane-based company, Vita Snax. The other co-director was Trevor Munnery of Unlimited Public Relations (UPR), a consultant to the Association of Liquidpaperboard Carton Manufacturers (ALC). For his part, Munnery denied any links with MOP or Alana Maloney, but refused to answer questions on his links with Janet Rundle. Janet Rundle, in turn, said that she didn't know Munnery.[37] Gerard van Rijswijk, the Executive Director of ALC, threatened to sue *The Courier Mail* if links were made between his organisation and MOP. He also denied any knowledge of links between UPR, Munnery and Maloney or Rundle.[38]

With MOP's public credibility wounded, MOP withdrew from high-profile public campaigning and opted for behind-the-scenes lobbying instead. In August 1995, six months after being outed, MOP lobbied the National Food Authority (NFA) to launch an inquiry into the effects of UV radiation on milk in plastic containers in supermarkets.[39] It was a claim similar to that played out in the courts in the United States a decade earlier. In 1984, the Paperboard Packaging Council (PPC) hired Ogilvy & Mather Public Relations to halt carton milk packaging's annual three to five per cent loss in market share to its plastics rivals. One of Ogilvy & Mather's strategies was to 'create and publicise a consumer affairs' issue based on scientific studies that milk in paper is more nutritious [and] better tasting', though they didn't resort to creating a front group.[40] Plastics manufacturers took legal action and won a permanent injunction against the paperboard manufacturers over claims on the effects of light on milk quality.[41]

A legal win in the United States, though, made little difference to MOP's plans in Australia a decade later. In late September 1995, MOP formally applied to the NFA to amend the Food Standards Code to protect the vitamins in pasteurised milk from degradation through exposure to light.[42] At first the NFA were non-committal and requested additional information, including a copy of MOP's articles of association.[43] Rundle indicated the organisation was not incorporated, even though she had claimed the group had 10 000 members.[44] On the same day, van Rijswijk issued a media release announcing a street protest in Perth by 'banner waving teenagers', with their sign proclaiming 'I want my milk in cartons please'. It was, he said, 'part of a campaign by ALC (Australians Love Cartons) to promote the advantages of buying milk in cartons'.[45] The NFA turned a blind eye to MOP's informal status and decided that the issue warranted further investigation.[46] Both MOP and the ALC argued that, as a minimum, milk in plastic containers should be labelled to include a warning about the effect of light on milk quality. They also wanted the food standards code amended so that greater protection be given to milk 'against photo-degradation'.[47] However, the tide was running against MOP and the ALC.

Three-quarters of the submissions, mainly from dairy groups and plastics packaging companies, opposed MOP's application.[48] One plastic manufacturer, Prepac, included in its submission a copy of a major newspaper advertisement titled *Buy plastic, Bye-Bye vitamins* that had been run in New Zealand by the carton board manufacturer, Tetra Pak, which it cited as evidence that 'Tetra-Pak are prepared to fight very aggressively to defend their sales'.[49] On 1 August 1996, the NFA's project manager and principal legal adviser contacted Rundle to inform her that it was proposed her application be rejected.[50] In a last desperate flurry of activity, van Rijswijk faxed off a four-page memo reiterating the major points of their submission. MOP also protested.[51] But the NFA dismissed Rundle's request for a public hearing, and, having failed to win an inquiry and with its public credibility crippled, MOP finally folded.[52]

For those in the know, MOP had demonstrated both the potential and limitations in the use of a PR-driven front group to damage a commercial rival. However, the use of 'astroturf' groups, a termed coined in the United States to describe fake grassroots groups, wasn't confined to a struggle for market share in the packaging industry.

Running interference

In 1997, Seph Glew and his business partner, Paul Tresidder, bought the old Arnott's Biscuits factory site in the Sydney suburb of Homebush, just a hop, skip and a jump from the site of the 2000 Olympics. Glew and Tresidder's company, Kirela Pty Limited, had grand plans to redevelop the property into a huge $250 million office, entertainment and retail complex that would vie for customers with Westfield Holdings Burwood Centre a few suburbs away. But before Glew could proceed, his company needed the site to be rezoned from industrial land to one that allowed the development of office space, restaurants and retail developments.

A few months after lodging their rezoning application with Concord Council in early 1998, they received a copy of a brochure that had been distributed among local residents by the North Strathfield Resident Action Group (NSRAG), warning that the developer's plans for a shopping complex would cause a major increase in traffic and even drug dealing. In common with many small local residents groups, NSRAG was not incorporated, but more puzzling was that no one locally had ever heard about the group. Soon other newsletters were in circulation, one authorised by a 'Mr. K Mason', which listed a phone number, but Glew's attempt to contact him was unsuccessful. By a stroke of luck, however, a council officer mentioned that she had written to the residents group and had been contacted by a Ken Hooper, who had left his contact details. Glew unsuccessfully tried to make contact with Hooper.

Frustrated by his inability to find out who was behind the campaign against his proposal, Glew did a company search and hit pay dirt. Ken Hooper was listed as one of two shareholders in the PR company, Hooper Communications. Hooper, who had been a high-level media adviser to state Liberal leaders Nick Greiner and Kerry Chikarovski, had gone into the PR industry. In a bid to flush Hooper out, Glew faxed him a draft copy of a brochure he proposed distributing in the local community. In response, Hooper's solicitor warned that any damage to Hooper or the company's reputation from the publication of the brochure could result in a substantial damages claim. The letterboxing efforts of NSRAG ceased but a new group, Sydney Independent Retailers (SIR), emerged. Their brochure claimed that Glew's proposal would 'threaten the viability' of existing retail outlets, cause 'traffic chaos' and result in 'Cabramatta-style drug haunts'. This time, however, it was authorised by Hooper from his

Woollahra address. Why would a PR consultant from leafy inner-city Woollahra be all that interested in a development in Homebush?

Glew launched legal action in the Federal Court of Australia under the Trade Practices Act provisions outlawing false and misleading conduct. He argued that the covert campaign was likely to constitute a breach of the Act, and accordingly sought access to key documents to enable him to determine whether further legal action was merited. Glew had included a colleague of Hooper's, Jim Photios, as a respondent to the legal action. After the legal action was launched, Photios had approached Hooper's client, the shopping centre developer Westfield, and sought legal indemnity for his role in the covert campaign. After being rebuffed, Photios turned to Glew and agreed to testify in return for indemnity against legal action. In a sworn affidavit, Photios spilled his guts.

Attached to his affidavit was a 'highly confidential' May 1998 memo from Hooper that revealed the scheme to create a front group to mask Westfield's role in the operation: 'This week we will undertake to obtain a Post Office Box, as a contact point for flyer reference for local residents and will issue the first of a series of flyers, designed to establish a legitimate protest group.'[53] Hooper had also outlined his political strategy to mobilise local residential opposition to the proposal and direct it at the local Labor Party member of state parliament, John Murray, and the Mayor of Concord Council, Peter Woods. Hooper also bragged that he had been involved in blocking other retail developments at Parklea, near Blacktown, and at Hornsby, as well as in a campaign in Bondi. The court granted Glew's application for access to documents.

As the legal action gained momentum, Westfield Holdings was forced into an embarrassing backdown. Where it had earlier denied any connection with Hooper, Westfield Chairman Frank

Lowy, who had just been made a Companion of the Order of Australia, apologised on behalf of the company.[54] 'We have been guilty of a lack of transparency and openness, and that is a matter of great regret and embarrassment to the company', he said. 'Steps have been taken to ensure that activities of this nature do not occur again.'[55] Westfield revealed that they had previously hired Hooper to work on eleven separate local grassroots campaigns against rival retail developments, or to provide 'background assessments about opposition to Westfield's development proposals'.[56] Despite the apology, Westfield continued to fund Hooper's legal defence.

In July 2004, Westfield forked out $3.5 million to settle Glew's legal action, but without admitting guilt.[57] In the aftermath of the court win, Glew was inundated with people telling him of their experiences with suspect community groups. 'There were dozens of people who told me of their experiences, some bringing in boxes of documents', he said.[58] But Glew's court win was something of a pyrrhic victory. Despite Concord Council agreeing to the rezoning, the NSW State Government had imposed restrictions on the project, banning the development of a cinema complex and substantially reduced its scale. The outing of Westfield's front group may have caused some short-term embarrassment, but the planning restrictions stayed in place. In 2004, though, Westfield got a taste of its own medicine when the Concerned Residents and Businesses Against Centrepoint Overdevelopment took out full-page ads opposing Westfield's plan to redevelop Centrepoint. One of the members of the group, retail giant David Jones, admitted that they contributed to the group, but wouldn't disclose how much.[59]

While some in the PR industry were aghast at the front group operations, Ian Kortlang, a prominent Australian PR practitioner, was more worried about how visible it had become. 'People may decide the family pet needs to be put down, but they don't like seeing it strangled in front of the grandchildren', he said.[60] Westfield's embarrassment was limited, though. Not long after the Hooper debacle, Westfield contributed $100 000 to fund the Environmental Council of Sacramento (ECOS) in California, which joined with another group, South County Citizens for Responsible Growth, to run a legal action against a rival development.[61] As a result of the lawsuit, the project was temporarily canned, but later proceeded.[62] Westfield's Peter Lowy defended funding legal actions taken by community groups. 'We have a responsibility to our shareholders to protect and grow our assets. If somebody else is trying to develop there, we will be aggressive in both fighting them and attracting that retail demand', he said.[63]

In early 2006, Westfield funded a group in California called Arcadia First!, which opposed the development of a major retail mall adjacent to Westfield's Santa Anita mall.[64] In May 2006, two months after Westfield obtained land entitlements to allow the company to expand its Southcenter project in Oregon, Westfield funded the establishment of Alliance for South End. A Westfield lawyer, Peter Buck, established the group which, on the first day of its existence, launched three separate legal appeals against the development of a retail development in Renton, Oregon.[65] However, Westfield's use of the tactic has generated resentment. 'We are going to take a stand against a bully', one Westfield opponent stated at a public rally.[66] But using a community front had its limits; one of its legal bids to stop the development was rejected on the basis that the non-profit group did not have legal standing to object.[67]

•

While issues management and crisis management enthusiasts extol the socially useful benefits of their model of how PR should work, the reality is less enticing. The insistence of the food industry to be free to advertise to whomever they like, irrespective of age, is hardly an example of an adequate response to rising levels of obesity. McDonald's issues management style has included resorting to oppressive lawsuits, for many years evading responsibility for the deaths and injuries from the outbreak of Legionella originating from its Fairfield outlet, and only making changes to its menu and marketing when Morgan Spurlock brought the obesity issue into sharp relief. AANA, a trade association of which McDonald's is a member, threatened to mobilise the media companies dependent on its advertising revenues as a part of a lobbying campaign against restrictions on advertising. Just as issue management campaigns have been used to thwart community pressure for changes in public policy, covert campaigns have also been used by companies against their commercial rivals. Far from narrowing the gap between public expectations and the performance of corporate and government agencies, all too often issues management and crisis management has only succeeded in exacerbating it.

THREE
PUSHING DRUGS

In the heart of the Sydney suburb of Ryde—Australia's drug industry alley—50 marketing managers and PR advisers from major drug companies, including Pfizer, Bristol-Myers Squibb, Novartis and GlaxoSmithKline, pondered the industry's poor public standing. The drug industry representatives—used to hustling everything from drugs for guys struggling with their love life to life-saving cancer treatments—were depressed. 'I am appalled by our reputation', Group Vice-President Far East Region for Schering Plough Rod Unsworth told a room of industry heavy-hitters, discussing 'reputation management' at the third Australian Pharma Marketing Congress in May 2005. Unsworth warned of the potentially fatal consequences of the Australian drug industry's defensive posture. 'If we say we are going to just look after the opinion leaders and we don't give a damn about the public, we are dead. And if we let the debate be about price, we are dead', he said.

The marketers in the industry, Unsworth warned, 'will tell you time and time again sell the benefits, do not get into areas of weakness'. The problem for the drug industry is that it has numerous 'areas of weakness' and little public credibility. With low credibility and a ban on the 'direct-to-consumer' advertising of prescription medicines, drug industry PR campaigns rely heavily on the widespread use of 'third parties'. To realise its potential, the drug industry needs a receptive environment— apparently independent doctors willing to champion and prescribe drugs, 'patient' groups that can lobby governments, and media to help push new 'breakthrough' drugs, and a media thirsty for 'good news' stories. The industry not only wants government regulators to approve and pay top dollar for new and purportedly 'innovative' drugs, but also to back away from strict enforcement of restrictions on how they are promoted. It is an industry where the boundary lines between marketing, lobbying, PR and advertising are blurred at best.

Not surprisingly, with so much of its marketing conducted behind the scenes, the industry has been tainted by revelations of drug companies' largesse towards doctors, the withholding of data on life-threatening side-effects, its shadowy involvement in patient groups, and massive drug recalls. The biggest controversy of them all was the recall in October 2004 of Merck Sharp & Dohme's anti-inflammatory drug Vioxx after US authorities revealed an increased risk of heart attacks after just 18 months of use. In Australia, Vioxx probably caused several thousand additional heart attacks among its 300 000 consumers.[1] The death toll attributable to the drug is unknown, but several hundred seems to be a conservative estimate. 'It killed more Australians than the Bali bombing and we are spending billions on anti-terrorism projects but we are not doing anything about drug advertising', says Dr Peter Mansfield from the drug industry watchdog group, Healthy Skepticism.[2]

The global drug industry, which generated revenues of more than US$608 billion in 2006, is the world's most profitable stock market sector. According to IMS Health, the leading drug industry market analyst, the United States alone accounts for just under half the world's total drug consumption. Australian drug sales represent only 1.3 per cent of the global market, but $7.8 billion in sales is still a welcomed contribution to the coffers of the global drug companies. But against the backdrop of controversies, some in the Australian drug industry pragmatically think that courting the 'key opinion leaders' is probably the best they can hope for. Corporate Affairs Manager for Bristol-Myers Squibb, Michael Moore, told the conference that the industry had built 'third party support' among 'our key stakeholders in government, among the medical profession and the health consumer representatives'. However, he was far from persuaded that the industry should or could win over a sceptical public:

> Whether that wins the hearts and minds of Joe Public out there, I don't think it will, and, at the end of the day, I don't think it matters so much because we will still sell product whether or not Mum and Dad in the suburbs like pharmaceutical companies.

It is a sentiment that is common in the drug industry.

An internal drug company market research document, unearthed by a UK parliamentary committee, stressed the importance of 'third parties' in reaching potential customers, which the drug company dubbed the 'missing millions'. The company analysis stated:

> Strong perception exists amongst missing millions that any communication or information provided needs to be from a credible source, eg. GP, 'medical organisation', patient group— NOT outwardly a drug company—stigma attached to pharmaceutical companies that they'd just be doing it to sell drugs, not seen to be patient focussed.[3]

Two central themes promoted by the drug industry are that doctors act as independent agents free of drug company influence, and that the industry has a 'strict' voluntary code of conduct that polices marketing promotions. Drug industry self-regulatory codes are designed to look good, but how effective are they?

As part of its investigations into the operations of the British drug industry, the UK House of Commons Health Select Committee obtained access to 49 boxes of marketing and PR records from five global drug companies: GlaxoSmithKline, AstraZeneca, Pfizer, Eli Lilly and Wyeth. Of particular interest to the committee was the question of the degree of compliance with the Association of the British Pharmaceutical Industry's (ABPI) Code of Practice. The consultants who reviewed the documents noted that 'building long-term, sustainable relationships with various stakeholders, including journalists, key opinion leaders (KOL) and well respected medics and academics emerges as pivotal in dealing with such negative publicity and when conducting PR activities generally'.[4] The code emphasises the need for member companies' communications to be 'objective' and 'balanced', but the consultants noted that PR campaigns featured sponsored 'key opinion leaders' who were expected to counter controversies over product safety in ways that were 'frequently neither objective nor balanced'.

Codes of misconduct

In Australia, a story screened in August 2001 on Channel Nine's 'Sunday' program, revealing that Pfizer had sponsored a Sydney Harbour cruise for doctors, replete with scantily clad dancers, sent shock waves through the industry.[5] In a bid to head off the controversy over its promotional practices aimed at doctors, the drug industry volunteered to adopt a tougher regime of self-regulation. For any industry under sustained public pressure, self-regulatory codes are a more palatable option than government regulation. They can preclude the adoption of tougher regulatory standards where misdemeanors are often played out in full public view, where records are accessible via freedom of information legislation, and ministers and officials are accountable to parliament and its committees. More importantly, the development, interpretation and enforcement of standards are open to greater industry influence than would otherwise be the case.

In 2002, the peak drug industry group, Medicines Australia, submitted a draft code governing the marketing of drugs to the Australian Competition and Consumer Commission (ACCC) for approval. After submissions from interested parties, the ACCC proposed to approve the code, subject to several proposed amendments, the most significant of which would require all member companies to publicly disclose planned sponsorship of events and travel for doctors, 'to ensure that benefits are not provided which might affect doctors' prescribing habits'. Despite the denials of doctors, research indicates that drug company gifts and subsidies pay off handsomely. Of course, if the door to our doctor's surgery featured a big panel stating 'this doctor is sponsored by ____' with a long list of drug companies underneath, we would doubt the independence of the advice being given to us. But drug industry gift-giving and doctors gift-taking is something deemed too delicate for patient's eyes.

Not surprisingly, the drug industry reacted with horror to the ACCC's proposed amendment, fearing that being required to publicly provide details of forthcoming events would spark more critical publicity. 'Uninvited parties (such as the media)', they complained, could 'attend educational meetings for ulterior purposes. This risk could deter doctors from attending.'[6] The Australian Medical Association (AMA) claimed that the disclosure of doctors' interactions with drug companies could 'expose doctors and pharmaceutical companies to public derision by people with unfounded prejudices', and objected to the inference that wining, dining and free travel could influence a doctor's prescribing behaviour.[7] However, in a meeting with the ACCC, the AMA flagged that they could live with a condition that disclosed details of the events, but only after they were over. It was a concession the drug industry was quick to pooh-pooh, suggesting the AMA didn't realise 'the enormity of the administrative burden' it would impose on the drug industry.[8]

Instead of backing the public's right to know about potential conflicts of interest, the ACCC meekly accepted the drug industry's counter-proposal of a three-member panel, to be known as the Code of Conduct Monitoring Committee (CCMC), to sample materials promoting drug industry 'educational' events and report its observations in the annual report on the code.[9] After the code came into force in January 2003, the CCMC sought copies of invitations to events covering only six classes of drugs. It was deluged with material on more than 4700 'educational' events targeting doctors, with an average of 40 events per week in 2005 alone.[10] But despite the staggering number of events, none were investigated for any possible breaches of the code. However, the committee did caution member companies against the inclusion of 'pictures of chefs or food' or hotel venues on invitations. A majority of the committee even dismissed the suggestion that holding 'educational' meetings at wineries and restaurants could be considered extravagant or inappropriate.[11] The following year the committee's comments were more opaque. The unnamed venues, they wrote, 'reflected the professional standing of the audience'.[12]

The code also provides for complaints over drug advertisements and other promotional activities. Since Medicines Australia's code receives the ACCC's blessing, close to two-thirds of the complaints have been made by rival drug companies, while individual doctors and healthcare professionals were the next largest group. Of course, the drug companies are those with most to gain from a successful complaint, and have the capacity to follow through on a complaint. Health professionals, individuals and academics, on the other hand, do it in their own time and for the public benefit. More puzzling is the relative inaction of the Therapeutic Goods Administration (TGA), the government regulator. Even though the TGA has the power to act independently, it now defers to the Code of Conduct Committee convened by Medicines Australia. As a complainant, the TGA, which is entirely funded from fees from drug industry 'clients', has submitted just a handful of complaints a year. Drug companies have lodged four times as many complaints as the TGA.

Just over a third of complaints result in adverse findings, with the most common penalty involving no more than the withdrawal of the offending promotional material. In a submission to the ACCC, the drug industry claimed that the penalty that worries drug companies the most is being directed to issue corrective letters or advertising to doctors. Where fines are imposed, they are commonly for less than $25 000, a puny amount in the world of drugs. For example, the Australian government spends more than $1.1 million *per day* subsidising consumers' access to Pfizer's cholesterol-lowering drug, Lipitor. Medicines Australia defends these low fines on the grounds that they are comparable to potential penalties under state-based fair trading laws and the Trade Practices Act. It is a misleading comparison, as drugs are regulated under the Therapeutic Goods Administration Act, which provides for fines of up to $200 000 and suspension or withdrawal of marketing approval. Even though populist talk-radio shock jocks and politicians talk up mandatory sentencing for individuals who are repeat offenders, the Code of Conduct Committee is very forgiving of recidivist drug companies. In the eyes of the committee, repeated offences by the same company only matters if it involves a repetition of exactly the same breach of the code.

There are major procedural problems with the code, too. Companies are represented by senior staff and lawyers, while health professionals and individuals are largely left to fend for themselves. The committee, unlike a court of law, does not have the power to require documents to be produced to assist complainants. Complainants are even required to agree to keep adverse findings confidential until an appeal process is completed. The drug industry body bizarrely claims that 'it would be an abuse of process to release information about a complaint before the complaint was finalized'.[13] In the real-world judicial system, cases are conducted in open court, proceedings can be reported, and the public release of initial judgements is not contingent on an aggrieved party first having an appeal heard. For the drug industry, there are real PR benefits of its own system. Even if the committee makes adverse findings against one or more companies, they are released in one batch every six months. Even then, it is rare for the media to notice the appearance of a new report buried in the backblocks of the Medicines Australia website, the arrival of which is unannounced by a media release.

In late 2005, Medicines Australia submitted an application to the ACCC for a renewal of the code. With a few minor tweaks, the drug industry felt sufficiently confident to request it be approved for five years. In August 2006, the ACCC re-authorised the code for three years, with only one significant change. A little over a month before finalising the code, the ACCC proposed that companies be required to submit a monthly report detailing each 'educational' event it organised for doctors, the venue, the purpose of the event, the hospitality provided, the number of attendees and the total cost of the function. To ensure a level of transparency, the industry would be required to post the details on a website every six months. Once more, both Medicines Australia and the AMA were horrified. Disclosure of this infor-mation, Medicines Australia complained, 'impugns the reputation of the medical profession' and is 'by implication, an apparently baseless denigration of the character of MA industry executives'.[14] The drug industry was also nervous about the additional workload involved in collating the information on an estimated 700 events a month, even though it is hard to imagine that adding a one-line summary into a spreadsheet is anything other than a tiny fraction of organisational effort. The drug industry also complained that the information could be 'misused' by the media or consumer groups.[15] Of course, the only way this information could be used is in public debate over the appropriateness of drug companies subsidising the 'education' of doctors. For its part, the AMA argued that disclosure may deter drug companies from organising such events and doctors from attending them.[16] This time, the ACCC held firm and rejected the hand-in-hand protests of doctors and drug companies. But before the ACCC announced its decision, health journalist Ray Moynihan revealed in *The Australian* and the *British Medical Journal* that in July 2005 Roche spent approximately $65 000 on a dinner at a top Sydney restaurant for 300 cancer specialists.[17]

When the ACCC announced its approval for the revised code, the President of the AMA, Dr Mukesh Haikerwal, complained that the amendment was a 'knee-jerk' reaction to revelations about Roche's largesse.[18] An unnamed Medicines Australia spokesman told *The Australian* that the first time they heard about the amendment was the same day that the story on Roche's conference dinner broke.[19] Both the AMA and Medicines Australia statements created the impression that the amendment was the arbitrary reaction of the ACCC to one media story. But both the AMA and the drug industry had been fully aware of the proposed change well before Moynihan's story was published. Medicines Australia had made two submissions and met with ACCC staff twice to discuss these exact changes, and the AMA had made a written submission on the proposed amendment two weeks before Moynihan's story appeared.[20,21] The drug industry's feigned howls of protest had nothing to do with surprise and everything to do with making a legal challenge against the ACCC's decision seem somehow defensible. A spokesman for Medicines Australia, Paul Cross, from the Canberra-based PR firm Parker & Partners, declined to comment on the discrepancy between their expressed concerns and their prior knowledge of the ACCC proposal.[22] Behind the scenes, though, Medicines Australia was canvassing its options. The Chairman of Medicines Australia, John Young from Pfizer, sent a memo to member companies, suggesting that members 'should weigh up the likely negative public perception of the industry' if it decided to appeal the ACCC's decision. The unpalatable alternative would be 'the potential ongoing negative publicity that may occur every six months when the required report of educational meetings is published'.[23] Three weeks later, they announced they were appealing the ACCC's decision. A subsequent communications plan by Parker & Partners, which was also leaked to *The Age*, described the rejection of the ACCC's disclosure proposal as creating 'a long-term political problem' for the industry.[24] 'While the current government is in principle opposed to compulsory regulation, we cannot presume the political circumstances will not force their hand. In addition, the Labor Party will almost certainly look to compulsory regulation as a part of their policy platform for the next federal election', the plan stated.

The objection of both the drug industry and the AMA begs the obvious question: if doctors aren't influenced by the food, travel and accommodation subsidies and the cost of these is not excessive, why the secrecy? The director of Healthy Skepticism, Peter Mansfield, argues that the accusation is not that doctors are corrupt, but that receivers of gifts usually want to recipro-cate the favour. He said:

We are not saying that it influences all of the people all of the time but clearly it influences enough of the people enough of the time to provide a good return on investment. We know there are wide variations in prescribing patterns by doctors and we know that exposure to drug companies is a key factor that predicts the difference in prescribing patterns.[25]

Mansfield's vision is that doctors should simply emulate the standards expected of sporting umpires and judges. 'Umpires and judges don't receive gifts and we need to move towards that', he said.

Hard sell

Bill Curtis, the founder of the Sydney-based advertising and medical communications company Curtis Jones Brown, views adverse coverage of 'disease awareness' campaigns as indicative of the industry's reputation problem. He told the Australian Pharma Marketing Congress:

Why is it that disease awareness advertising, principally on television, is seen as the nasty dark subversive work of an industry that shouldn't be allowed to do this? Answer. Because we are seen to be that sort of industry: manipulative, dark, menacing.[26]

Ideally, the drug industry would like to be able to promote prescription drugs through 'direct-to-consumer' advertising via ads in newspapers, radio on television and websites. The media companies Fairfax and News Limited, which are suffering from declining classified advertising revenue, are receptive to the idea. Despite acknowledging the potential for advertising to manipulate emotions to sell drugs, Fairfax spokesman Bruce Wolpe said the company would support a relaxation of the rules. News Limited was similarly inclined.[27] At present, the only OECD countries to permit it are New Zealand and the United States. In the absence of being able to undertake open-slather advertising, the drug industry has funded 'disease awareness' campaigns via corporate-friendly patient groups. The formula is simple: identify a disease or condition, argue that it is under-diagnosed, and that under-treatment is very costly to society. Often this promotion is done by funding an existing patient group, or if none exists, creating one. To enable the media to provide coverage without having to do any legwork, a patient and a doctor are often identified as frontline media talent and a video news release made to help sell the good news story that a treatment is available for the condition. An annual week named after the disease and hosted by the patient group can help break through the normal news clutter. In some cases, a full-scale television or newspaper adver-tising campaign is launched. Before a flood of potential patients reaches the offices of doctors, a separate, but largely invisible, campaign has been rolled out to help entice doctors to prescribe a new drug.

The drug industry was a latecomer in teaming up with patient groups. Initially, the industry's attention was captured when, in 1987, ACTUP, the US AIDS activist group, targeted both the drug industry and government regulators for their sluggishness in responding to the AIDS crisis. Slowly the drug industry turned its mind to enlisting citizens and patients as lobbyists for favorable government decisions on approvals and the all-important pricing deals. In January 2000, a $500-a-copy report by a former drug industry executive, Fred Mills[28], reviewed the global state of play in drug companies working with patient groups. Based on infor-mation provided to him by drug companies, Mills noted some of the pitfalls for non-profit groups:

> The perception that industry-patient group collaborations can lead to unwelcome publicity is the principal reason holding

many potentially fruitful relationships back. Despite this, groups are biting the bullet and some of the early efforts at partnerships have been very worthy and mutually beneficial.

Casting his eye Down Under, Mills noted that both Eli Lilly and Janssen 'have very good contacts with Australia's Schizophrenia Fellowship, the largest patient group for schizophrenia in Australia'. Now known as the Mental Illness Fellowship of Australia, the group acknowledges Janssen-Cilag, which markets the antipsychotic drug Risperdal, as a 'foundation sponsor'.

Where many of the initial drug industry 'partnerships' were with relatively small groups, the extraordinary sales of Pfizer's Viagra changed industry views on what was possible. In Australia, Viagra gained approval for sale from the TGA in September 1998, subject to the addition of warnings of potential side-effects, such as heart attacks in patients using other medications. Approval for sale is one thing, and being included in the government subsidised drug list, the Pharmaceutical Benefits Scheme (PBS), is another matter entirely. For Pfizer, the stakes were high. Unsubidised Viagra cost $70 for a four-pill pack. Subsidised, it would cost most consumers $20, and cheaper still for concession card holders. The cost, though, would be borne by taxpayers, with the tab initially estimated to reach as much as $200 million.

In June 1999, the Pharmaceutical Benefits Advisory Committee (PBAC), which decides whether a drug should be included in the drug subsidy scheme, rejected Pfizer's application on the grounds that it would benefit few medically. Pfizer was not amused. Six months later, it launched legal action in the Federal Court against the committee and its individual members. In March 2000, the court dismissed the drug company's appeal and ordered it to pay the Commonwealth's legal costs. The following month Pfizer lodged a further appeal. However, even a favourable ruling would only allow it to have its case before the PBAC reheard. Pfizer decided to supplement its legal manoeuvres with a little grassroots lobbying by contributing $200 000 to Impotence Australia (IA) for a 'disease awareness' advertising campaign on impotence, with some behind-the-scenes help from Hill & Knowlton. The advertisements did not disclose Pfizer's funding, but their role was soon revealed in separate articles in *Australian Doctor* and the *Australian Financial Review*. IA's Executive Officer, Brett McCann, conceded that he 'could understand that people may have a feeling that this is a front for Pfizer'.[29] 'Without their funding we wouldn't be able to do the work we do with men and their partners—that's the bottom line, we couldn't do it', he said.[30]

Aside from the initial embarrassment over the covert role of the drug company, there was little long-term damage, as few subsequent news stories ever mentioned the corporate funding behind the non-profit mask. Pfizer was successful in its second legal round, so it went back before the PBAC.[31] But the drug industry's success in having a drug company representative included as a member of the PBAC made only marginal difference.[32] The committee approved Viagra being added to the PBS, but only for men with one of ten specific medical conditions. IA was less than happy, with McCann publicly arguing for unrestricted access.[33] Worse news was to follow for Pfizer. In February 2002, the then Minister for Health, Kay Patterson, rejected the committee's recommendation. Once more, McCann objected.[34]

One Pfizer promotional ad, however, went too far when it claimed that 'one in three men have erection problems', a claim parroted in some media stories. The study wasn't a survey of the general population, but only of those who visited a doctor. Even then, those in the group had an average age of 71 and only had erection problems 'occasionally'. Following a complaint by an academic to the CCMC, Pfizer was fined $10 000, less than the cost of one large newspaper advertisement.

Pfizer wasn't the only company having promotion problems. With the marketing success of Viagra, other companies muscled in on the 'erectile dysfunction' market. Eli Lilly introduced Cialis and GlaxoSmithKline and Bayer introduced Levitra. The changing market saw IA add new sponsors to its cast of credits. In a joint media release, IA, Bayer and GlaxoSmithKline unveiled a 'Men's Health Initiative' to be championed by the well-known actor, Gary Sweet. The 'performance pack initiative' involved mailing samples of Levitra to 11 000 general practitioners around the country to coincide with media appearances featuring Sweet. In *Pharmaceutical Marketing*, a global trade magazine, two PR industry executives argued that the careful use of celebrities could boost media coverage, 'particularly when you do not have a strong news story'. But they warned, celebrities needed to be carefully 'managed':

> Are they going to stay on message, or is there a possibility that they could be involved in a scandal in advance of your launch? It may be sensible not to involve them in 'off the cuff' questions from journalists. Try to pre-plan interviews so your celebrity is not caught off guard.[35]

As a result of Australia's ban on direct to consumer advertising, Sweet wasn't supposed to mention Levitra by name, but in one radio interview he did.

Drug regulator TGA thumped its chest when asked by the ABC's 'Media Watch' about the apparent breach of advertising standards. Breaches could attract fines of up to $200 000 or, in the worst case, revocation of marketing approval, the TGA sternly warned.[36] The TGA lodged a complaint with the drug industry's code of conduct committee over the Levitra website, but not about Sweet's naming of the drug. The committee upheld the complaint, but, as it often does, imposed no sanction beyond the withdrawal of the offending material.[37]

Pfizer's success with Viagra and IA spurred other drug companies to spend more effort courting patient groups. After a few years of off-again, on-again discussions between the drug industry and the Consumers' Health Forum of Australia, the peak health charities group, the two set to work drafting guidelines on effective collaboration. The underlying principle of the guide, which was developed with funding from a coalition of eleven drug companies, is that patient groups can retain their independence while simultaneously accepting drug company funding. In the supporting notes to the guide itself, the drug industry explicitly noted that one of the benefits of funding non-profit health groups is the prospect of 'securing support when applying for Pharmaceutical Benefits Scheme listing of medicines'.[38] The groups—which span patient groups, traditional health charities and consumer groups—all had different ideas about where to draw the line. A few insisted that any funding compromised their independence. Others argued that drug company funds should be quarantined to funding specific projects. Others wanted core funding from sponsors. Faced with disagreement between the groups, the guide's steering committee hedged its bets. The antidote to concerns about corporate funding compromising non-profit groups' independence, they suggested, could be overcome by gaining funding from *more* drug companies. It is a suggestion that asks non-profit groups to regard the notion of maintaining strict independence as being a decidedly unfashionable relic of the 20th century.

The guide also leaves it to non-profit groups to decide whether the public should be informed about who was sponsoring whom. The guide, however, makes clear that a quid pro quo for corporate cash is an expectation that public criticisms of drug companies will be muted:

Effective relationships may influence the way in which public criticisms of partners may be made. It is an act of courtesy to advise the other party of a particular position that will be taken publicly, but the parties should still enjoy the right to free expression of views. Parties should agree about the way in which differences of opinion will be handled in the media.

Despite considerable moves to require disclosure of drug company largesse towards doctors, patient groups have been largely off the radar. However, Helen Hopkins, the Executive Director of the Consumer Health Forum, has flagged that drug company sponsorship of travel or 'hospitality' for patient group representatives is an 'emerging issue'.[39] 'So far as we know, it is an occasional phenomena [*sic*]', she said.[40]

The problem though, is that with neither patient groups nor drug companies required to disclose funding or other support, no one has a clue as to the magnitude of the problem. One global review of patient groups found that, while many patient groups accepted drug company funding, few included conflict-of-interest statements on their websites. Of the eleven Australian patient groups reviewed, only four had their annual report on their website, but none of these revealed the percentage of income from drug companies.[41] 'We would like to see some more transparency in all these arrangements', Hopkins said.[42]

There are significant risks to the public from compromised patient groups. The more non-profit groups become dependent on drug company cash, the more they will emphasise the over-medicalisation of conditions when non-drug treatments may be more effective. Perhaps even more worryingly, when a drug has worse-than-expected side-effects, patient groups that should be playing the role of a watchdog may avoid barking for fear of irritating a sponsor.

I can't see clearly now

Sometimes the decision of a drug company on the other side of
the world results in boosting the prominence of a new patient
group in Australia. By 2003, Novartis Ophthalmics was keen to
organise the Australian launch of Visudyne, a drug to treat macular
degeneration, a condition that degrades the quality of vision and
predominately affects those over 50. However, it found that there
was little awareness of the condition among the target population
or doctors. Novartis turned to the Sydney office of Edelman, one
of the largest global players in the healthcare PR sector, to raise
the profile of the condition. In an article contributed to the trade
magazine, *Pharmaceutical Executive*, Nancy Turett, the president
and global director of Edelman's health practice, explained that
'the heart of PR is third-party credibility. Third-party messages
are an essential means of communication for validating scientific
credibility, for legitimizing products, for building brand and
disease awareness, and for building defences against crises'.[43] Not
surprisingly, a central Edelman strategy for Novartis was funding
a credible 'third-party' patient group in Australia.

According to an Edelman document, US$80 000 was allocated
to the little known Sydney-based, Macular Degeneration
Foundation (MDF), with a further US$90 000 to cover expenses.
To help ensure visibility for the campaign, Edelman set about
creating Macular Degeneration Awareness Week and recruited
the entertainer Kamahl—the singer appeared in a community
service announcement distributed to radio stations, and was
included in a video news release distributed to television stations.[44]
Edelman was later pleased to note that three-quarters of all the
media stories tracked in its media monitoring echoed the drug
company's key themes.

It is not surprising that a patient group would appreciate
greater attention for a potentially serious condition, but how

safe is its sponsor's drug? On its website, MDF advises that after the Visudyne treatment:

> minor changes in your vision are very common and usually settle by the third week. Do not expect an improvement in your vision. You may continue to lose vision in the first 6 months of treatment. After this the vision tends to stabilise.[45]

Novatis Australia's mandatory three-page consumer information sheet that accompanies the drug describes potential side-effects as affecting only 'a few people'. However, it notes that the drug 'has caused a severe decrease in vision shortly after treatment in a small number of patients. Partial recovery of vision was observed in some of these patients'. The same company is far more explicit in disclosing the potential risks to US customers. There, the company's mandatory information sheet runs to thirteen pages. 'Severe vision decrease', it states, has been reported in one to five per cent of patients within the first week, with only 'partial recovery of vision' in some patients. Novartis also warns that other side-effects, including severe vision loss, anaemia, pneumonia and gastrointestinal cancers, were reported in between one and ten per cent of patients, and at a rate greater than those tested with the harmless placebo in the drug trials.

The PR beauty of drug companies funding third parties is that 'patient' groups aren't bound to publicise the information regulators require their sponsor to give to customers. With many consumers turning to the Internet as an important source of information on their health and possible treatments, the MDF are doing no favours for those afflicted with the disease by under-stating the potential consequences of using Visudyne. In this instance, instead of being an independent group that puts the interests of patients first, the foundation is pushing a drug that may make both the eyesight and overall health of some consumers worse. Instead of demanding that regulators require Australian consumers be given the same information as is routinely given to US consumers, the foundation has remained mute.

When it comes to gaining approval of new drugs, PR companies aim to coordinate the lobbying efforts both of doctors, who are deemed 'product champions', and patients demanding the treatment. To the untrained eye, media coverage of new drugs appears to be largely spontaneous when it really is part of a carefully crafted plan. Ahead of the public launch of a heroin treatment drug, Subutex, in March 2000, Reckitt Benckiser, the diversified company that manufactures the drug, hired Reed Weir Communications (RWC), a small specialist drug and biotech PR company based in Sydney, to handle the PR campaign. For Reckitt Benckiser, the key to its success was gaining approval from the PBAC, which would determine if the drug would gain access to the PBS. Just in case the application was rejected, RWC prepared a fall-back plan.[46] The first stage of the plan, RWC later wrote, would be to send letters to the private addiction treatment clinics, 'expressing disappointment at not having achieved a subsidy and re-inforcing the commitment to dialogue with Government to reverse the decision'. They also anticipated that they would need some grassroots lobbying muscle ahead of a resubmission. 'RWC would encourage triallists, drug users seeking treatment and private clinic directors to write a personalised letter to encourage a reversal of the decision', they wrote in a submission nominating their campaign for a PR award.

In the end, plan B was unnecessary as the PBAC approved the company's application. Ahead of its marketing launch, RWC selected a national network of nine 'high-profile clinicians as spokespeople', and facilitated media training for them to ensure they 'relayed key messages in every interview'. For the company, the launch worked a treat and, with PBS approval in the bag, there was no need to activate the backup plan. Other companies, though, take a different tack. In recognition of the importance of sales teams, the Australian Pharmaceutical Research, Innovation & Marketing Excellence Awards were launched in June 2005. At the inaugural gala dinner, Pfizer Australia took out the first prize in the 'marketing campaign' category for its campaign promoting Lipitor, a drug to treat high cholesterol levels. In 2005, Lipitor was the world's biggest-selling drug, reaping US$12.9 billion for Pfizer. In Australia, Lipitor is the most prescribed drug on the PBS, with the federal government forking out $433 million in 2004–05.[47] To win the award, the company was required to demonstrate how its marketing prowess helped 'to improve or to maintain the product's performance'.[48] However, the details of the winning company's submissions remain a closely guarded secret. Pfizer's spokesman, Craig Regan, also emphasised their submission was not for public eyes.[49] In the world of drug pushing, awards are to be admired by peers, not scrutinised by the public.

One novel strategy for promoting Lipitor involves not overtly pushing the drug at all. The Lipitor Institute sounds like it might be housed in a quaint sandstone cottage, but it exists solely in cyberspace. Three times a month, in cities around Australia, practice managers and doctors front up for a weekend small business management skills workshop at a five-star hotel. After a session on cardiology case studies, the doctors settle in for workshops on financial management skills and an 'on-the spot financial health check on their surgeries', all courtesy of the Lipitor Institute.[50] Call the Institute itself, though, and you won't get a cardiologist or a business trainer, but be pointed in the direction of Sara Turner from DDB Remedy, the healthcare unit in the advertising company DDB. Turner herself is not allowed to speak to journalists on just what the Institute does, but Craig Regan, Pfizer's Media Affairs Manager, can.

Regan, a former adviser to Australian government ministers, including Philip Ruddock, explained that the courses 'are very popular and we see that the doctors love it'.[51] Why would a drug company spend tens of thousands of shareholders' money running basic business management courses? 'It is obviously good for us to be well thought of by doctors...It doesn't involve products so we can't be criticised for pushing one drug over something else', he said. As for how many doctors attend or the role of DDB Remedy, Regan wasn't prepared to say. 'We're declining to provide further specific information that might be useful to competitors', he wrote in an email.[52]

Peter Mansfield from the drug industry watchdog, Healthy Skepticism, believes there is method in Pfizer's apparent generosity. 'Pfizer will have done research on what doctors appreciate having help with', he said. In the United Kingdom, two drug industry researchers subdivided doctors into four categories, with one being tagged the 'entrepreneurs (wolves)'.[53] The purpose of the Lipitor Institute, Mansfield believes, is to creating a sense of rapport with the entrepreneurial 'wolves' so that they agree to see company sales representatives. 'It is not that it has a direct effect on prescribing. The main point of gifts is to obtain access for their reps so they can use the techniques that work on those individuals', he said.[54]

Another marketing award winner was Novartis Pharmaceuticals Australia, which picked up the award for the launch of Elidel, a prescription cream used to treat the skin condition eczema. In an interview after receiving the award, Joseph Hartzell from Novartis's marketing team was upbeat: 'The PR in particular was very, very powerful. We got lots and lots of press'.[55] Novartis had every reason to be pleased with the uncritical media coverage they got. 'Most importantly, Elidel does not bring with it the worrying side-effects of common steroid creams and ointments, such as skin thinning', the freebie Melbourne commuter paper *MX* confidently predicted.[56] Channel Seven's 'Today Tonight' breathlessly reported in October 2003 that 'a medication called

Elidel, taken orally or in a cream, hoses down the itch and stops the scratch factor without steroids' side-effects'.[57]

Behind the PR blitz was Burson-Marsteller, which had been commissioned by Novartis to hype the product 'to drive patients to their doctors to request Elidel and ensure healthcare professionals suggested Elidel as a treatment option'.[58] It worked, with the original sales targets set by Novartis being exceeded. However, the same month that Novartis collected its marketing award, the first warnings about Elidel's potentially serious side-effects started to emerge. In Australia, the TGA warned that its US counterpart had received ten reports of cancer in children and adults using Elidel. The drug remained on the market, but the Australian government regulator cautioned that its use should be for as short a period as possible.[59] By January 2006, the US Food and Drug Administration had stepped up its warning, explicitly cautioning against use of the drug on children under two.[60] Even though the FDA are worried about the drug, photos on Novartis's Eczema Control website continue to include those of a young baby—well under two—with the caption: 'I don't like sleepless nights'. In the eyes of the Australian regulator, the original approval for use on babies over three months remains in place. In the PR-driven media, there is silence about Elidel's side-effects.

Pfizer's fickle philanthropy

Pfizer Australia's Manager of Government Affairs, David Miles, recounted at a drug industry conference that in the period between accepting his job as Pfizer's Australian lobbyist and his first day of work, he tallied the comments people made to him about his career choice. According to Miles, who had worked as an adviser to Liberal Senator Nick Minchin, 90 per cent of the feedback consisted of comments such as 'you are going to join the dark side' or 'the evil empire'. Among PR practitioners, philanthropic contributions have been a long-standing way to help soften the image of a corporation and buy support. Pfizer, the world's largest drug company, was one that needed some image softening.

In 1999, the Australian arm of the company wanted to develop a 'cause-related marketing' project with a non-profit group to tie into the company's image-enhancing efforts based on its 150th anniversary in September that year. Pfizer turned to Cavill + Co, a Sydney-based consultancy that specialises in designing programs that 'have integrity, longevity + are strategically sound' between corporations and non-profit groups. Company founder Hailey Cavill sought out the Royal Life Saving Society Australia (RLSSA) as a potential partner to run what was initially to be a three-year program. The practical goal was to reduce the death toll by drowning of children under the age of five. Dubbed 'Keep Watch', the RLSSA's goals were all about saving lives. On the other hand, Pfizer's dominant interest was in using the project to change how the company was perceived, with five of the company's six project objectives being image-related. First and foremost was using it 'to demonstrate Pfizer's corporate positioning: Life is our life's work (i.e. to demonstrate this as a commitment and action rather than just words alone)'.[61]

The project had specific target audiences in mind—the government, health professionals and its own employees in particular. To help achieve this, RLSSA produced radio and television community service announcements, produced hundreds of thousands of brochures and posters for distribution to general practitioners' offices, pharmacies and childcare centres. For a company like Pfizer, community service announcements—which television stations air without charge for recognised charities—are a boon. Not only is the company's philanthropic work promoted, it is done at a fraction of the cost of running advertisements in its own name. In December 2004, the company and charity were seeking to enlist federal politicians as 'Ambassadors for Toddler Safety'. The aim was to have ambassadors act as 'a community contact point and distribution centre for information on preventing toddler drowning'. For Pfizer, though, it potentially opened up contact with a range of politicians and their staff who had the potential to influence their business. After the ambassadors launch, though, the six-year program came to an end. 'We mutually decided it was time to move on and do something different', said Pfizer spokesman Craig Regan.[62]

Pfizer's concern about deaths from drowning was tested when, just weeks after the federal Parliament House launch of the 'Ambassadors for Toddler Safety', the tsunami swept through East Asia and parts of Africa, killing approximately 300 000 people. The World Bank estimated that the tsunami destroyed the homes and livelihoods of a further two million, creating a humanitarian disaster of unprecedented scale. Around the world, there was a massive response. The generosity of citizens put companies such as Pfizer under enormous pressure to make a substantial contribution. Pfizer—which had global sales of US$52.5 billion, with net income of US$11.3 billion that year— was ranked as the world's seventh-largest corporation. In a series of announcements, Pfizer committed itself to contribute a total of US$20 million in cash and US$60 million worth of medicines to the tsunami relief and rehabilitation funds. However, six months later, Miles told a drug industry conference that the general view among drug companies in Australia initially was that contributions to the appeal would not be publicised. Then, he recounted, callers to talkback radio programs in Australia demanded to know what the industry was doing. After Medicines Australia publicised various company contributions, Miles said talkback radio callers argued that even more should be contributed. According to him, the reaction was, 'Well, if you can give $60 or $70 million, why can't you give $100 million? Or why can't you do $120 million?'

'We would be better off giving five million and shutting up', Miles said, only half-jokingly. 'As soon as you get into big numbers people think you can double or triple it.'

•

Were the talkback radio callers who expected Pfizer to do more being unreasonable? US$20 million may sound like a lot, but it was less than a day's profit for Pfizer, and less than the top-five company executives were paid in salaries, bonuses and stock that year.[63] The US$60 million worth of medicines was an inflated figure, too, as it was calculated on the wholesale price—on which the company still makes a profit—not on the much lower marginal cost of production. Just how miserly Pfizer's contribution to the tsunami relief efforts were was illustrated when the CEO of Pfizer at the time, Hank McKinnell, was given a US$180 million golden parachute to leave the company in February 2007.[64]

Miles' candid comments on Pfizer's philanthropy are symptomatic of why the drug industry has a reputation problem. Group Vice-President Far East Region for Schering Plough, Rod Unsworth, who appeared on the panel alongside Miles, thought the industry could look to other industry sectors for inspiration on how to rebuild its public and political credibility. 'I spend a bit of time in Canberra talking to people', he told the conference. 'The one industry that is ahead of us by a long way is the tobacco industry... The tobacco industry runs a better government campaign and public relations exercise in Canberra than we do. Now that scares the hell out of me', he said.

FOUR
KILLING THEM SOFTLY

Promoting 'corporate social responsibility' (CSR) reports and programs as a panacea to public disquiet about corporate misbehaviour has become one of the growth areas in the PR industry. PR companies have formed specialist CSR practice groups, headhunted former activists as consultants, and extolled the necessity for companies to invest in CSR reputation-management programs. *CSRWire*, an online news service for corporate social responsibility devotees, proclaims that 'CSR integrates the interests of stakeholders—all of those affected by a company's conduct—into the company's business policies and actions. Corporate Social Responsibility embraces two main concepts—accountability and transparency'.[1] The idea that companies are listening and responding to the concerns of their critics seems appealing at first glance, and is an invitation to us to suspend scepticism. After all, surveys reveal most Australians want companies to behave responsibly, but we harbour the strong suspicion that they don't.[2]

There are those in PR who are keen to hitch a ride on the corporate CSR bandwagon as a way of rehabilitating the reputation of the PR industry. Former Public Relations Institute

of Australia (PRIA) national president, Lelde McCoy, told one
PR industry conference that the growth of CSR and reputation
management work offered the possibility of creating a 'less hostile
operating environment for our organisations'.[3] But within the
ranks of PR, there is scepticism about the contradiction between
PR companies hyping the virtues of transparency and accountability to clients while being secretive themselves. In a *PR Week*
survey on CSR, one anonymous participant commented on 'the
irony that one part of a communications business could
pronounce on CSR while another division represented Third
World dictators'.[4] Scepticism aside, however, CSR is viewed by
many in the PR industry as just another issues management tool
to help quarantine public criticism of their clients to the margins
of public debate and forestall the imposition of government
regulation.

At the heart of CSR is the proposition that companies should
decide who to talk to, what to listen to and what to disclose.
Instead of putting citizens in the centre of a democratic process
to determine binding standards for *all* companies, CSR expects
citizens to voluntarily cede power and let PR professionals decide
standards that *only some* companies should embrace. Despite all
the hyping of 'stakeholder' involvement and the verification of
social reports, neither amounts to much when companies are
in the driver's seat.

When British American Tobacco (BAT) was contemplating
producing its first corporate social responsibility report, its UK-
based Corporate and Regulatory Affairs director, Michael Prideaux,
sketched the benefits of the process as being to build 'credibility'
and establish a 'robust platform on which to build a reputation
communications campaign'. He wrote:

> The process will not only help BAT achieve a position of
> recognized responsibility but also provide 'air cover' from

criticism while improvements are being made. Essentially it provides a degree of publicly endorsed amnesty. In addition, it will provide access to important stakeholders and opinion-formers that, until now, have proved difficult to engage.[5]

But sometimes it was impossible to avoid public humiliation.

In mid-June 2006, Justice Jim Curtis from the Dust Diseases Tribunal of New South Wales ruled that British American Tobacco Australia Services' (BATAS) destruction of scientific records relating to the health effects of smoking, under its Orwellian-sounding 'document retention policy', was for 'the purpose of a fraud' under the New South Wales Evidence Act.[6] 'If BATAS was not selectively destroying scientific documents prejudicial to its position in future litigation, how is it that lawyers rather than scientists were assigned to judge the value of research material?', he wrote in the judgement. BATAS had been hoping that its legal team could persuade the tribunal that it didn't need to pay part of the $200 000 compensation costs for the death of Alan Mowbray, a motor mechanic who had worked for transport services company Brambles Australia. After Curtis's damning ruling, which cleared the way for a discovery of documents and a full trial, BATAS opted to negotiate an out-of-court settlement.

Three weeks later, British American Tobacco Australia (BATA), the parent company of BATAS, succeeded—in conjunction with other major Australian corporations—in persuading a parliamentary inquiry to embrace its preferred standards for 'corporate social responsibility' reporting. Instead of a mandated minimum for reporting against social, environmental and other parameters, BATA argued that companies should be left to their own devices to determine what to disclose. The role of governments, BATA argued in its submission, should not be in setting minimum standards for CSR reporting, but in providing incentives for companies to embrace social reporting. In essence, BATA prefers an 'all carrots, no sticks' approach. To demonstrate its social reporting credentials to the parliamentary committee, BATA attached a thick wad of the various social reports dating back to 2001–02, along with grandly titled documents such as its 'Statement of Business Principles'. BATA was keen to reassure the parliamentary committee that the 'stakeholder' consultations undertaken in preparing the reports were convened by independent facilitators, and that the reports are verified by a suitably qualified auditor. The sub-text was that, if you don't trust the corporation, then you can trust the process and the credibility of the big-name facilitators and auditors. BAT's latest global report alone runs to 230 pages. In addition, there are the social reports being churned out by BAT's subsidiaries in 32 other countries, too.

For global companies, collecting, analysing and synthesising data across numerous operations and countries is an expensive and management-intensive process. Why would companies spend millions undertaking such a time-consuming process? Companies or industries that are on the nose struggle to attract and retain good staff, shareholders become restive, and media can be more inquisitive. A manager with BATA, Kate Hogben, explained at a PR conference that BAT's reputation affected its ability to 'gain a "seat at the table" with government'.[7] If executives aren't taken seriously by government, companies are vulnerable to being ignored altogether.

BAT isn't the first company to travel the social reporting road. In the 1990s, the traditional corporate philanthropy approach was viewed as woefully inadequate after a series of high-profile scandals. Nike was widely dammed for buying products from overseas contractors exploiting cheap labour. In response, Nike and others in the clothing and footwear industries devoted much greater attention to developing, overseeing and reporting on new labour standards of suppliers and their sub-contractors. Shell was another company that was profoundly traumatised in 1995 by its unsuccessful attempt to dump the disused Brent Spar oil platform in the Atlantic Ocean and its seedy involvement with the Nigerian military dictatorship, which executed Ken Saro-Wiwa and eight other environmentalists. In response, Shell launched a major PR program, which impressed some in CSR circles.

If high-profile activist campaigns were pushing corporations from one direction, the growing influence of ethical investment funds was exerting pressure from another. Fund managers were demanding much more detailed information to enable them to decide which publicly traded companies to invest in. Companies that had traditionally relied upon the annual report as their primary communication tool were being deluged with detailed surveys on their social and environmental policies and practices. Getting the tick of approval from funds such as UK-based FTSE4Good and the US-based Dow Jones Sustainability Index was viewed as important to help reassure wary investors and suspicious activists.

BAT's enthusiasm for social reporting was spurred on by the determination of the World Health Organization (WHO) to curb the climbing global death and injury toll from the tobacco epidemic. WHO estimates that tobacco-related deaths are likely to rise from the current five million per year to ten million by 2025, with most deaths occurring in developing countries. When the former Norwegian Prime Minister, Gro Harlem Brundtland, took over as Director General of WHO in July 1998, she made clear her determination to ensure that the negotiation of a Framework Convention on Tobacco Control was completed by end of her term in May 2003. In May 1999, the World Health Assembly—convened under the aegis of the WHO and comprising representatives from 191 countries—voted unanimously to support the negotiation of a convention that would bind signatories to implement strategies to curtail tobacco's deadly toll. This was an alarming development for BAT. It was still a highly profitable company, but each year its sales volumes slipped a little further. If the long, slow decline of tobacco consumption in developed countries was cause for concern for BAT, even more worrying was the looming prospect of an effective global convention that was legally binding on signatory nations, including the expanding markets in less developed countries.

With a 15 per cent share of the global tobacco market and operations in over 180 countries, BAT is the world's second-largest private tobacco corporation. In 2006, it sold 689 billion cigarettes and generated total revenue of £23.9 billion ($52.3 billion). Based on WHO estimates, the UK-based Action on Smoking and Health calculated BAT was responsible that year for as many as 750 000 deaths. Not long after negotiations commenced, it was apparent that the convention was likely to back the policies the tobacco industry hated most—bans on advertising and promotion, support for tax increases, and protecting people from exposure to second-hand smoke. The global tobacco industry—dominated by companies including BAT, the US-headquartered Philip Morris, and Japan Tobacco International (JTI)—was facing its biggest-ever crisis. Its preferred focus—on voluntary measures, industry-controlled youth smoking initiatives that had little effect, and 'safer' cigarettes—looked likely to get short shrift. An internal 1999 BAT memo sketched how politically isolated the tobacco industry had become. WHO, Gro Harlem Brundtland, the World Bank, and health ministers were all assessed by BAT as 'hostile', with only finance ministers and tobacco growers, the UN Food and Agriculture Organization and the World Trade Organization being listed as 'allies'. Even worse for the tobacco industry was the WHO's determination that tobacco companies would be excluded from direct involvement in the negotiations of a convention.

An internal BAT assessment accepted that a binding convention was inevitable, and that BAT needed to concentrate on 'lobbying and reputation management'. 'The question we need to ask is: Can the tobacco industry move itself ahead—fast enough and far enough—of the WHO agenda to negate the need for the convention and enhance its reputation in the process?', one memo asked.[8] In BAT's view, its best strategy was to try and limit their losses:

> We need to consider a set of policy changes we consider necessary to convince our priority stakeholders that sensible economic, political and public health goals can best be achieved via a co-operative tobacco industry, rather than one that is in permanent conflict with the WHO.

BAT's memo noted that their campaign activities to date had been 'aimed at maximising opposition' to the WHO's Tobacco Free Initiative proposals, including unidentified 'initiatives to publicise through academics and think tanks, the implications of global governance for world trade and national sovereignty'. BAT wanted to organise 'third parties' to deliver its message, but without leaving any fingerprints.

BAT's social reporting project emerged in the hope that it could help mobilise allies, court moderate community groups, and deflate the momentum towards a tough binding convention. One internal document, titled 'strategy for launching "sensible regulation"', stated that the objective was to 'strengthen BAT's position as a responsible and visionary company on the back of our call for "sensible regulation" and thereby strengthen our leverage vis-à-vis the WHO'.[9] In its more optimistic moments, BAT hoped that if its campaign gained sufficient traction it would be able to contain the tobacco convention to a 'principles only' declaration that would leave ample flexibility for the tobacco industry. In one memo, written after a meeting with the accountancy firm KPMG, BAT noted 'the publication of a social report is to a large extent an inevitability'.[10]

Getting down to business

On a sunny September morning in 2001, a small group gathered in the sixth-floor conference room at the Museum of Contemporary Art in Sydney's fashionable distrcit of The Rocks. The task of the handful of people assembled in the museum's smoke-free room was to canvass ideas on how to make BATA a socially responsible company. BATA's PR company at the time, Jackson Wells Morris (JWM), was politically well-connected and boasted substantial experience when it came to advising corporate clients, but had little experience organising a 'stakeholder' consultation process. So BATA hired Laurel Grossman and her colleague, Mathew Wilson, from the Melbourne-based Centre for Stakeholder Research (CSR) to convene a series of meetings around Australia. CSR described its mission as being to 'facilitate dialogue...to reconcile differences and encourage mutual development and growth which will, in the long term lead to a sustainable future'.[11] BATA knew that to entice any of its critics to participate in the process, it would need to create an expectation that the process would be fair and rigorous. As bait, it promised to respond in writing to all issues identified by those attending its social report meetings, and these would be incorporated into the final report. As further reassurance, BATA emphasised that the whole process would be verified by a global audit company, Bureau Veritas.

As with many PR programs for multinational companies, those in Australia were working from a global template. BAT's London head office hired the Tarrance Group, a US-based PR and polling company with a history of working for tobacco clients, to develop a 'stakeholder classification mapping' system for use on a country by country basis. Using this system, in-country social report managers were required to screen potential invitees. But BAT did not disclose the system to those invited to attend, and has not made the mapping system public. However, some of the details were later to be found buried in the first social responsibility report published by BAT's Sri Lankan subsidiary, the Ceylon Tobacco Company (CTC). The report reveals the stakeholders who were 'deemed to have a high business impact' were further subdivided according to where they were on a spectrum of views ranging from 'sympathy,' 'neutrality' to 'hostility'. Stakeholders were then categorised according to whether they were considered to have a high, medium or low 'degree of flexibility' with respect to tobacco issues. An accompanying chart in the CTC report revealed that 'hostile' stakeholders were expected to either have a low or medium level of 'flexibility', but would be substantially outnumbered by those classed as 'neutral' and 'sympathetic' participants. The CTC was the only one of the initial fourteen BAT social reports to divulge details of the Stakeholder Mapping and Classification System. It seems that was too transparent for the liking of BAT's head office, and no further details have been released.

Unknown to those invited to the meetings around Australia, Grossman's CSR had prepared a Stakeholder Mapping and Classification Report for BATA in May 2001.[12] Even without knowing about the report, Australian tobacco control advocates boycotted BATA's meetings. The core tobacco control activists knew, based on their own experience and from the industry's own internal documents, that BAT supported voluntary measures precisely because they wouldn't dramatically reduce tobacco consumption.

Their scepticism was well justified. Publicly, BAT had insisted that stakeholders could discuss any issues they wanted, without the outcomes being predetermined.[13] However, a 'social reporting process diagram' later disclosed by BAT's Sri Lankan subsidiary, Ceylon Tobacco Company (CTC), revealed that one step in the global social reporting process was to 'select and prioritise issues and scope' before even commencing the first 'dialogue' meeting.[14] Curiously, it was a step omitted from the near-identical diagram in BAT's global social report.[15] Well before the first 'dialogue' meeting commenced, BAT globally had also identified three priority theme areas of 'risk information and understanding', 'risk reduction' and 'business integrity'. In its report, CTC explained that BAT United Kingdom had identified six core platforms that all the participating 'end markets'—BAT-speak for country subsidiaries—were 'to adopt as topics for discussion in stakeholder dialogue'. These BAT UK-identified topics included the demonstration of 'commitment to combating under-age smoking', and the promotion of 'sensible' regulations governing the manufacture and marketing of tobacco products, and the demonstration of good 'corporate conduct and accountability'.[16]

Another critical aspect of BAT's social reporting was the selection of facilitators who would lend the process an air of authenticity. In Australia, BAT hired Susan Halliday, who had recently completed a term as the Howard Government-appointed Federal Sex Discrimination Commissioner and, before that, had been the Assistant Director of the Business Council of Australia. In other countries, similarly high-profile individuals were recruited, including a former bishop in the United Kingdom, media commentators and presenters in Argentina and Hungary, a 'media executive' in Uganda, and a former High Court judge in Zimbabwe. Despite all the money and effort invested, BAT's process floundered. In Australia, for example, the meetings were so poorly attended that BATA refused to even disclose the number who turned up. The story was similar elsewhere. But having committed itself to the process, BAT had to roll out the reports, with the overarching global report among the first. In a low-key event in London in May 2002, BAT's then Chairman, Martin Broughton, launched the company's inaugural 81-page global social report. Anticipating scepticism, Broughton used one of his punchiest lines up front: 'This is a serious piece of work; it is not a "PR" document.'[17]

BAT claimed that its social responsibility report was drafted in accordance with the Global Reporting Initiative (GRI) guidelines as well as AA1000, another social reporting standard promoted by the UK-based group AccountAbility. The GRI guidelines state in the 'society' section that corporate reports should contain information on 'consumer health and safety'. One of the core indicators, the guidelines state, is 'existence and description of policy for preserving customer health and safety during the use of products and services'. While BAT's global social report disclosed that three of its employees had been killed and 37 involved in serious accidents during 2001, it omitted any estimate of the number of people who had been killed or seriously affected by consuming its products.[18] In fact, in its initial 2001 report, BAT ignored half of the indicators recommended by GRI. For BAT, the beauty of voluntary guidelines is that they are unenforceable, with no penalty for non-compliance.

In Australia, BATA's social report process was suspended in March 2002 when Victorian Supreme Court Justice Geoffrey Eames ruled in favour of dying smoker Rolah McCabe, who was suing BATAS for damages. The destruction of BAT documents had compromised the ability of McCabe's legal team to discover relevant information to such a degree that Eames proceeded straight to awarding damages against the company. (Later that year, BATAS won their appeal against Eames's decision.) When BATA's report emerged in March 2003, it echoed much of the content of its parent company. 'Our credibility and sincerity is often questioned and we need a process that is widely regarded as being transparent', BATA's Chairman, former New South Wales Premier, Nick Greiner, wrote in the foreword to the 154-page report.[19] Across the front cover, in case anyone wondered about their good intentions, were emblazoned the words 'openness, transparency, listening, responding, accountable, engaged, understanding'. Despite the flowery language, Greiner and his colleagues could not even concede that nicotine is addictive, instead preferring to describe it as 'a naturally-occurring substance in the tobacco plant which is thought to have a mild stimulant effect'.[20] The report also avoided acknowledging the devastating health effects of the tar created when tobacco is burnt, stating merely that it 'consists of many different chemical constituents and classes of constituents'.[21]

Around the world, stakeholders who had participated in good faith soon discovered that BAT had no intention of listening to what they had to say. BAT Malaysia was told that that the company should 'consider eventual cessation of all marketing (i.e. advertising and promotion) efforts of cigarettes—even to adults'. For the company, however, this was unacceptable. 'The suggestion to stop marketing directly to consumers is currently beyond our responsible marketing targets', they bluntly wrote in their response. BAT's subsidiary in Argentina, Nobleza Piccardo, reacted in similar fashion when confronted with 'unreasonable' demands from its stakeholders, who insisted that Nobleza Piccardo should quit the manufacturing of toxic cigarettes within ten years.

While BAT was developing its social report, it was also busy with parallel initiatives that it hoped would kill off the tobacco control convention. BAT hoped that a convention that put public health ahead of free trade would be found to be in conflict with World Trade Organization (WTO) rules. To press its case, the Chairman of BAT, Martin Broughton, invited the WTO Director-General, Mike Moore, to join him at the Rugby World Cup final in Cardiff on 9 November 1999.[22] To BAT's delight, Moore accepted. An internal BAT memo revealed that the purpose of the invitation was not to watch the rugby, but to 'create a platform for dialogue on the WHO Tobacco Free Initiative's impact on WTO principles'.[23] 'A smoker and former NZ ally, Moore may prove key in helping to resist calls for the WHO's TFI proposals to be built into the WTO system', the memo to Broughton stated. BAT's best-laid plans, though, came to nought. Shortly before the meeting, Brundtland gained an undertaking that the WTO wouldn't intervene in the tobacco control convention. In letters to Broughton in April 2000 and again in October 2000, Moore was the bearer of bad news: 'The WTO does not have any influence over the tobacco negotiations taking place in the World Health Organization. Unfortunately there is nothing I can say with reference to your submission to WHO on its proposed tobacco convention.'[24]

Globally, BAT had another card it hoped would pre-empt the parties to the tobacco control convention from adopting binding standards on policies the industry feared most, such as a ban on advertising. At a meeting on 1 December 1999 in Geneva, BAT, Philip Morris and JTI agreed they had to make some concessions to the WHO. In September 2001, BAT and several other tobacco companies unveiled an international voluntary code for marketing, grandly titled *International Tobacco Product Marketing Standards*. According to BAT, these new 'globally consistent international marketing standards' represented a 'raising of the bar' and 'establish a benchmark for the industry world-wide'. But a leaked memo from a Wall Street tobacco analyst for Credit Suisse First Boston Group punctured BAT's hype. It was the analyst's view that the major companies were trying to counter the WHO standards, and was sceptical that the proposed standards represented a 'raising of the bar'.[25] 'In many countries the existing laws or industry codes are already more restrictive than the provisions of the international marketing standards', the analyst noted.

Despite the best efforts of the US government and the tobacco industry, the Framework Convention on Tobacco Control was adopted in May 2003. Undeterred, BAT in Australia and elsewhere continued churning out ever-bigger social reports. But, what hasn't been reported is significant. Late in 2005, it was revealed that BAT had been secretly operating a tobacco plant in repressive North Korea.[26] For four years of its social reporting blitz, BAT had successfully concealed an entire business operation.

In Australia, BATA dropped using Grossman's company, preferring instead KPMG's Ethics and Sustainability Advisory Service. Just as the release of BATA's first social report was stalled by the controversy over its 'document retention' policy, their second report, which was originally due out in March 2006, was caught up in the fallout from the ruling in the Dust Diseases Tribunal. But BATA still ducks and weaves when it comes to protecting the health of consumers. When the federal government proposed the introduction of graphic photos on cigarette packs featuring health impacts such as mouth cancer, BATA mailed tobacco retailers packs of 200 sign-on letters for customers objecting to the changes, to be sent to the federal Minister for Health, Tony Abbott.[27] The new standards were introduced, but, in deference to the lobbying campaign, the size of the image was reduced from the proposed 50 per cent of the pack cover to 30 per cent. But even when the new standards came in, BATA had a trick up its sleeve. On the inside of the cap of its Winfield brand, BATA printed the word 'Anyhow', made famous by actor Paul Hogan in a 1970s television advertising campaign.[28]

BATA has also objected to proposals for a ban on tobacco products being on display at point of sale in shops, and opposed taxation increases. Nor has BATA opted to protect those who don't choose to smoke. In what has proved an effective rearguard action, BATA has encouraged opposition to bans on smoking in pubs from the Australian Hotels Association. Even though the company concedes that 7 per cent of Australian bushfires originate from cigarette butts, it has also opposed the mandatory introduction of 'fire safe' self-extinguishing cigarettes. Nor can it bring itself to disclose how many customers die from consuming its products. With BATA selling in excess of 11 billion cigarettes in 2005, representing 45 per cent of the market, it stands to reason that it is responsible for approximately the same percentage of the smoking-induced death toll. If social reports are all about revealing the inner workings of the corporate conscience, the deaths of more than 8500 deaths of BATA-loyal customers don't appear to trouble the company much. For the indicator requiring disclosure of measures to preserve customer health, all BATA could bring itself to state is that 'we comply with all local laws and regulations. All of our tobacco products carry a government health warning, as required by law.'[29]

It would be nice to think that for all their slickness, no one would be taken in by social reports, let alone from a tobacco company. After all, if a notorious tobacco company can pull off a corporate makeover with a social report, any company could. But some have been persuaded by them. BATA was included in the 2005 Corporate Responsibility Index, published by the *Sydney Morning Herald* and *The Age*. The index is based on corporate self-assessments, which are then reviewed and scored by the accountancy and consulting company, Ernst & Young. Even though BATA ranked as among the six worst performers out of the 27 companies in the index, exactly where it ranked was not made clear to readers. Its ranking was further obscured by the inclusion of a bold tick of approval for BATA in the index table graphic, which the key explained meant it was in the 'less than 75%' category, the lowest possible rung. If parents were sent their children's school reports with the lowest category being less than 75 per cent, the odds are that the *Sydney Morning Herald* would help lead the ensuing uproar. University of Sydney public health professor Simon Chapman asked, in a letter to the editor of the *Sydney Morning Herald*, 'why so coy in giving the actual score?'[30] It was a good question, but one that drew no response and no change to the scoring of the subsequent annual supplement.

Even if BATA's report had relatively little impact on the course of the negotiations of the global tobacco convention, some readers of its reports were impressed. The Dow Jones Sustainability Index (DJSI), an index of stock exchange listed companies that claims to track performance of 'the leading sustainability-driven companies', was first launched in 1999. The index is designed by Sustainable Asset Management (SAM), an Australian and Swiss investment research company, to assist subscribing investment managers—such as those managing pension funds—with the selection of more socially responsible companies. The DJSI boasts that it has 60 subscribing investment companies in 14 countries, with $6.1 billion under management.

For the first three years of its operation, it shunned the tobacco sector. BAT's social report, however, changed all that. SAM was so impressed with BAT's social report that in September 2002 it announced that both the UK-registered BAT and BAT Malaysia would be included in its 2003 index, and have been retained ever since. SAM's summary enthused that BAT:

> has an excellent overall sustainability performance compared to the industry average, and is clearly positioned among the best in its industry... BAT's performance in the social dimension is outstanding compared to its industry, especially in external stakeholder relationship management and public reporting.

Even though SAM waxed lyrical about BAT's social reporting, some company insiders were despondent. Speaking at an international PR conference in October 2005, the head of Corporate

Communications for BAT, Fran Morrison, complained that tobacco companies were viewed as an 'axis of evil', and that the company's CSR reporting process had actually increased journalists' scepticism towards the company.[31] 'We suffer from out-and-out demonisation. One journalist said tobacco producers were terrorists', she said.[32]

Morrison's career path is typical of many in PR. After having worked on many of the leading news and current affairs programs for BBC, she moved into the world of corporate PR. When Shell's reputation went down the tubes in 1995, it was Morrison who had carriage of Shell's 'Way Forward' communications strategy, which was designed to rehabilitate the public standing of the company. Her experience in helping salvage Shell's image made her an attractive recruit for BAT. In considering an offer from BAT, Morrison has written that she wanted to find out more about the allegation that the company had concealed the risks of smoking, 'because I could not have worked against a dishonest background'. Morrison found reassurance. 'It didn't take me long to realise there is no "smoking gun". I was struck by how sound BAT's positions are and felt strongly that they deserved to be better understood', she explained.[33]

The low road

BAT's enthusiasm for social reporting—which is seen as a 'reputation management' approach with a distinctly European flavour—is not shared by others in the tobacco industry. The world's largest private tobacco company, the US-headquartered Philip Morris (PM), has avoided social reporting altogether. PM has traditionally taken a more typical US-style approach to insulating itself from the shift in social attitudes by courting potentially powerful allies. In a March 1985 memo, Hamish Maxwell, the CEO of Philip Morris International (PMI), reported that:

> a number of media proprietors I have spoken to are sympa-
> thetic to our position—Rupert Murdoch and Malcolm Forbes
> are two good examples. The media like the money they make
> from our advertisements, and they are an ally that we can and
> should exploit.[34]

Another PMI executive elaborated on Maxwell's point: 'As regards
the media, we plan to build similar relationships to those we
now have with Murdoch's News Limited with other newspaper
proprietors. Murdoch's papers rarely publish anti-smoking articles
these days.'[35]

Murdoch grew so close to PM that in August 1989 he was
elected to the company's board, a position he held until 2002.
But courting the powerful is a strategy that can be sustained for
only so long if everyone else grows more hostile. In 1995, the
company developed what it proposed as a ten-year-long program,
dubbed Project Sunrise, to reverse the public, media and political
hostility to the company. It was, one document stated, 'designed
to enhance the position of Philip Morris as the reasonable/respon-
sible industry leader and work to give the company a legitimate
"seat at the table".'[36] One step in its corporate makeover was a
name change to Altria for the parent company. An internal email
from November 2001 explained that the company hoped to take
advantage of the name change to shift the parent company's
media profile away from tobacco to more socially acceptable
topics. 'We can begin to focus attention away from tobacco, and
on to compliance, responsibility, philanthropy, environment etc,
all the things we want Altria to be identified with', the email
stated.[37]

In another document, Joshua Slavitt, the policy issues director
in PM's issues management department, recommended the
company 'utilize the company's corporate philanthropic efforts,
specifically support for education and nutrition programs—to

establish good-will with anti-tobacco elected officials and community activists. Encourage these groups to deliver our messages.'[38] One program that evolved from this strand of thinking was for PM to position itself as a champion in efforts to counter domestic violence. As so often happens, a PR program created in corporate head office overseas was taken up and adapted for rolling out in Australia.

In February 2003, the Office of the Status of Women (OSW) convened a conference in Melbourne on the impact of domestic conflict and violence. The keynote speaker at the conference was Dede Bartlett, the founder of PM's domestic violence workplace programs and a board member of the US-based Corporate Alliance to End Partner Violence. Simon Chapman, professor of public health at the University of Sydney posed the question: 'Why on earth is the Office of [the] Status of Women colluding in all this?'[39] It was a question answered a few days later in a Senate Estimates committee hearing, where expenditure by government agencies is open for scrutiny by senators. PM (Australia), it turned out, was the major sponsor of the conference, covering the costs of the venue, catering, invitations and conference resources. It also had a representative on the business working group that put the conference proposal and program together.

Senator Trish Crossin asked the OSW representative, Ms Rosemary Calder, whether 'you would see this as a Common-wealth activity that Philip Morris sponsored or would you see this more as the Commonwealth sponsoring a Philip Morris activity?' Before Calder could respond, Senator Eric Abetz intervened to state that the arrangement was a 'partnership'. To help publicise the conference, which was pitched at the business community, the OSW spent $30 260 hiring the PR company Quay Communications to talk the event up.[40] A few months earlier, OSW had spent $128 700 hiring another PR company, Write Communications, which boasted media personality Ita

Buttrose as a 'consulting director'. Their role was to publicise the visit of Kim Wells, the CEO of the US-based Corporate Alliance to End Partner Violence at a series of other events aimed at the business community in Melbourne and Sydney.[41]

While the treasure trove of internal tobacco industry documents is unique in allowing scrutiny of the real story behind the CSR facade, there are indications that the faux embrace of social responsibility extends to other industry sectors too. In Australia, the long notorious mining giant Rio Tinto has been a leading player in the CSR scene, and was one of the early supporters of the Corporate Citizenship Research Unit at Deakin University.[42] Like BAT, Rio Tinto has a comprehensive system for evaluating what material is included in its reports. But as impressive as their reports appear, a critical question is how they decide what should be *excluded*.

In January 1999, the Indonesian gold mining company Kelian Equatorial Mining (PTKEM), a 90 per cent Rio Tinto-owned subsidiary, buckled to community protests and initiated an investigation into a range of alleged human rights abuses, including the deaths in mysterious circumstances of two mine opponents. In its next social report, Rio Tinto said nothing.[43] Among CSR devotees, having a social report audited is supposed to be reassurance for any sceptics. 'Knowledge that there is independently verified social audit information around will give journalists confidence that if they present a corporation's side of the story, they're not just falling for expensive spin', wrote Steve Hilton and Giles Gibbons in their book on the virtues of CSR, *Good Business*.[44] Rio Tinto's report was reviewed by the auditing company, Arthur D. Little, who approved it. However, its auditing technique was based only on a sampling system of the information provided to it by the company. Even after the *Australian Financial Review* revealed, in a front-page story, that the human rights investigation had confirmed a number of instances of sexual abuse, Rio Tinto ignored disclosing the findings in its next report.[45] It is inconceivable that senior managers were unaware of the controversy, but obviously they decided that it was a sordid tale best concealed from the company's global shareholders.

There are other dirty secrets Rio Tinto prefers kept under wraps. In response to a shareholder resolution filed by US pension funds in 2003, the US-based Freeport-McMoRan confirmed that it directly funded the costs of Indonesian military units based near its huge gold and copper mine in West Papua. Freeport had funded part of the costs of a 2000-strong military, notorious for their human rights abuses, to the tune of $5.6 million for 2002 and $4.7 million for 2001.[46] When Freeport finally revealed it was funding the military, Rio Tinto had a 15 per cent direct share in the company, as well as being a 40 per cent joint venture partner in expanding the mine. (Rio Tinto has subsequently sold its shareholding.) The payments—which were omitted from both Freeport and Rio Tinto's audited social and environmental reports—have been condemned by human rights and environmental organisations.

Five years later, the *New York Times* revealed that Freeport staff collaborated with Indonesian military intelligence officers in monitoring the email and phone calls of environmental activists concerned about the mine. Jane Perlez and Raymond Bonner reported that Freeport had designed a system to intercept email messages by 'establishing a bogus environmental group', which required people to register online and provide a password. 'As is often the case, many who registered used the same password for their own messages, which then allowed the company to tap in', they reported. Not surprisingly, both Freeport and Rio Tinto declined to comment on the report.[47] Nor do their social reports mention other lobbying activities Rio Tinto have participated in, including meetings with Australian Embassy officials in Jakarta wanting representations to ensure security forces deal with small-scale miners on their mine sites.[48] Nor has Rio Tinto disclosed their lobbying efforts against Australian government policies supporting an expansion of renewable energy.[49] Even at a smaller scale, Rio Tinto's transparency has its limits. After a few years' break from funding the Melbourne-based think tank, the Institute of Public Affairs, the company is once more shovelling cash into the group's coffers. Despite volumes of data available in its social reports on partnerships with numerous non-profit groups, there is nary a mention of its funding of a think tank. Nor are they willing to even discuss the matter, having not responded to a request for an interview.

Turning over a new leaf?

Within the world of PR, the US-based PR consultant Peter Sandman is famous for his formulation that 'Risk = Hazard plus Outrage'. While he doesn't badge his advice with the CSR tag, some of the core half dozen strategies to manage community 'outrage' in Sandman's toolbox include the necessity to 'acknowledge prior misbehaviour', 'acknowledge current problems' and 'bring unacknowledged concerns to the surface'. In a January 2006 internal memo to the beleaguered board of AWB—the Australian wheat trader facing an inquiry into $300 million paid in kickbacks to the Iraqi military dictator, Saddam Hussein—Sandman noted, 'I tell my clients: Especially when stakeholders are paying close attention, you must either keep embarrassing facts genuinely secret or wallow in those facts. Acknowledging them only reluctantly and under pressure is a losing strategy.'[50] In a presentation in 1998 to an Australian mining industry conference, Sandman cautioned companies about embracing his suggestion that they needed to 'acknowledge your prior misbehaviour' too enthusiastically. 'I don't chiefly mean things you have done that nobody knows you have done and when we find out you will go to jail', he said. 'If there are any of these, I urge you to seek legal counsel before you seek communication counsel. I'm talking about negative things on the public record.'

If Sandman, who is considered an evangelist for more transparency than many of his clients are willing to accept, cautions clients against real transparency, it is not so surprising that CSR reporting amounts to little. While it can be a useful management tool to ensure more systematic attention to issues, a rough rule of thumb is that the more controversial a company is, the more likely it is that the CSR reporting and advisory processes are a PR mechanism designed to control public debate rather than inform it.

CSR initiatives, such as voluntary social reporting, offer little prospect that shareholders or citizens will be told about things that companies want to be kept secret. Instead, companies would rather only tell us what we already know, and even then, only if it suits their purposes. There is one powerful reason companies won't disclose more: there is no penalty for concealing their most egregious sins. Enticing 'stakeholders' into participating in corporate advisory processes is also about subtly shifting debates away from conflict between fundamental values to discussing the 'common ground', but only in a forum where the committee composition can be stacked in favour of the sponsor's interests. And so, what is often touted as a 'win–win' solution, in reality, usually requires the more critical participants—who are in a minority—to lower their sights and define mitigation, rather than prevention, as a 'win'. Even where strong recommendations are made, the sponsor is free to discard those that don't suit its interests. As numerous recent corporate scandals have revealed, the disclosure of corporate sins has come not from companies themselves, but through the efforts of assertive community-based activists, nosy journalists, public-spirited leakers, and court proceedings that have prised open files. Minimum mandatory reporting standards would be a useful additional tool to increasing corporate accountability and raising performance standards, while voluntary standards leave too much to the whim of executives and their PR advisers.

·

Part of the art of PR professionals is to raise expectations about what a corporate social responsibility program can deliver as a way of enticing wary non-government organisations to become involved in the first place. There is a flip side, though. Speaking at a PR conference in late 2005, Geoff Allen, the Chairman of the Allen Consulting Group, recounted that, while he considered the CSR move 'very valid', he had seen its downside within corporations too. Some staff who built up strong relationships with consumer and environmental groups, he said, 'get occupational myopia' and 'effectively go native with the counter-parties'.

'They separate themselves from management, they lose effectiveness, they lose influence and I've seen them lose their jobs simply because they have just gone too far to the other side and lost a sense of what the corporation is there for', he said.[51] In the eyes of most CEOs and senior executives, making money, after all, comes ahead of corporate social responsibility.

FIVE
BATTLE TANKS

'It's a little bit like my yacht club' is how Mike Nahan, the former veteran activist with the Institute of Public Affairs (IPA), described the process of hand-picking members for the Melbourne-based think tank. 'We go out and say "would you like to become a member" and they do.'[1] The IPA, however, is not in the business of organising genteel sailing trips for its 54 members.

Since its formation in 1943, the IPA has been the spear carrier for those within corporate Australia willing to fund and promote ideas for restructuring the economy and weakening the power of the unions. If the term 'think tank' conjures up an image of studied reflection on weighty topics, the reality could hardly be further from the truth. The IPA unashamedly sees its role as being to clear the way for supporting politicians and officials to implement policies deemed too politically toxic to touch.[2] Central to its strategy is trading on its self-description as being 'independent' to help amplify what would otherwise be a marginal dissident voice by utilising relationships with friendly media commentators and political movers and shakers. Within the world of PR, corporate-funded think tanks have long been seen as arm's length 'third-parties' that, with some—usually secret—

funding, will advance a sponsor's message. In this guise, think tanks are more like a non-profit PR firm. Where PR consultants crave public invisibility, the IPA needs a high-profile visibility to survive and thrive. Corporate contributors are treated more like clients than the average financial supporter. But like most PR firms, they seek to keep the details of who is paying them secret.

In 1993, Burton Yale Pines, the former senior vice president of the Heritage Foundation, one of the largest US think tanks, described the role of think tanks as being 'the shock troops of the conservative revolution'.[3] The military analogy is apt. Think tanks are the intellectual equivalent of battle tanks, which rely on a combination of speed, defensive armour and offensive firepower to overwhelm opposition forces. Battle tanks are noisy beasts, too. The IPA's impact comes, not from appearing in peer-reviewed academic journals, but from its willingness to eschew the cautiousness and caveats that characterise traditional academic work. An IPA staffer can deliver a snappy provocative policy prescription consistent with its free-market ideology. Certainty and controversy sells.

While there are other bigger, better-funded think tanks, such as the Sydney-based Centre for Independent Studies (CIS), which boasts three times as many staff, the IPA is the noisiest. In 2006 alone, the IPA had 196 opinion columns—an average of almost four a week—appearing in newspapers across the country, including *The Age*, the *Australian Financial Review*, the *Herald Sun*, *The Australian*, *The Courier Mail* and the rural newspaper, *The Land*.[4] And lots of arm's-length noise is just what the IPA's deep-pocketed funders, predominantly major corporations, are looking for. Notorious companies, such as tobacco corporations, would be unlikely to attract a receptive audience if they stood on a street corner with a megaphone. However, a little funding routed via a think tank enables the policy agenda of corporate funders to be projected to a broader audience with more credibility than if they did it themselves. For politicians and political staffers, the IPA is a meeting ground for like-minded policy buffs. For the media, the allure of the IPA is their accessibility, sound-bite savvy, and as a source of free copy for opinion pages. What the IPA lacks in terms of the volume of work produced relative to a university, they make up for in superior hustling.

For most of the post-Second World War period to the 1980s, Australia has been governed by Liberal–National Party coalition. When conservative federal governments are in power, think tanks often struggle to maintain relevance. Despite the rise of new social movements through the 1960s and 1970s, the scope of the IPA's vision remained largely fixed on its foundation agenda of industrial relations and economic policy. It was as though the rise of consumer, health, social welfare, environmental, Aboriginal, women's and peace movements had gone unnoticed. The election of Margaret Thatcher as British Prime Minister in 1978 and Ronald Reagan as US President in 1980 re-energised the relatively small global network of conservative think tanks. Suddenly, policies such as privatisation and union-busting were firmly on the agenda. In Australia, the political landscape was more confusing. In the late 1970s and early 1980s, a wave of conservative state governments—in NSW, Victoria, South Australia and Western Australia—fell to be replaced by Labor governments. Federally, Malcolm Fraser's reign ended with the election in March 1983 of the Labor Party led by Bob Hawke. Policy debates that were previously advanced by lobbying ministers in the corridors of power were forced into an oppositional extra-parliamentary role. The rather stodgy right-wing think tanks, which had previously been on the margins of political debate, assumed a new importance in the conservative movement. The IPA's old guard were replaced with some of the high-fliers of the corporate world. Hugh Morgan, the Chairman of Western Mining Corporation (later renamed WMC), became IPA Treasurer in 1982.

Morgan is one of the few corporate leaders who combines personal charisma, a commitment to free market activism and an ability to shake money loose from the big end of town. Not long afterwards, Rupert Murdoch joined the IPA's Council, and News Limited became one of its most generous supporters.[5]

Within a few years, the number of corporate subscribers had almost tripled. Corporate funds flowed and the IPA began to expand. More effort was devoted to presentation and the marketing of its views to the mainstream media, and a new generation of staff was recruited. Rod Kemp, the son of the founder of the IPA, was appointed as Executive Director. In 1987, Gerard Henderson, a former adviser to John Howard, was appointed as the Director of the NSW Institute of Public Affairs, although two years later he parted company to set up his own company-cum-think tank, the Sydney Institute. Even though economic and industrial relations policies remained the IPA's main focus, slowly they broadened their field of view to encompass cultural issues such as education, the role of the churches in public policy debates, and 'bias' at the ABC. But in other areas, the IPA was slow to react. It wasn't until 1989 that the IPA created its Environment Unit, which for a few years was headed by Ron Brunton, a one-time analyst with the intelligence agency, the Office of National Assessments.[6] (In 2003, Brunton was appointed as Commissioner of the ABC by the Howard Government.)

The newfound corporate supporters proved to be a fickle lot, though, and the flush of new funding soon receded. Other think tanks were struggling too. In March 1991, the IPA amalgamated with the Perth-based Australian Institute for Public Policy (AIPP), with its Executive Director, John Hyde, heading up the merged think tank. At the following year's annual general meeting, Hyde bemoaned that the financial base of the organisation was becoming 'more fragile as we lose companies and individual members'.[7] Earlier that year, the organisation had convened a navel-gazing Future Directions Seminar, at which, Hyde reported, the board and staff 'decided to try to position the image of the IPA where misrepresentation was more difficult.' In Hyde's view:

> To be persuasive, arguments and imagery must strike sympathetic chords, this is not to say that a large audience should agree with what IPA spokesmen propose—it is after all IPA's role to lead debate and the first requirement must be to be correct.

Throughout the 1990s, the IPA struggled for relevance, and even the election of the Howard Government in 1996 did little to revive its flagging fortunes. The once influential Tasman Institute bailed out of the think tank game and merged with a consultancy company. There were also new players in the political landscape competing for the ear of government. Business lobby groups, such as the Business Council of Australia (BCA), the Minerals Council of Australia (MCA) and the Australian Chamber of Commerce and Industry (ACCI), were now more adept at representing their views directly to a more receptive government. The corporate merger mania of the 1990s also took its toll. Some companies that had once been rusted-on IPA supporters, such as North Broken Hill (NBH) and AMP, were taken over, and the chief executives of the merged companies opted to cut off funding. In contrast, the Sydney-based CIS flourished, in part reflecting Sydney's rise as Australia's corporate capital, but predominantly because of the staying power of its founder, Greg Lindsay.

Dealing with those pesky NGOs

For major corporations, how to respond to the rise of community-based activist groups has long been a vexed question. Strident counterattacks all too often backfired, while hoping that activist groups would simply fade away had proven equally unsuccessful.

The idea of tighter regulation of non-profit groups is a high-wire act for free-market think tanks, which are non-profit groups that are often reliant on government-bestowed tax concessions, and are secretive about who funds them. In 1980, the Heritage Foundation drafted a detailed blueprint, *Mandate for Leadership*, for the incoming administration of Republican US President Ronald Reagan. As part of their vision for the Reagan revolution, they identified the need to undermine the growing credibility of activist groups and eliminate any government financial support for them. Once in power, the Reagan Administration proposed a Presidential Executive Order, named A-122 Cost Principles for Non-Profit Organizations, under which any organisation attempting to 'influence a government decision' would be deemed ineligible for any government funding, even if advocacy activities were funded from other sources. The far-reaching nature of the proposal galvanised the formation of the National A-122 Coalition, which, over the next three years of high-profile campaigning, succeeded in defeating the proposal. With its broad-brush approach defeated, companies were left to fend for themselves.

In 1994, Philip Morris (PM), the world's largest private tobacco corporation, pondered how to undermine the growing strength of Californian tobacco control groups. An internal PM strategy proposed to run a campaign to 'regulate charitable health organizations'. What they wanted to do was to compulsorily direct non-profit groups away from public advocacy and lobbying, and into less politically effective areas such as research. Its strategy for rolling back the California tobacco control movement suggested: 'Cap administrative costs, salaries, lobbying expenditures; establish minimum percentage of funds for research.'[8] The strategy failed. When the Republicans won the majority in the US House of Representatives in 1994, led by Speaker of the House Newt Gingrich, a coalition of conservative think tanks and activist groups dusted off their plans to weaken the role of advocacy groups. A leading conservative activist, Grover Norquist from Americans for Tax Reform, told a journalist: 'We will hunt [these liberal groups] down one by one and extinguish their funding sources.'[9] This time, they hoped to achieve their aims by mounting a stealth attack to ram a bill, titled Stop Taxpayer Funded Political Advocacy, through Congress. When the details of the draft legislation were leaked, this scheme, too, wilted. Inside PM, though, the dream lived on.

In a 1995 strategy dubbed 'Project Sunrise', PM sketched a decade-long plan to counter what it referred to as the 'anti-tobacco industry' or 'ATI'.[10] In one document outlining what it referred to as its 'Fair Play' strategy, PM noted that 'the Antis draw their strength from their funding, their credibility in public opinion, and in their unity. Our primary strategies focus on impacting each of [these] sources of strength.'[11] Joshua Slavitt, the policy issues director in PM's issues management department, flagged the need to divert funding away from advocacy efforts that 'are causing the most harm to the company'. Slavitt also suggested the company should 'recruit other industries and organizations that are interested in curtailing the efforts of consumer advocacy organizations'.[12] Like earlier plans, little came of PM's scheming to undermine their critics funding.

If the idea of curbing the influence of activist groups that caused corporate discomfort first emerged in the United States, the interest in the concept was global. Throughout the 1980s and until Nelson Mandela was released from prison in February 1990, Shell was in the spotlight for its refusal to withdraw from South Africa, which was racially segregated under its policy of apartheid. It was scrutiny the company resented. In Australia, it fell to Anthony Adair, Shell Australia's Public Affairs Manager, to defend the company from criticism by the anti-apartheid movement. After Mandela's release from prison, the oil giant came under increasing pressure from environmental NGOs.

Despite the failure of other attempts at limiting the role of NGOs, Adair felt that he 'couldn't let the issue slide'.[13] In the early 1990s, he raised the issue in the Business Council of Australia, which contracted former *Bulletin* journalist Tim Duncan to prepare a paper for internal use on what could be done about the rise of NGOs.[14] The issue went quiet until, in 1995, Shell was humiliated by a Greenpeace campaign that blocked the company's attempt to dump the disused Brent Spar oil platform in the Atlantic Ocean. Adding to Shell's woes was the backlash against the company over its campaign against novelist Ken Saro-Wiwa, who was executed, along with eight others, on trumped-up charges by the Nigerian military dictatorship in November 1995.

In 1997, Adair retired after a 25-year stint with Shell. 'I'd had enough of Greenpeace, the Uniting Church and various Marxists and Stalinists and people who were making my life unpleasant', he said.[15] In retirement, as a Senior Associate at the Shell-supported Sydney-based CIS, Adair crafted a proposal to curb NGOs influence with a code of conduct. In Adair's view, activist groups had been too successful in raising public awareness, including over Union Carbide's Bhopal disaster in India, the Chernobyl meltdown in the former USSR, the Exxon Valdez oil spill disaster in Alaska, and Nestlé's promotion of infant milk formula in developing countries.[16] In particular, he took aim at some of activist groups' most effective tactics—civil disobedience and electoral campaigns. Adair proposed that NGOs should be required to ensure 'full disclosure of financial information, including sources of funding' and the 'application of funds'.[17] Any NGO that sought funding, tax concessions, involvement in service delivery or public policy would have to be a signatory to the code. Adair then let the issue slide and moved on to pursue his other interests.

In September 2000, the IPA took up where Adair left off and convened a 'Corporate Affairs Forum', which aimed to discuss '"coal face" issues of concern to corporate affairs executives' and to provide 'direction for the IPA's newly established NGO Project'.[18] It was the inaugural forum at which former Labor minister turned IPA staffer, Gary Johns, canvassed his ideas for curbing activist NGOs. Soon afterwards, the IPA launched a specialist newsletter, *NGO Watch*, edited by former PR practitioner Don D'Cruz. The IPA thought they had spotted a way of attracting high-paying corporate subscribers wanting early-warning information about activist campaigns. It flopped. With few corporate subscribers, the October 2002 edition was the last. 'There weren't enough buying the product', Johns later said.[19]

Setbacks aside, the idea of muzzling outspoken advocacy groups was gaining traction in the corridors of power. In July 2003, Federal Treasurer Peter Costello released a draft Charities Bill, which proposed that, if seeking 'to change the law or government policy' was the dominant purpose of a non-government organisation, it would be considered sufficient to warrant withdrawing a group's tax-deductibility status. Tax deductibility makes little difference for minor donors, but for major contributors and foundations it can be crucial. In the face of uproar over the Bill, Costello retreated and dropped it. But Costello's full-frontal approach has been replaced by the Australian Tax Office launching a series of investigations of the tax status of non-profit groups.[20]

Meanwhile, the IPA was in a financial fix on how to fund its NGO project. Corporate income remained relatively stagnant and the IPA's policy of not accepting government funding limited its options. Their luck turned, though, when, in late 2003, the Minister for Family and Community Service, Amanda Vanstone, spotted an opinion column by Johns extolling his idea of establishing standards for NGOs. Staff in her office contacted Johns to see if the IPA were interested in some government funding for a consultancy project aimed at establishing a 'protocol' for vetting NGOs that gained direct or indirect support from government.[21] They were. While their website boasted that they had a 'no government funding' policy, they dispatched a funding proposal. Central to John's argument was the idea that lobby groups are displacing unorganised citizens, which he complained 'tend to be run as non-member organisations, preferring supporters without voting rights'.[22] To counter this, they proposed that, before NGOs were granted high-level access to government officials, funding or be included on committees, they should have to pass a series of threshold disclosure tests. Information to be disclosed to government would include 'their source of funds, their expertise, their membership and the means of electing their office holders'.

At a meeting of the Prime Minister's Community Business Partnership Program in mid-December 2002, after what a departmental memo described as 'strong support' from Amanda Vanstone, who was chairing the meeting, a major grant for the IPA was approved.[23] The Prime Minister's Community Partnership duly provided $54 268 for the project, with Johns and Lobbyist John Roskam billing their time out at $1200 and $850 per day respectively. Subsequently, the Department of Family and Community Services (FACS) laughably defended awarding the IPA the contract without going to tender, on the grounds that the project required 'independent or impartial research/assessment by an independent organisation'.[24] A series of parliamentary questions also probed, as one departmental staffer put it, the 'credentials' of the IPA to do the project. Uncertain of how to respond, FACS forwarded the questions to Johns for his input.[25]

Despite the IPA framing their concern as being the displacement of citizens by all organised lobby groups, their public advocacy on the issue singled out environmental, human rights and aid organisations for criticism while remaining mute on the impact of the far more numerous, better-funded and better-connected business lobby groups. Internal Department of Foreign Affairs and Trade comments provided to the IPA as part of their consultancy project, which were released under the Freedom of Information Act to The Wilderness Society, revealed that when it came to climate change, departmental representatives had 'regular' meetings with major industry groups, and only 'occasionally' met with environmental groups.[26] An internal AusAID briefing note on the IPA's draft proposal was pointed: 'Overall this is a disappointing, simplistic, information-gathering exercise to validate their original proposal to develop and implement a system of public disclosure and reporting about Department/NGO relations'.[27]

The IPA's final report, which proposed collating and disclosing data on most departmental relationships with NGOs, generated little support from government agencies wary of more work for little gain. The IPA's champion Vanstone had been moved on in a ministerial reshuffle, and there was no sign that her replacement, Kay Patterson, had much interest in the project. A submission to Cabinet, noting the report but taking no action, was approved. With the outcry against Costello's proposals still fresh in their memory, the Government Communications Unit initially suggested the report be buried by releasing it on a Friday. In the end, ministerial scheduling problems meant it was not released until mid-week, but it was largely ignored by the media and NGOs alike. Even the IPA was only told about the release of the report the morning after it occurred. A departmental adviser noted that Roskam 'became quite agitated' at the missed media opportunity, and flagged that he would complain to the minister's office. According to an internal FACS email, Roskam stressed their enthusiasm to see the report recommendations implemented, to which the officer noted 'we didn't tell him it's not really a priority'.[28] But the IPA is known for its persistence.

Even though Don D'Cruz and Gary Johns left the IPA after former Liberal Party adviser and Rio Tinto lobbyist John Roskam took over the think tank's reins in July 2005, the NGO project rolled on. Roskam commissioned a report from Ross Fox, a policy adviser to Victorian Liberal Senator Michael Ronaldson. If a broad frontal attack on NGO's had gone nowhere, this time they opted for precision. Tucked in among seemingly innocuous proposals, packaged reassuringly as 'strengthening' civil society and ensuring 'accountability', were measures designed to have non-profit groups that participated in election campaigns or organised civil disobedience protests stripped of tax-deductibility. Fox specifically singled out The Wilderness Society for mention over its electoral campaigns. Non-government groups said nothing in response to Fox's proposal, but Queensland Liberal Senator Brett Mason took the issue up in the Senate, again specifically targeting The Wilderness Society. 'This is a shopfront for political advocacy', Mason said.[29] Within Liberal Party ranks, the view was that it was time The Wilderness Society was nobbled once and for all. The Forest Industries Association of Tasmania, dominated by the logging company Gunns, had also written to federal ministers, arguing that The Wilderness Society should be stripped of their tax-deductible status because they had campaigned against the coalition in the 2004 election. Not long afterwards, the federal Minister for the Environment, Ian Campbell, confirmed that he was pursuing the matter.[30] Gunns, however, which had campaigned for the government and been a major party donor, was showered with government funds to help investigate the construction of a new pulp mill in northern Tasmania. However, the first group to fall victim to the IPA's campaign was not The Wilderness Society but the Sydney-based overseas aid watchdog, AID/WATCH.

The Australian Taxation Office (ATO) advised the group in October 2006 that their tax-deductible status had been removed because they had been 'trying to procure changes in Australia's

aid and development programs' and were involved in political
activities. 'Political purposes, which include a purpose of seeking
changes to government decisions and propagations of a particular
point of view, are not charitable', the ATO wrote.[31] In particular,
the ATO took exception to AID/WATCH urging supporters to
write to the government to put pressure on the Burmese military
dictatorship, delivering an ironic 60th anniversary birthday cake
to the World Bank and raising concerns about the Australia–United
States Free Trade Agreement.[32] It is a ruling that must have pleased
the IPA but for them it is a double-edged sword, as their own
tax-deductible status is also vulnerable.

Do as we say, not as we do

Shortly after the IPA publicly launched its NGO project, Mike
Nahan the then Executive Director of the IPA was challenged
on how the group was funded. 'The IPA has in place an extensive
mechanism that separates its funding from its activities', he wrote.
What exactly the mechanism was he didn't specify, except to
stress that 'except for me, our spokesmen have no involvement
with, or detailed knowledge of, our fundraising'.[33] Why do
companies fund think tanks like the IPA? In part, a little corporate
cash funnelled into the IPA allows them to amplify what would
otherwise be a self-interested voice. In 2004, the IPA's website
proclaimed that it 'seeks to promote general interests rather than
sectional ones', airily suggesting that it can accept funding from
self-interested parties without any impact on its independence.
'Unlike some other institutions, we do not accept government
funding, nor are we beholden to, or the mouthpiece for, any
particular section of the community or any particular economic
activity or group', it boasted.[34]

After details of the IPA's contract with the government became
public knowledge, it was criticised for the contradiction between

its advocacy of transparency for other NGOs while embracing secrecy itself. 'We take that on board', Nahan said in August 2003, promising complete donor disclosure in its 2003 annual report. 'We will list all our major supporters by name and level of funding'.[35] It was a deft PR move, shifting disclosure far enough off into the future in the expectation that the pledge would soon be forgotten. (The IPA's 2003 annual report made no disclosure of corporate donors.) For a while, it worked. Shortly after Roskam started as Executive Director, he was asked about the pledge and backtracked. 'It's not for us to reveal our supporters', he told *The Age*. 'Whether we like it or not, the Australian democracy is not so sophisticated that companies can reveal they support free market think tanks, because as soon as they do they will be attacked.'[36] These days, Roskam opts to leave it to companies to disclose their support for the IPA. Secrecy suits the interests of both the sponsor and the sponsored. Funding companies, which currently contribute approximately 60 per cent of the IPA's $1.2 million dollar budget, include those from mining, oil, tobacco and energy industries.[37] But sometimes its advocacy alienates even them. Earlier this decade, the mining giant Rio Tinto cut off funding when the IPA's strident criticisms of Aboriginal organisations coincided with efforts by the company to build bridges with Aboriginal leaders. In the end, though, it was a short-term setback. 'Rio Tinto are back on board', Roskam said in May 2006.[38] For their part, Rio Tinto refuse to disclose how much they are contributing or what exactly they are funding.

One little understood aspect of the IPA's budget is the importance of allowing funders to earmark support for the work of specific 'units'. Of the IPA's $1.2 million income in the 2006 financial year, just over $504 000 was earmarked for spending on specific projects. As a non-profit company, the IPA is exempt from income tax and, until late 2006, wasn't eligible to receive tax-deductible donations. Prior to Costello granting this concession, for a company to claim a contribution to the IPA against tax it needed to be able to demonstrate that its contribution is related to income-earning activities. Irrespective of tax-deductibility, within companies, managers want to be able to defend their budget decision against bottom-line outcomes. 'Corporations increasingly have a much shorter run view of the public policy process and that makes it hard for us too because companies say "John how does this contribute to my bottom line tomorrow"', Roskam said.[39] Despite touting itself as 'independent', the IPA risks financial oblivion if its policy work doesn't deliver what corporate executives need. For example, the IPA's NGO work has specifically singled out groups like The Wilderness Society and Greenpeace, and argued they should lose their tax-deductibility status. Do Gunns and the pesticides and genetic engineering company Monsanto fund the NGO unit? 'I won't comment on Gunns but in relation to Monsanto in the past they have not been very significant sponsors actually', Roskam said. Gunns CEO John Gay confirmed that the company had sponsored the project until approximately late 2005.[40] What about Esso Australia, a subsidiary of Exxon? After all, in the United States the company funded a shadowy non-profit group to campaign to have Greenpeace's tax status revoked.[41] Exxon in Australia, however, declined to comment. Shell was similarly unresponsive in discussing their funding of think tanks. Asked in late 2006 if Gunns, Esso and Monsanto had funded the project, Johns didn't disagree: 'I don't think that's inaccurate.'[42] However, he added the caveat that he didn't know the details of the project funders.

If, as the IPA's Don D'Cruz once claimed, corporate sponsorship of activist non-government groups is akin to 'protection' money, surely corporate funding of the IPA is the flip side of the coin, with the think tank funded to run interference on corporate critics. Roskam concedes the point: 'I agree with that point that it's protection', he said.[43] 'But I define protection money in a different way in that it is actually protection from the excesses of NGOs in the same way it is protection from the excesses of government'.[44] Roskam himself also has a substantial personal interest in persuading companies that they should contribute to the IPA. With a base salary in the $100 000 to $140 000 range, he can earn a bonus of up to 50 per cent based on performance against the think tank's 'key performance indicators', which 'will be substantially related to the achievement of financial goals'.[45]

There are other problems with the secrecy surrounding think tanks funding. One argument advanced by Johns for NGO transparency was that both shareholders and citizens 'need to know about NGOs who seek to access their resources'.[46] It is a fair point, but do shareholders have a right to know if their money is being given to think tanks like the IPA? Roskam acknowledges that the IPA's secrecy contradicts the standards others should abide by, but has no intention of changing tack. 'Corporates can't be seen to be supporting a free market think tank because their shareholders don't like it', he said. Which begs the question of whose interests they claim to be defending. Johns also argued that when groups seek the ear of government, the question must be asked 'is the NGO well-governed?'.[47] It's a good question but one which the IPA doesn't take kindly to being asked about itself. From among its 54 members, those elected to the board each year tend to be an eclectic mix of captains of industry, corporate PR practitioners and academics. An examination of six years of the IPA's annual reports to late 2006 reveals that Bill Clough attended none of 38 board meetings in that period. (He is no longer on the board.) Harold Clough fared little better, managing time for only five of 39 over the same period. How is it that board members who never or rarely attend still manage to hold down a seat on the board of directors of the company for so long? 'I'm not going to talk to you about our internal governance arrangements', Roskam tersely responded.[48] Was it because Clough Engineering, a Perth-based engineering and construction company, was a major financial supporter? Roskam would only confirm that the publicly listed company was well known as 'key supporter' of the IPA.

In a guest lecture at Parliament House, Gary Johns argued that one test of a non-profit group being granted access to government should be its ability to demonstrate that the group has a verifiable list of members 'that distinguishes members—people with voting rights—from supporters'.[49] It is a test the IPA itself fails. On its website, it promises that for $55 anyone can become a general member. However, anyone paying their dues would discover that they are simply a financial supporter without any voting rights. The IPA's corporate structure limits its members to 54, who are selected by staff and the board. 'We market it as membership but technically they are not and it is something we are aware of', Roskam said. Even with only 54 hand-picked members, there is little active participation. In 2005, only a dozen or so turned out for the annual general meeting. Despite all the controversy over who funds the IPA, Roskam insists that the IPA never tailors its research findings to match a sponsor's interest. But where does the think tank draw the line in what influence a donor has on a project? 'It can get very up close and friendly, certainly. We can't and won't guarantee the direction that we go in but it varies from issue to issue', he said.[50]

Line rental

One issue the IPA have taken a keen interest in is the debate over the regulation and ownership of Telstra, the telecommunications giant that was majority government-owned until the bulk of the government-held shares were sold in late 2006. Over recent years, IPA staff have churned out a series of opinion columns in leading national newspapers, letters to the editor,

articles in its own magazine, a backgrounder on telecommunications,[51] and submissions to government inquiries touching on
Telstra's interests. In early 2001, the IPA's then Executive Director,
Mike Nahan, railed against the Australian Competition and
Consumer Commission (ACCC) 'micro-managing' Telstra and
the telco industry.[52] When in the 2001 election campaign, the
Opposition Labor Party stated its opposition to the further
privatisation of Telstra, the IPA's Jim Hoggett popped up with
an opinion column in *The Australian* denouncing Kim Beazley's
policy.[53] In another opinion piece published on the think tank's
website, Gary Johns argued for full privatisation and against any
further regulation of Australia's largest company.[54] When there
was widespread public debate about the quality of Telstra's service
in regional areas, the IPA's Andrew McIntyre extolled the virtues
of the telcos's service. He wrote in an opinion column in *The
Australian*:

> I don't think I have seen so many Telstra phone booths
> in my life; in every single town and, it seemed, on every
> single corner. In the remotest, most unlikely places, the
> familiar phone booth, with microwave link and solar
> power, a fully automatic and autonomous phone,
> complete with instant dial tone, infallibly works as reliably
> and as clearly as my phone in the city.[55]

When the telco was criticised for a sub-contractor outsourcing
information technology jobs to India, Nahan jumped to Telstra's
defence.[56] When the Productivity Commission issued a draft
report floating the possibility that Telstra be split to separate its
retail and wholesale functions to increase competition, the IPA
reacted with a critical submission. 'The IPA sees this as an unnecessary and largely retrogressive step', it argued. Within the IPA,
the role of being Telstra's defender was shared around. However,
in late 2004 the IPA appointed Chris Berg as the head of the

telecommunications and media unit. The ACCC, he complained soon afterwards, were subjecting the telco to 'overly aggressive regulations'.[57] Berg co-authored a submission to the Productivity Commission urging the full privatisation of Telstra.[58] In one column, Berg complained that mobile phone use, 'as with smoking, is being subjected to heavy handed social regulation and legislation'. His particular gripes were with the ban on using mobile phones in cars and restrictions on airline passengers making calls.[59]

The IPA's enduring enthusiasm for Telstra was finally explained in February 2004 when the Senate representative of the Minister for Communications, Information, Technology and Arts, Rod Kemp, answered a question from the Labor Party Senator Kerry O'Brien.[60] Kemp—who had worked at the IPA for seven years prior to entering parliament in 1990—explained that Telstra had funded the IPA to the tune of more than $165 000 over the preceding five financial years.[61] Despite the notional IPA policy of not accepting government funding, it seems that taking money from a majority government-owned company was fair game.[62] For its part, Telstra states that its 'community sponsorships, partnerships, grants and awards aim to provide real benefit to our communities', but initially refused to discuss its funding of the IPA. Rod Bruem, from Telstra's National Media Office, explained to the author that the company wouldn't disclose details of any current funding of think tanks unless required to by parliament.[63] However, documents subsequently obtained under the Freedom of Information Act shed light on the intimate relationship between the IPA and the telco company. 'We have been keen to draw out the shortcomings of some ACCC decisions and approaches that have adverse ramifications for business and have been in the forefront of the debate on privatization', Nahan wrote in a funding pitch in late 2004 to Bill Scales, Telstra's managing director of Corporate and Human Relations.[64] Berg, Nahan assured Scales, 'is developing material, which we intend to publish, demonstrating the benefits of forgoing regulation'.

Noting that in 2000 Telstra had funnelled $50 000 into the think tanks coffers compared to the previous year's $9000, Nahan begged Scales to double the company's contribution. Of course, he noted, he'd be willing to meet Scales to 'discuss the past and future nature of the IPA's work'.[65] In a follow-up email, Nahan flagged that a funding proposal he'd like to prepare would be for 'market based solution [*sic*] to rural environmental issues and specifically water markets and corporate governance'.[66] Appended to the funding pitch was a list of IPA newspaper columns, dominated by attacks on the ACCC's regulation of telecommunications and a smattering of submissions on Telstra-related issues. Despite Nahan's plea, Telstra's contribution remained unchanged.[67]

In mid-August 2005, Roskam met with Telstra's Group Manager of Regulatory Public Affairs, Julia Foley, to discuss the think tank's plans, and the following week sent her a copy of the IPA's work program for the telecommunications and media unit. It was, Roskam noted, 'derived from the things that we talked about'. Needless to say, it was Telstra-friendly.[68] Entertainment and communication, the think tank wrote, 'should not be micro-managed by regulators'. They also opposed Telstra being constrained by community and universal service obligations to provide a basic standard of service. Nor did the IPA favour an 'open access' regulatory regime that would require Telstra to provide access to its fibre-optic broadband network for other telecommunications companies wanting to sell competing retail services. The work program stated, 'A major aim of the IPA will be to change the "accepted wisdom" in Australia that access regulation is appropriate to the telecommunications sector'. They also opposed the regulatory regime imposing access standards for the aged or those living in rural areas. 'The IPA will emphasise the positive effects that a sensible policy framework would have, not just for the technology literate users, but for all members of the community', Roskam wrote.[69] Close collaboration between Telstra and IPA staff was not a new development either. In a letter to Nahan in September 2001, Telstra's then Group Manager of Public Affairs, Andrew Maiden, noted that he had recently met with the IPA's Dr Jim Hoggett, 'to discuss projects for the forthcoming year'.[70] The following year, Maiden commended Nahan on the 'fine contribution to public debate on public policy matters of interest to Telstra' by the IPA and Hoggett in particular.[71] (Both the Centre for Independent Studies and Gerard Henderson's Sydney Institute also receive Telstra funding.)

The IPA's enthusiastic defence of Telstra raises important questions about all involved. It is extraordinary that at a time when it was a majority government-owned company that Telstra funded a think tank to run a mutually discussed campaign that included attacks on the government's own corporate regulator, the ACCC. In none of the pro-Telstra columns and letters did IPA staff publicly disclose that their organisation received funding from the company or disclose the funding link when making submissions to parliamentary inquiries. Telstra's Rod Bruem concedes disclosure would be best. 'I think all think tanks should disclose how they are funded and let's be open about it,' he said.[72] The IPA's willingness to tailor their workplan to suit their Telstra interests begs the question of what they do when more than a measly $9000 a year is on the table.

Water wars

Publicly undisclosed contributions from corporate funders are not a new issue for the IPA. When a parliamentary standing committee launched an inquiry into water management in Australia, the committee was deluged with more than 180 submissions. One of the recurrent issues was the need for better management of water in the Murray–Darling river system. Murray Irrigation Limited (MIL), Australia's largest private irrigation company and an opponent of increased environmental river flows, made a submission. The IPA didn't make a submission, but it didn't stop them playing a major role in trying to derail the allocation of 500 megalitres for environmental flows in the Murray River. For its interim report, the committee turned to a December 2003 IPA Backgrounder, *Myth and the Murray*, by the Director of the IPA's Environment Unit, Jennifer Marohasy, and a consultancy report for MIL by Dr Lee Benson, both of which argued that concerns over the health of the Murray River had been exaggerated. Marohasy and Benson were invited by the committee to participate in a 'scientific roundtable' with two CSIRO scientists and another from the CRC for Freshwater Ecology. The committee preferred Benson and Marohasy's scepticism, and quoted them extensively in support of their recommendation that plans for increasing river flows should be put on hold.[73] The only dissenting voice was Labor member Dick Adams, who challenged Marohasy's take on the science in a minority report.

In wasn't until three months after the committee released their report that the *Australian Financial Review* revealed MIL had contributed $40 000 to the IPA.[74] The IPA neither disclosed the contribution on its website, in Marohasy's backgrounder, or when called to discuss the issue before the committee. Not surprisingly, Adams indicated he would have liked to have been informed of the conflict at the time. The then IPA Executive Director, Mike Nahan, claimed that the think tank's work on the Murray was not influenced by the donation. Marohasy stated that she didn't take 'an interest in who funds IPA', while MIL would neither confirm nor deny its contribution to the IPA.[75] Even though Roskam is now happy to identify MIL as a donor, he concedes that disclosure would have been consistent with what the IPA argued others should do. 'We are aware of that and we'll keep that in mind for the future', he said.[76] But the IPA is used to riding out short-term embarrassment. Within a fortnight of Roskam's concession, Marohasy featured as a commentator on Michael Duffy's ABC Radio National program, 'Counterpoint'. The water extracted from the Murray River system by irrigators, she asserted, was simply the water that one would have 'naturally spilt out across the great flood plains of the Riverina'. She got in a direct plug for MIL, too. In the 1990s, the company, she said, had donated water savings back to a wetland working group.[77] Duffy asked for no disclosure and Marohasy volunteered none.

MIL's General Manager, George Warne, describes the company as 'great supporters' of the IPA. 'They come and speak to our board every two or three years for support for a specific project that they think may have relevance given our battle over natural resources management', he said.[78] On one occasion, he said, MIL paid to cover the costs of a round of speaking engagements in January 2004 by Marohasy to meetings with irrigators.[79] For Warne, the benefit in funding the think tank is that often their policy ideas end up being embraced by both Labor and Liberal parties. But the interests of MIL and the IPA don't always match. The members of MIL were adamant opponents of the plans by the federal, New South Wales and Victorian governments to privatise the Snowy Hydro scheme in mid-2006. When MIL raised the issue with the IPA, Roskam says he explained their support for privatisation was unshakeable.[80] But, if nothing else, MIL's sponsorship appears to have had the effect of the IPA remaining mute. Among the torrent of articles and controversy over the proposed privatisation, the normally voluble think tank was mute.

Fronts of fronts

At a conference on public relations for mining industry staff in 1996, Mike Nahan fielded a question from the floor on how he would counter a campaign being run by a group like Greenpeace. He observed that 'you have to have groups outside industry associations—industry associations have limits on what they can do'. Nahan then warmed to the question:

> Make sure that the tough things are said—farm it out and let other people say it...Greenpeace is basically a ratbag organisation. I'd say develop a countervailing ratbag organisation. If you have left wing organisations and right wing organisations one tends to cancel out the others...you have to assist fund a variety of individuals, such as universities, and a variety of organisations.[81]

Even though the IPA generates lots of media noise, it has a wafer-thin support base on the ground. Without the capacity to mobilise a grassroots constituency, the issues raised by the IPA often sink without trace. To fill the void, the IPA cooked up a plan to convene a conference in Ballarat to coincide with the 150th anniversary of the Eureka Stockade in December 2004, as a prelude to launching a new group 'to counter the environmental movement'. The marketing pitch was simple: appropriate the nationalistic imagery of the Southern Cross, call it the 'Eureka Forum', and cast a corporate-funded think tank's conference as the rebellion of the little people against environmental tyranny.

The Eureka Forum was an event pitched at individuals and local industries, but with enough scope to justify support from the big corporate types. 'Environmental fundamentalism is denying farmers, foresters, fishermen, prospectors, miners, beekeepers, 4WD (four-wheel-drive) enthusiasts and others access rights, property rights, water rights. It is also generating excessive

red tape and harming the environment', the IPA proclaimed in
its promotional material. But if the Eureka Stockade was open
to anyone who wanted to join in, the IPA wanted to vet who
could sign up for their rebellion: 'The IPA reserves the right to
select attendees'. The keynote address, titled 'Environmental
Fundamentalism', was given by Jennifer Marohasy, who argued
that bans on broadacre clearing of woodlands in Queensland,
restrictions on water use in the Murray–Darling Basin, and mora-
toriums on genetically engineered food groups are evidence of
'environmental fundamentalism'.[82] As with most IPA events,
luring journalists to appear on the program is part of the formula.
Michael Thompson, a journalist with *Queensland Country Life*,
spoke at a breakfast function. Acting as master of ceremonies
for the Eureka Forum was Tim Lee, a journalist with the ABC's
national rural affairs television program 'Landline'. Even though
Lee had told the IPA that he would be attending in a private
capacity only, they proceeded to promote him as being from
'the ABC'.[83]

A little over two months later, the IPA had settled on the
outline of its new seemingly independent offspring. Its name,
the Australian Environment Foundation (AEF), mimicked that
of the mainstream environment group, the Australian Conservation Foundation. Marohasy registered a web domain for the
new group, and business registration forms were filled and filed
with the Australian Securities Investment Commission (ASIC),
listing the IPA's Collins Street office as both its registered address
and principal place of business. Nahan and Marohasy were
identified as two of the six company directors, with others
including Kersten Gentle, the Victorian organiser of the timber
industry's front group, Timber Communities Australia. On World
Environment Day, 5 June 2005, the new group was launched,
not in the Collins Street offices of the IPA, but in the northern
NSW town of Tenterfield. AEF proclaimed that its 'focus will be

on making decisions based on science and what is good for both the environment and for people'. Marohasy, who was listed at the time as chairwoman of the AEF, sought to downplay the role of the IPA, stating that she was involved in an individual capacity only.[84] Shortly afterwards, the registered office address shifted from the IPA's Collins Street office to the home of one of its office bearers.

Those involved in the AEF resent the accusation that it is a front group for the IPA. However, IPA Executive Director John Roskam describes it as 'very simply an extension of our work on the environment, agriculture, genetically modified crops and water issues'.[85] So why would the IPA bother creating a new group that was simply campaigning for the same policies? The separation, Roskam said, was simply because the skills required to run a membership-based group are different from those the IPA has. In a bid to project a reassuring image, AEF announced that former television gardening personality, Don Burke, was the Chairman of AEF. Burke asserted the group's independence: 'We have no-one who is setting an agenda for us, we're not getting money from any particular group or whatever.' As for ties to corporate-funded groups such as the timber industry-funded Timber Communities Australia, Burke said, 'I wouldn't tolerate that in any group that I belong to ... nor would I tolerate payment coming in from groups that want us to change'.[86] However, by the time of its inaugural national conference in Brisbane in September 2006, AEF had enthusiastically embraced corporate funding.

During the conference, the sponsors—which included Monsanto, Murray Irrigation Limited, the Gunn's-dominated Forest Industries Association of Tasmania, and cotton company Auscott—were repeatedly thanked for making the conference possible. The presenter of ABC Radio National's 'Counterpoint' program, Michael Duffy, who covered his own costs to attend the event, was on hand to offer words of encouragement. Duffy noted that environmentalists 'are always proposing changes... and unfortunately journalists and even people who read newspapers like the idea of doing something'. The 'problem', as Duffy saw it, was that 'people like us often believe that we don't need to do anything'. One possible solution, he suggested, could be for the AEF to propose 'things that don't involve doing much'.[87]

AEF's policy line seems predictable. The few voices of moderation at the conference were from the transient guest presenters. Their suggestions that the existing system of National Parks was a good start, that the evidence demonstrating climate change is solid or that the logging industry would have to give ground, were humoured, but not embraced. Despite the reassuring language of balance and relying on science, the mood of the conference was dismissive of the idea of ratifying the Kyoto Protocol, in favour of logging native forests, supportive of considering nuclear power, and even hosting a nuclear waste dump. With less than a hundred members and tentative corporate support, AEF is struggling financially after only a year in existence. The Brisbane conference alone accounted for over three-quarters of its 2006 expenditure.

•

The effectiveness of think tanks like the IPA owes much to a simple set of principles: obscure the funding source behind the advocacy, court journalists with impressive-looking research and ready-to-roll talking heads, and dovetail advocacy in with allies in the media and politics to develop an 'echo chamber' effect. Even though a common maxim in journalism is to 'follow the money', comparatively few do when it comes to the think tanks that are increasingly shaping public debate. More surprising, though, is that it is rare for the journalists or the editors of the opinion pages of the newspapers to request disclosure of their potential conflicts of interest. It is hardly surprising that the IPA, despite its faux-enthusiasm for transparency, is reluctant to openly disclose which corporations fund it. It is, after all, in Roskam's words, in the 'protection' business. But within the burgeoning global network of free-market think tanks, there is disquiet about the rise of think tanks that see themselves as little more than corporate mouthpieces. In late 2005, John Blundell, the Director-General of the UK-based Institute of Economic Affairs and someone with impeccable credentials as a pioneer of the free-market think tanks, lashed out at what he dubbed 'wonk whores' and the trend to companies effectively buying advocacy support. 'Large cheques come attached to particular policy recommendations and senior corporate types sit on committees ready to "candle-snuff" dangerous ideas', he told *The Times*.[88]

SIX
TOXIC PR

The dark thunderclouds rolling across the wintry sky of Melbourne's western suburbs on 21 August 1991 were an ominous portent of things to come. In the heart of the vast Coode Island chemical complex, a flame flickered for just four seconds at the foot of storage tank number 80. Then all hell broke loose. A ball of flame shot 50 metres into the air, the earth shook and staff in the nearby administration building later described the sound as like the roar of a jet engine. Seconds later, the 15-metre high tank, propelled by the 280 000 litres of the toxic chemical acrylonitrile it dumped behind it, took off like a space-bound rocket. It flew through the air on a ten-second journey covering approximately 50 metres before finally crashing back to earth between the administration building and the station where chemical tankers came to fill up.[1] As cladding from the tank crashed to the ground, it brought down the powerlines supplying the complex. Without power, the alarm system was crippled. Tank 80's flight ripped apart the fire fighting system connected to it. One of the few defences left to contain the burning chemicals were the high earthen bund walls that had been constructed around the tanks to contain their contents in just such a worst-case scenario. Two minutes after tank 80 lifted off, tank 81 rocketed skywards too. It soared up a hundred metres, spilling 132 000 litres of toxic phenol along its path before crashing back to the ground, narrowly missing a tank containing more than two million litres of benzene.

The Coode Island tank farm was soon like a scene from a war zone. Some empty tanks just crumpled and melted from the intensity of the fires. Others exploded, their lids hinging back to reveal a fireball to the clouds. Debris from one exploding tank would rain earthwards smashing into other tanks. A tanker truck, loaded with 40 tonnes of benzene, went up in a ball of flame. Fed by an ever-expanding cocktail of chemicals, the raging fire generated a pall of black smoke, which, fanned by the westerly wind, soon arrived in Melbourne's central business district. City workers and residents were directed to stay indoors, close the house up, place towels under the doors and listen to the radio in case evacuation was necessary. Office air-conditioning units were turned off to avoid sucking the toxic air into buildings. Victoria Police scrambled its helicopter to track the plume of toxic smoke while Environment Protection Authority staff frantically monitored the air quality on the ground. After passing through Melbourne's business centre, the smoke wandered over to Richmond before a wind change pushed it across to the Yarra Valley.

When Coode Island went up, Colleen Hartland was working in Victoria's Parliament House as a pantry hand. After a chemical fire three years earlier at United Transport, a transport depot several hundred metres from Coode Island, Hartland and other residents had banded together to form the Hazardous Materials Action Group (HAZMAG). HAZMAG built a strong following, demanding that Coode Island be moved out of inner-city Melbourne. Soon after Tank 80 took off, Hartland was told by journalists in Parliament House about the unfolding disaster. HAZMAG's worst fears had come to pass.

If the United Transport fire had been a wake-up call, the chemical industry had chosen to slumber on. Even though Terminals Limited ran the Coode Island tank farm, it was the company's owner, Burns Philp, that called the shots. Soon after Tank 80 took off, Burns Philp called in the PR firm Hill & Knowlton to manage the crisis. The then Managing Director of H&K Australia, Brian West, later said that, within ten minutes of being called, the company had someone in Burns Philp's head office and, not long afterwards, someone else at the burning tank farm. 'When everyone else was running away we were going towards it, but because we knew police media liaison, we were able to get access to that site to start dealing with the management of the company', West said.[2]

For two-and-a-half hours, nearly half of all Melbourne's fire-fighters battled the inferno. It was horrible work. The crests of the containment walls were so narrow it was difficult to traverse the extinguished ponds without slipping down towards the foam-covered stew of chemicals contained within the bund walls. But getting along the top of the bund walls was the only way to access the still-burning pools of chemicals. By evening, most of the fire had been subdued, but not before it stretched firefighters' resources to the limits.

Before daylight had faded, a senior Burns Philp executive, Alex Awramenko, issued a media release stating that Terminals were assisting authorities bring the fire under control and were keen to 'establish the cause' of the fire.[3] It was a textbook crisis management move aimed at establishing Terminals early on as responsible, cooperative and accessible to the media. One thing Hill & Knowlton knew from experience was that it is always better to say something, no matter however bereft of substance, than leaving the field to be occupied by those likely to be far more critical. For Terminals, the public perception of the origin of the disaster mattered immensely. Proven negligence could potentially jeopardise insurance claims and result in prosecution for breaches of legislation. Public pressure could also force the government and regulators to insist that the whole Coode Island chemical complex be relocated outside Melbourne. Or, at a minimum, the government would insist on tougher standards and more rigorous enforcement. If, on the other hand, the fire was perceived as something entirely beyond the control of the company, the long-term impact would be significantly less. West later explained that in a crisis like Coode Island, companies needed to make sure that 'you are clearly seen to be in the victim box not in the culprit box. It makes a big difference as to how you are perceived and reported in the short term and how you are ultimately viewed in the long term.'[4] But companies can't plausibly position themselves as victims by issuing media releases proclaiming their innocence.

Later that evening, Victoria Police convened a media conference. At it, Chief Superintendent Brett Hume from the Metropolitan Fire Brigade revealed an unconfirmed report suggesting the fire had been caused by lightning. Up the back of the media conference was a representative of Hill & Knowlton. In a memo, later obtained as a result of a Freedom of Information request by the author, they noted Hume 'said a lightning strike could have been the cause (which fits into your statement)'.[5] It is unclear who this memo was addressed to, though it appears to have been to Burns Philp's Alex Awramenko. In a pitch to snare a share of the next morning's radio coverage, Terminals dispatched a media release at midnight, reiterating that the cause of the fire 'is still being investigated'.[6] However, by morning, Terminals plant manager Denis Wadeson was certain, informing the head of the police investigating team, Senior Sergeant Alex Robertson, that lightning had caused the fire.[7] For Terminals and the chemical industry, the prospect that the origin of the disaster was a freak act of God rather than incompetence of a chemical company was about as good as it could get.

The next morning, the industry faced a more immediate challenge, with Premier Joan Kirner scheduled to visit the chemical complex with the media in tow. To the relief of Terminals, rather than committing the government to moving the entire chemical complex, Kirner announced that a review panel would assess all chemical storage options at Coode Island and elsewhere. But the crisis was not yet over. A small fire at tank 69 had resisted all attempts to extinguish it. When senior Metropolitan Fire Brigade officers were meeting at Coode Island that afternoon, Tank 69 exploded. It was as though the disaster of the day before was being replayed. More tanks exploded in flame, and chunks of metal flew through the air. The lid from one tank crashed to ground, narrowly missing a group of firefighters. A piece of shrapnel smashed through the windscreen of a firefighting tanker, luckily unoccupied at the time. It took four more hours before the fire finally succumbed. The fire was out, but large sections of Coode Island lay in ruins. Eighteen storage tanks had been totally destroyed or seriously damaged, and a further 15 damaged. The repair bill was estimated to be more than $20 million. The impact on the health of emergency workers was unknowable, but more than 120 firefighters and 90 police complained of ill-health from the smoke.

The fire had also been a catastrophe for the public credibility of the chemicals industry, and the concerns of HAZMAG had been vindicated. Graphic aerial footage of the exploding tanks had been screened around the world, with stories leading every CNN international bulletin for 48 hours. In an attempt to regain lost ground, Terminals announced they had appointed Dames and Moore, an engineering and environmental consultancy, to inquire into the fires. Work on the investigation had already commenced, they reassuringly stated.[8] Not surprisingly, residents, the Opposition Liberal Party, local government leaders and the Victorian Trades Hall Council urged the relocation of chemical storage facilities. Robertson, from the City West Criminal Investigation Bureau of Victoria Police, announced that a task force with representatives from a number of agencies had been formed to prepare a brief for a Coroner's Office investigation into the fires.[9] Joan Kirner beefed up her stance, too, announcing that all or part of the Coode Island complex would be moved.[10]

In a bid to defuse the growing political crisis, Terminals adopted a conciliatory stance. It flagged that it 'would give full consideration to not rebuilding or replacing the damaged tanks' at the chemical complex.[11] In a fax to Burns Philp, Mary Clark, a Hill & Knowlton consultant, sought to reassure the company that all was not lost:

> We had to combine our strategies; announce the possible non-rebuilding of the plant (to keep government and unions happy as well as the community)...I apologise for not making sure you saw this but I believe it is all legally watertight and no irrevocable commitments have been made.[12]

Clark sought to soothe the jangled corporate nerves by recounting that an AAP journalist had commented to her that their approach 'seems like a very responsible attitude'. 'This is the desired effect of this strategy', she wrote.

Behind the scenes, Terminals had some bridge-building work to do with others in the chemical industry. Six days after the fires erupted, the industry gritted its teeth and decided to present a united front. A 'highly confidential' Hill & Knowlton memo reported that Clark attended a strategy meeting of the Australian Chemical Industry Council at which they agreed that both would 'follow the strategy that the chemicals industry would carry the weight of the publicity'.[13] In a bid to placate the hostile public, the Bulk Liquids Industry Association ran reassuring full-page advertisements in major newspapers, thanking the firefighters and the Victorian Government, but opposing the relocation of Coode Island. Rather than place ads in the papers of the most affected suburbs, Hill & Knowlton figured that private one-on-one briefings for the editors would be more effective.[14] However, no matter how reassuring the statements from the industry were, the question that worried them most was what had caused the fire. The lightning strike theory was ditched soon after Channel Seven broadcast security camera footage from a premises adjoining Coode Island. From the footage, Hill & Knowlton noted, 'it does not appear that a lightning strike occurred prior to the explosion'. Despite having earlier backed the lightning strike theory, the internal Hill & Knowlton memo stated that 'as policy we did not allege that a lightning strike caused the fire simply because it has not been confirmed'.[15]

The lightning strike hypothesis had other problems for Terminals, as it was unclear whether its insurance policy even covered such events.[16] In the face of uncertainty, Terminals' media release criticised 'ill-informed commentators' for 'advancing opinions on the circumstances surrounding the explosion and subsequent fire whilst investigations have not been concluded'.[17] Even though Police had told Hill & Knowlton they didn't want them interfering in the morning media conferences, they kept in close contact with the police media unit.[18] Less than two weeks after the fires, a Hill & Knowlton memo noted 'H&K maintaining good liaison with head of police investigation squad Alex Robertson'.[19] A few days later, *The Age* reported that Robertson was considering the possibility that the cause of the fire could have been sabotage.[20] It was as if a kite was being flown to test the winds.

Almost six weeks later, police convened a sensational joint media conference featuring Victoria Police officers and Metropolitan

Fire Brigade personnel, at which they announced that the cause
of the Coode Island fires was sabotage. According to police, the
stainless steel pipes on Tank 80 had been cut by saboteurs using
oxyacetylene equipment. Robertson claimed the saboteurs started
a small fire intended as a protest and, when it grew larger than
intended, they had run out a fire hose in an attempt to douse
the flames, then grabbed their oxyacetylene gear, stuffed it in a
backpack and escaped without anyone seeing them. The evidence,
Robertson pronounced, was 'conclusive', and that in order to
track down the culprits, they were appointing a 20-person
taskforce to investigate the sabotage.[21] In a media statement,
Robertson stated that 'the culprits have endangered hundreds of
innocent members of the community'.[22]

The media went into a feeding frenzy. The front-page headline
of *The Age* headline proclaimed 'Hunt for Coode Island saboteur'.
The tabloid *Herald Sun*'s journalists, John Silverster and Craig
Dixon, reported that detectives on the case would 'check the
radical environmentalists and groups of individuals with perceived
grievances against the storage plant'. The only hint of scepticism
came from the Secretary of Trades Hall Council, John Halfpenny,
who called on police to reveal evidence to back up their claim.
Having announced the conclusion before completing inquiries,
the head of the taskforce, Inspector Sharp, backtracked and
invoked the need for secrecy. Sharp said that police would not
be releasing further details, as it would adversely affect the investigation, and mysteriously claimed that no individual, group or
organisation was being investigated.[23] If the claims made by
police seemed nonsensical, they passed without scrutiny. One of
the spillover effects was that the public hearings on the fire that
commenced the following week were entirely overshadowed.
They also forced ABC TV's influential 'Four Corners' program
on the Coode Island fires, set to air a few days after the police

media conference, to soften its critique and incorporate the sabotage claims.

Four years later, Hill & Knowlton's Brian West insisted that they had no prior knowledge that Robertson would allege sabotage, and that the claim took them 'by surprise'. When pressed, West suggested the author speak to Rob Masters, from Hill & Knowlton's Melbourne office. As set out in a witness statement to the Administrative Appeals Tribunal (AAT) in a Freedom of Information appeal, the author recounted Masters stating:

> We had close liaison with Police prior to the press conference where we had them do the upfront work to save the company being in the focus too much, we didn't want to be seen to have our head up... If the company said this sort of thing then people would be inclined to be a bit sceptical about how credible it was.

In a statement to the AAT, Masters agreed the statements attributed to him were 'broadly consistent in general theoretical terms' with the advice he would provide to a client, but rejected the suggestion that Hill & Knowlton had liaised with police about promoting the sabotage theory.[24] Hill & Knowlton's Mary Clark also submitted a statement that she had only become aware of the police's sabotage theory after media contacted Terminals, seeking a comment. Terminals, she wrote, 'indicated clearly that they did not support the theory of sabotage'.[25]

Hill & Knowlton's story was contradicted, however, when documents obtained in the course of the AAT proceedings revealed a letter from Terminals to the Minister for Police and Emergency Services, Mal Sandon, stamped 'confidential', which had been written the day after the Victoria Police media conference. In it, Terminals General Manager, Eric Olufson, wrote that the week before the police went public, Terminals 'requested and were granted a lengthy meeting to express our views on some of the evidence he believes pertinent to the theory of sabotage'.[26] Victoria Police claim they have no record of the meeting. But there was no attempt to criticise the sabotage theory at all. Terminals' letter to Sandon simply stated that 'we are not in a position to make comprehensive supportive statements' about the sabotage theory.[27] On a draft copy of the letter, a handwritten preamble to this sentence, not incorporated in the final version, stated 'although we are not discounting the theory'. A media statement issued by Terminals the same day blandly confirmed that sabotage was 'one of several theories which have been investigated'.[28] Clark later amended her statement to the AAT. 'My advice to Terminals was to disassociate [sic] the company as quickly as possible from the theory of sabotage, without being critical of the police. Neither Hill & Knowlton nor Terminals supported or promoted the theory of sabotage at any time,' she wrote.[29] But this was contradicted by another document also obtained in the AAT case. On a cover note to a copy of Terminals's media release on the sabotage claims, Clark wrote to Channel Nine's television news reporter, Hugh Rimington, '...it is worth saying (if you want to) that Terminals considers sabotage to be "one of several possible causes of the fire", but that they will be continuing their investigations into all other possible scenarios...'[30]

If Terminals were being publicly coy, a spokesman for the Bulk Liquids Industry Association felt no such constraints, telling the media they were shocked at the suggestion of sabotage.[31] The day after the police media conference, the Australian Chemical Industry Council (ACIC), of which Terminals was a member, held a day-long crisis meeting for chemical plant managers from around the country. ACIC's spokesperson, Rudi Michelson, told the media 'we are in a state of amazement that one of our plants has been sabotaged'.[32]

In the days after the police media conference, Colleen Hartland received a number of phone calls from plumbers ridiculing the claims made by police. 'They all told me that it wasn't possible for oxyacetylene to cut those pipes', she said. There may have been a fatal technical flaw in the police claims, but it made little difference. In one day, Victoria Police had destroyed much of HAZMAG's hard-won public credibility. Journalists kept their distance, and members of the public who didn't have personal knowledge of the groups were wary. For Hartland, worse was to come. In the month following the police media conference, she received obscene phone calls to the point where she avoided answering the phone. The tyres on her car were slashed when it was parked outside her Footscray home. Hartland was so convinced that she would get a visit from police, she wryly recalled that she cleaned up her house. She needn't have bothered, as the 20-person Operation Coode never even contacted her or interviewed anyone in any of Melbourne's major environmental groups. The issue soon died down and the media circus moved on.

In June 1992, more than eighteen months after the initial sabotage claims, the Department of Labor and Industry and Victoria Police announced that the fire had been caused by a lack of maintenance.[33] Exhaustive forensic tests on metal pipes and other equipment seized from the site had shown that there was no criminal involvement. The Department of Labour and Industry had consulted metallurgists and concluded that the failure of the pipe at the base of Tank 80 was more likely to have been caused by general wear and tear and the age of the pipes than foul play.[34]

Victoria Police decisions, though, are fickle. In April 1994, over a year and a half after discarding the sabotage theory, the police revived it once more for the benefit of the Coroner's hearing. In a brief submitted to the Coroner, Detective Senior Sergeant Alexander Robertson claimed that the pipe had been cut by a 'high energy cutting process', and designated the cause of the fire as 'suspicious'.[35] Witness statements and evidence given under cross-examination exposed massive holes in Robertson's theory. Tony Del Monte, an operator employed by Terminals Limited, stated that just minutes before the fire started, he had walked past the very site where it was claimed the saboteurs had been at work.[36] Denis Wadeson, the site manager at Coode Island, along with other witnesses, acknowledged that the cutting wheels and welding rods found at the base of Tank 80 were probably from the construction of the tank or earlier maintenance work. Numerous witnesses, including Wadeson, told the inquiry that oxyacetylene cannot cut stainless steel pipes.[37]

The 'conclusive forensic evidence' that police had relied on for the original sabotage theory was a report produced by Robert Barnes of the Victoria Police State Forensic Science Laboratory. Barnes, along with Bruce Cannon from the Welding Technology Institute of Australia, argued that the lack of oxidation on the spatter on the remaining pipe led them to conclude that it had come from a flame-cutting process within days of the fire.[38] Other experts called on by the Coroner's Office disagreed. Metallurgists from RMIT and those engaged by Terminals agreed that the 'spatter' was 'caused by extreme heats and an actual bubbling or rising of certain elements of the metal to the surface'.[39] Nor could the Occupational Health and Safety Authority replicate the damage to the pipe with cutting and grinding tools or oxyacetylene.[40] But even if the pipe had been cut by 'saboteurs', it couldn't have caused the explosion. Terminals staff gave evidence that the pipe was empty, having been washed out after the last delivery of chemicals three months earlier. Even if there had been phenol in the line, the Occupational Health and Safety Authority concluded that little would have escaped, as it was just above its melting point and any leakage would have quickly solidified on the pipe and ground. Even if it had leaked, the air temperature would have to have been at least 78°C to reach ignition point, but it was only approximately 15°C at the time of the fire.[41]

Robertson's fire hose claim didn't stack up either. Evidence provided by Terminals employee Wadeson was that the fire hose was run out by Terminals staff.[42] Indeed, Victoria Police's Senior Sergeant Jouning, who was assisting the Coroner, explained that just three weeks after the fires, the Victorian Operations Manager for Terminals Ltd, Rob Bennett, told detectives that he had helped run out the hoses.[43] Jouning also revealed that police received this information five weeks *before* they held the media conference at which they claimed the fire hose had been run out by saboteurs. Nor could the Coroner find evidence to support the argument that a fire had burned at the base of the tank for some time prior to the explosion. The security camera footage showed the explosion followed by the tank taking off four seconds later, leaving no time for any saboteurs to escape incineration let alone run out the fire hoses. 'Add to this', the Coroner noted in her report:

> the difficulties in transporting oxyacetylene flame cutting equipment over the bund walls and the fact that there was no evidence of any such equipment found after the fire … and one sees the implausibility of every inference that might potentially arise from the metallurgical conclusions.[44]

When police first outlined their sabotage theory to a credulous media, Hill & Knowlton, Terminals and Victoria Police officers all knew of one or more fatal flaws in the hypothesis. But at the time that it mattered most, none publicly spoke out about what they knew. As a consequence, the public were deceived and a small group of citizens smeared and harassed for raising valid concerns about the location of a major chemical complex in the heart of Melbourne. For more than two years after Victoria Police launched their conspiracy theory, the government, departmental officials and the Coroner were to waste public resources investigating a hypothesis that was ludicrous from the outset. Perhaps more importantly, the consequences of having police so emboldened that they felt they could pursue a political agenda without suffering any consequence is disturbing. That there has been no internal investigation and no one disciplined hardly augers well. Victoria Police fiercely resisted my Freedom of Information application for documents on the Coode Island investigation and other allegations of eco-terrorism to such a degree that they suffered the largest-ever award for costs against an agency on a Freedom of Information case in the Victorian Civil and Administrative Tribunal (VCAT). Much of the power of the 'sabotage' accusation relied on journalists uncritically accepting a story fed to them by the police and then failing to follow up, except along predictably accusatory lines.

Journalism is often referred to as the 'first draft of history', but sometimes it is the only draft when the attention of the media wanders. When the sabotage accusation was initially disproved in 1992, it was little reported. When police revived the theory for the Coroner's inquiry and it was subsequently demolished, there was no coverage at all. Two years before Coode Island went up in flames, Tony Fitzgerald had warned, in his final report into corruption in Queensland, about the potential use of the media by:

> police officers and other public officials who wish to put out propaganda to advance their own interests and harm their enemies ... A hunger for 'leaks' and 'scoops' ... and some journalists' relationships with the sources who provide them with information, can make it difficult for the media to maintain its independence and a critical stance. Searches for motivation, and even checks for accuracy may suffer as a result.[45]

Tree muggers

By the mid-1990s, the logging industry in Australia was well and truly on the nose with the public. Julian Smith, from the advertising agency Ogilvy & Mather, told an advertising industry conference that, based on market research, the persona of the timber industry could best be summarised as being:

> I am a blue singleted, tattooed, seventeen stone bully. I work in the forests and I can't stand these bludgers who come in here and chain themselves to bulldozers and trees, so I drag 'em out of the way and give 'em a bit of a biff to go on with. I make a living raping the forests and I don't care about the future of the mess I leave behind. I just make as much as I can out of chopping down trees because it's a good lurk with a big quid in it while it lasts.[46]

Despite the logging industry having an appalling public reputation, all was not lost. Stewart Murrihy, a PR adviser for a proposed woodchip mill in Tasmania, explained to a national PR industry conference in 1995 that as soon as forests issues were in the media, public anxiety grew. 'So we really took the view that the key to the strategy was trying to keep it very low key', he explained.[47] While a low-key strategy was what the logging companies craved, they also embraced two other strategies to regain lost ground. The first was pouring funds and support into what has become Australia's longest-running grassroots front group—initially known as the Forest Protection Society (FPS) and later renamed Timber Communities Australia (TCA)—to put a community face on a logging industry message.[48] The second was playing the 'eco-terrorism' card, which had proven devastatingly effective following the Coode Island explosion. Hyping 'eco-terrorism' could not only help the logging industry publicly reposition any violence by loggers against environmentalists as a defensive response, but also be used to justify calls for police investigations of their opponents, and government measures to criminalise civil disobedience protests.

There was good reason for the public to view the logging industry as violent. In March 1986, the scene of logging industry contractors assaulting environmentalists at Farmhouse Creek in Tasmania had been broadcast internationally. Almost a decade later, the then Executive Director of the NSW Forest Products Association, Col Dorber, in a nationally televised interview, defended logging contractors assaulting environmentalists protesting against logging operations on the south coast of New South Wales:

> If we have to have a fight, if we have to physically confront those people who have opposed us for so long, then so be it ... I also say to people in the industry, if you are going to do that, use your commonsense and make sure it's not being filmed when you do it.[49]

In the ensuing public controversy, Dorber was widely condemned for his comments. Boral Timber resigned as a member of the industry lobby group, and Dorber apologised for his comments. He had his defenders, though. The then *Telegraph-Mirror* columnist Miranda Devine bemoaned that Dorber had apologised, and lashed out at Boral for 'deserting his cause'. Despite a lack of supporting evidence, Devine blamed environmentalists for damaging logging equipment, and cited this as justification for violence. 'It may not be palatable to say so publicly but violence can sometimes be good ... there comes a point in any disagreement when diplomacy ceases to be of any use. That is when violence has its place', she wrote.[50]

But pushing the storyline that damage to logging industry equipment was attributable to environmentalists had its limits. In March 1996, the NSW State Secretary of the Construction,

Forestry, Mining and Energy Union (CFMEU), Gavin Hillier, explained that South Coast logging contractors' equipment had been damaged during disputes over the unionisation of employees. He acknowledged that while environmentalists publicly got the blame, the contractors knew exactly who had vandalised their equipment:

> We know how to sugar trucks...and you break windscreens too because windscreen and tyres they don't get insurance for...but anything else you get insurance for. Every tyre is worth $2,000 to them. We had to hit them and hit them hard. And you [environmentalists] probably got the blame for it too along the track. I'm telling you now that they knew who it was, we told those contractors that you behave your fucking selves or the same thing will happen.[51]

If Hillier had revealed one of the timber industry's dirty little secrets, there was a deafening silence from peak industry lobby groups: no angry denunciation, no calls for police investigation, and not even a peep from the industry's compliant front group.

Barry Chipman is one of the long-standing activists of Timber Communities Australia (TCA). After working in a variety of jobs in and around the timber industry, in 1993 Chipman applied for a job as Director of the TCA in Tasmania. The contact on the ad was Robert Bain, the executive director of National Association of Forest Industries (NAFI).[52] At its launch in 1987, the logging industry had claimed that it would only be providing start-up funding for the group.[53] But as Chipman himself later acknowledged, the group is reliant on to industry funding. 'We could not function without that (financial) support from the companies and the industry', he stated.[54] Around the country, the TCA branches have been voluble defenders of the native forest logging industry's interests. On some occasions, its efforts have been dismal failures, such as its effort to prolong the logging of the rainforests of Fraser Island and elsewhere in south-east Queensland. In northern New South Wales and Western Australia, they have had some, though limited, impact. In other places, such as Victoria's East Gippsland, southern New South Wales and Tasmania, the TCA has been a significant player in perpetuating logging operations. However, the activities have sometimes got it into hot water.

In 1988, PR firm Network Communications distributed the strategy meeting notes of the FPS. Under the item of 'Long term program', the minutes recorded that:

> Robyn Loydell discussed activities by her group which involved taking over local environmentalist meetings, with the result that they became distracted from their ongoing campaign. Robyn's group actually controls the voting on several groups and could therefore vote to have them join the Forest Protection Society.[55]

When asked about the hypothetical scenario of a PR company hiring people to covertly infiltrate community groups to gather intelligence for a client, PR industry leaders are surprisingly relaxed about the idea. 'I wouldn't get terribly excited about it unless the information was misused. It would be like an investigative journalist getting in there to find things out and it is a question of how it is used', said Peter Lazar, a leading member of the College of Fellows, which overseas ethics issues.[56]

In an interview with the author in 1997, the then PRIA President, Tony Harrison, could see little wrong with the practice. At worst, he said, it was 'a grey area' where it was 'hard to give a definitive answer':

> But I think that if all you did was go in there and got some information that wasn't used to harm that organisation but

was used to give your client a better appreciation, then you'd find it hard to say that is unethical behaviour.[57]

A little over a year after Victoria's Police's Coode Island conspiracy theory, the FPS talked up the risk of 'eco-terrorism' once more. In January 1993, Steve Guest from the Victorian Association of Forest Industries flew to Tasmania with Sergeant Terry Walsh from Victoria Police's Special Branch. The ostensible purpose was to 'brief' timber industry leaders and Tasmania Police on the activities of the US-based group Earth First! and 'eco-terrorism'. After the briefing, police and timber industry leaders jointly fronted a media conference to express their alarm at the rise of 'eco-terrorism', even though none had occurred.[58] In the run-up to the March 1993 federal election, forestry issues were once more coming to the fore. Of particular interest was the likelihood that the Tasmanian Greens would win their first-ever Senate seat and potentially the balance of power, increasing the chance that the Labor Government would make concessions on Tasmanian forest issues.

Just two days out from polling day the election campaign took a dramatic twist. Early on a Thursday morning, a cheap explosive mix of fertiliser and diesel, along with a length of wire, was found underneath the railway track abutting the bridge over the Black River in North West Tasmania. The bridge adjoined a yard where logs were loaded onto the railway for transport to the woodchip mills further east. Hanging on the bridge that morning was a banner, which stated 'Save the Tarkine: Earth First', referring to Australia's largest area of rainforest wilderness. The media went into a feeding frenzy, fuelled in part by Premier Ray Groom pointing a finger at 'extreme' environmentalists.[59] Mark Addis, the Executive Director of the Forest Industries Association of Tasmania, chimed in too, stating that it was entirely consistent with what Earth First! people have indicated they are prepared to do.[60]

While the materials were made to *look* like a bomb, there was no way it could have exploded, as it didn't have a detonator. If it wasn't meant to explode, why would anyone bother? There were other telltale indicators that it was a hoax. If it were someone from Earth First!, why had the trademark exclamation mark been omitted from the banner? And how was it that an anonymous tip-off to one television station about the 'bomb' was to an unlisted number that was the dedicated 'police line'? But smears work in the absence of evidence, largely because too many journalists defer to authority figures, especially police. The next day, the front-page headline of the north-west Tasmanian newspaper, *The Advocate,* screamed 'Railway bomb: environment group linked', and the article confidently predicted that the 'international eco-terrorist group Earth First! has been linked with the potentially dangerous device on the TasRail line'. The Hobart newspaper, *The Mercury,* ran with the headline 'Explosives under rail line in green protest', though the following day it had to concede, after objections, that it had no evidence that the 'bomb' was associated with a 'green protest'. Once the ballots were cast and counted, the Tasmanian Greens narrowly missed out on winning the last Senate seat.

Six months later, Tasmania Police released a briefing note clearing environmentalists of involvement, while giving a more qualified exoneration to supporters of the timber industry.[60] Years later, a more emphatic memo from Victoria Police's Counter Terrorist Intelligence Section (CTIS) was obtained through a Freedom of Information request by Friends of the Earth. Written in July 1993, just four months after the 'bomb', CTIS noted that 'the device is considered [by Tasmania Police] to be an elaborate hoax and they have not ruled out the possibility that it may have been placed there by loggers in an attempt to discredit the Green movement'.[61] Even though Victoria Police knew by late 1993 that both the Coode Island and 'Black River bomb' 'eco-terrorist' claims were nonsense, it didn't deter Sergeant Walsh from teaming up once more with the logging industry to point an accusatory finger at environmentalists.

Walsh appeared at an October 1994 media conference hosted by the FPS in a Senate committee room in Parliament House, Canberra. In his presentation Walsh attributed non-prosecuted instances of damage to forestry and other property to environmentalists, dubbing them all 'ecotage'. He passingly noted the concern by environmentalists that there may be those in the timber industry perpetrating incidents to discredit the movement but was non-committal on the possibility.[62] However, Victoria Police's own false claims about Coode Island being 'sabotaged' didn't rate a mention and Walsh remained tight-lipped when asked by the author about them. There were other benefits of building a close relationship with police. At one PR conference, the head of NAFI, Dr Robert Bain, boasted that Victorian Special Branch police had infiltrated environment groups and passed information about the movements of protestors on to the timber industry.[63]

Bain might have been delighted with the fruits of courting police, but some officers were alarmed that the independence of police was being compromised. Early in 1995, Superintendent Haldane from the Bairnsdale CIB in Victoria noted that members of the FPS had attempted to align themselves with police. Officers 'having dealings with the FPS should do so in this knowledge and be careful not to compromise the impartial position of the force', he cautioned.[64] Several days later, Haldane followed up with another memo, which was later obtained under a Freedom of Information request by Friends of the Earth, indicating that he had received a tip-off that it was possible that contractors' equipment might be damaged 'by pro-logging interests in an attempt to discredit the anti-woodchipping and conservation movements'. Haldane sought to caution his CIB officers of jumping to the conclusion that environmentalists would be to blame.[65] Indeed, in the AAT Detective Sergeant John Weel from Bairnsdale CIB conceded that of twelve incidents of damage to logging machinery in forest areas in East Gippsland, there had been six prosecutions and convictions, none of which were related to environmental issues. Weel stated that the motivations ranged from rivalry between contractors, within families and general vandalism.[66] But there were good reasons to worry about the politicisation of police.

A complaint was made in 1991 to police against an environmentalist from the East Gippsland town of Bendoc because he had raised concerns that logging operations could be affecting the quality of the water supply of the town. Victoria Police's Counter Terrorist Intelligence Section determined that members of the 'radical green movement' were 'attempting to link forestry and industry to water degradation'. As a result they decided further inquiries were warranted and a note on the complainant should be kept in the file designated for potential 'eco-terrorists'.[67] The beauty of the myth of rampant 'eco-terrorism' and vandalism for the timber industry is that it can be used to justify anything. Following revelations in 2006 that a PR consultant to the forestry company Amcor, Derek Amos, had run a spying operation on environmental groups in Victoria, the federal Labor Party Spokesman on Forestry, Martin Ferguson, cited vandalism of logging contractors' equipment as a justification. He told *The Australian*:

> When you get screwdrivers jammed into the radiators of contractors' equipment and the workers have to sleep away from their families in their vehicles at night, there was a lot

of concern in regional communities about what some of the
environmental groups were doing to ordinary people and their
families.[68]

As with earlier reporting on Coode Island and the Black River
'bomb', Ferguson was not required to provide any evidence to
support his claim. Ferguson did not respond to repeated requests
by the author for an interview.

Political smears are one thing, but some timber industry
supporters have gone to extraordinary lengths to silence the
dissenting voices of protesters. With part of the Otway Ranges
forests comprising the water catchment for Geelong, and many
Melburnians having holiday houses along the Great Ocean Road,
it was always a matter of when, not if, the logging of the remnant
native forests came to an end. Faced with a sustained community
based coalition of local environmentalists and tourism operators,
major forestry companies were getting the message too. In
December 1998, Kimberley-Clark announced that it would no
longer source any of its timber feed from the Otways for its pulp
mill at Millicent in South Australia. The logging industry was
being squeezed by falling demand for logs and effective civil
disobedience protests that disrupted logging operations.

Ahead of another summer of protests expected to start in
mid-January 1999, logging industry supporters opted for a radical
strategy to end logging protests. The forests division of the
CFMEU and Belinda Murnane, the coordinator for the Otway
Forest Industries Information Group (OFIG), announced that
a public meeting would be held in Colac to develop measures
to counter 'greenies' blockading logging operations.[69] The convener
of the public meeting, the CFMEU's Jane Calvert, argued that
logging industry supporters needed a plan for 'peaceful direct
reaction' to environmentalists' civil disobedience. Calvert's 'direct
response', a police memo later revealed, included 'blockading

same [protestors] in the coups + videoing all their activities'.[70] It was a proposal supported by the meeting.[71] Addressing the meeting, which attracted approximately two hundred people, Chief Inspector John Robinson offered a little PR advice for the logging industry supporters. 'I stressed the need to minimise publicity and confrontation', he wrote in a diary entry, later obtained under the Freedom of Information Act.

The weekend after the meeting, a group of environmentalists visited the Beech Forest area and decided to set up a base protest camp on public land at the edge of Seaview Ridge Road. The following morning, a group of approximately 50 logging industry supporters arrived at the site and Calvert announced that the forestry workers and supporters were establishing a 'picket line' for 'health and safety' reasons, and that the 16 environmentalists would not be allowed to leave their campsite. When a number of individuals attempted to leave, they were herded back into the camp. Later that afternoon, Calvert announced that the only way that those blockaded into the camp could get out was if they signed a statement drafted by the CFMEU promising 'never to engage in any form of protest at a coupe or against a Forest and Forest Products/CFMEU worker and their workplace'.[72] To increase the pressure on the protestors, floodlights were set up to run all night. To power the lights, a generator was located next to the protest camp and its muffler removed. Chainsaws were repeatedly started up and brandished in the direction of those in the camp. Not surprisingly, the pressure began to take its toll. One of the protestors needed urgent medical attention, but pleas to allow her to leave were initially rejected until finally police called an ambulance.

Police continued to allow only food and other supplies into the camp, but no one was getting out. In an internal police memo, Victoria Police's Sergeant Merry noted that the CFMEU 'will not allow the greens to leave the area'. While outlining which shifts his officers would spend helping enforce the counter-protest, Merry advised that they 'will take no active role as to the legality of this picket at this stage'.[73] For five days, the environmentalists were imprisoned. The 'picket' was only lifted after several people managed to escape through the bush and raised the alarm. Media coverage, along with phone calls from Australian Greens Senator Bob Brown and family members to police commanders, finally had the effect of making police rethink their role as 'picket' line enforcers and bush prison officers. Two years later, eleven of the environmentalists initiated legal action for false imprisonment against the CFMEU and others. Eventually, in December 2004, Supreme Court Justice Ashley found in favour of some of the environmentalists and awarded them more than $210 600 in damages and other costs.

The decision is currently under appeal, with lawyers for the plaintiffs arguing that the damages were inadequate and unjustly denied to some. The potential outcome of the appeal has the CFMEU worried. 'The lawsuit could have the possibility of bankrupting the division of the union', said Michael O'Connor, the National Secretary of the Forestry Division of the CFMEU.[74] O'Connor refused to be drawn on whether the union had turned to the logging industry to help cover some of the $2.2 million it has spent on the case, insisting that he wouldn't comment on the case until the final decision has been handed down. Others were more forthcoming. On one of the 63 days of hearings on the case, a small delegation from NAFI sat up the back of the courtroom. They were there on a scouting trip to assess whether to financially support the CFMEU, though John Gay, the CEO of the Tasmanian logging company Gunns, preferred to explain that he was there 'just to have a look about'. However, Gay explained that the industry body agreed to financially support the union, although he was uncertain of the exact amount.[75]

The then head of NAFI, Kate Carnell, confirmed that NAFI had contributed funds and other support.[76]

•

While it is routine for PR issue and crisis managers to view police as just another group to be courted and hopefully mobilised as a credible 'third party', the very concept is alarming. The effectiveness of policing requires public trust and confidence that the enforcement of the law is based on an impartial assessment of the evidence and the even-handed application of the law. Politicised police, on the other hand, become agents of injustice, undermine the laws they have sworn to uphold, embolden vigilantism and deter citizens from being active participants in democratic debate. While some in PR embrace the use of coercive tactics others prefer selling the superficially appealing idea that activist groups should just sit down and talk things through with companies they have problems with.

SEVEN

WHEN CORPORATIONS WANT TO CUDDLE

Peter Sandman, one of the world's most influential but low-profile PR advisers, describes his work as being akin to that of an early childhood teacher: 'I don't think it is easily framed as spin-doctoring, it is much more like kindergarten—tell the truth, say you are sorry and share.'[1] If Sandman's clients find telling the truth and saying sorry hard enough, perhaps his most radical advice is to share decision-making with activist groups. Where most PR tends to rely on communicating to critics and their supporters indirectly through the media, Sandman wants clients to involve them directly. To do this, he advises clients to invite activists and critics into forums where they are provided with information, their advice is sought, and they are even encouraged to help set standards for their operations. 'Lure them into collaboration (by making the only alternative public unreasonableness and possible marginalisation). This is always worth trying, even if the group seems unlikely to prove willing. It can't hurt', he suggests.[2] The benefit of such 'engagement', he argues, is in getting 'external groups to face hard choices, and of out-sourcing controversial decisions that would have little credibility if made within the company'.[3] The flip side is that he urges activist groups to provide public support and encouragement when companies take their first tentative steps towards reform.

Central to Sandman's strategy is a classification of 'stakeholders' and, in particular, how much 'power' they 'can bring to bear'. In Sandman's analysis, the stakeholders that PR managers need to pay most attention to are those who have the greatest overlap between 'passion' and 'power'. Depending on how they rank in these two areas, the company can choose one of four strategies: deflect, defer, dismiss, or defeat.[4] (Sandman adds the qualifier that all the labels are 'exaggerations...but they capture something important'.) Stakeholders with power but no passion should be 'deflected', which involves 'keeping them out of the situation'. People with passion but no power, on the other hand, can be 'defeated'. Sandman suggests it is 'smarter to reach a compromise with them if you can', though he goes on to note that 'you can beat them if you have to'. And people with neither passion nor power are easier still. Just 'dismiss' them. The one occasion when Sandman says real reform is necessary is when dealing with people who have both high passion and high power. Those people, he says, are 'a force to reckon with', and the company will eventually have to 'defer' to their demands 'one way or another, to one extent or another'.

Sandman's analysis—part critic of corporate misbehaviour, part champion of activist groups—seems appealing. The medicine he prescribes his clients take—learning to love transparency, engaging with critics and treating them with respect, reducing hazard where the risk is real, and 'outrage' where it isn't—seems too good to be true. 'There is sometimes a risk', Sandman said, that a company:

> is willing to give up half a loaf but can't find anybody to take
> half a loaf. All it can find is people to accuse it of hypocrisy

because it's half a loaf...It is useful that there is someone
saying 'no it is only half a loaf, you asshole', but there has got
to be someone saying 'Wow, half a loaf'.[5]

In Sandman's analysis, which is shared by others in the PR
industry, the path to progress relies on NGOs prepared to cuddle
up with corporations and 'stake out the middle, not the extreme'.

Even if companies are reluctantly persuaded they have no
choice other than to get up close and personal with NGOs, it
requires advocacy groups to also embrace the idea. Enticing
NGOs to embrace 'engagement' with corporations involves selling
activist groups on the idea that financial independence from
business is a redundant 1970s notion, that collaboration with
industry is a superior, conflict-free and more effective form of
advocacy. NGO enthusiasts for 'engagement' with corporations
often rather smugly disparage the idea that they are being used
in a 'divide-and-conquer' strategy or that their independence is
compromised. But pick a social movement, whether it is
concerned with the environment, human rights, indigenous
rights, aid and trade or health, and divide-and-conquer strategies
are in play.

The reason the public supports watchdog groups is the belief
that they are fearless and independent advocates for the public
interest in a time when major political parties gravitate to what
their latest batch of polling defines as the 'centre'. Yet it is this
independence of non-government organisations that is at stake
with engagement with corporations. The term 'Stockholm
Syndrome' was coined in the early 1970s to describe the
phenomena of hostages sympathising with their captors. Whether
for financial reasons or growing personal ties to likeable corporate
executives, those enmeshed in engagement become more inclined
to believe the best of a company. When in doubt, they tend to
opt for silence rather than speaking out and letting the public

decide. Often engaged activists don't notice, or turn a blind eye to, the dual corporate game of speaking nicely to NGOs while lobbying behind the scenes to weaken existing regulations or undermine other campaigns. In many respects, the environmental group WWF Australia, which pulled in over $17.7 million in income in 2006, is an exemplar of corporate friendly activism, as it has espoused engagement for longer than any other Australian NGO. In 2006 alone, WWF Australia received over $886 000 from corporations. Internationally, WWF has a mixed reputation. Some national affiliates are notorious for the inclination of senior management to cut controversial deals and undermine grassroots activists. In other countries, WWF are widely respected by other groups as valued colleagues. WWF International, headquartered in Switzerland, has long embraced the role of mixing with the business elite, including those from the PR industry. In the late 1970s, Burson-Marsteller's (B-M) head of the Hong Kong office, David Mitchell, was appointed the head of PR for WWF International. As a result, the founder of B-M, Harold Burson, accepted an invitation to join the board. In his memoirs, Burson wrote that 'for five years I was on the WWF board amidst royalty and multi-millionaire industrialists'.[6]

In November 2005, Sandman flew to Alice Springs to speak at a Minerals Council of Australia's conference. This time, his trip was sponsored by Newmont, a global gold mining company dogged by controversies over pollution from a mine in Indonesia, and its attempt to develop the Lake Cowal gold mine in an internationally recognised wetland in central New South Wales. The day before Sandman's presentation, the conference got under way with a keynote presentation by Greg Bourne, the CEO of WWF Australia. When an Australian industry or company wants to 'stake out the middle' of a debate and 'engage' with an environmental NGO, WWF is usually the first port of call.

Bourne is no stranger to mining industry conferences. For more than three decades, he worked in senior positions in the multinational oil giant BP, including responsibility for oil and gas projects in the Middle East, South America and Papua New Guinea. At one stage, he worked, on secondment from BP, as the Special Adviser on Energy and Transport in British Prime Minister Margaret Thatcher's Policy Unit at 10 Downing Street, which included advising on the privatisation of the British Rail network.[7] After returning to the BP fold, Bourne worked his way up to become Regional President of BP Australasia, a position he resigned from in late 2003. He was subsequently recruited by WWF Australia's President, multi-millionaire Robert Purves, to take over as WWF Australia CEO in October 2004.

In his Alice Springs presentation, Bourne sketched his view that the business community divides into three: a rump of 'luddites' that flourish despite being laggards; the majority, which only respond to new imperatives when they have to; and the 'progressives', which he said 'need all the help they can get to be more bold'. WWF, Bourne told the assembled mining industry representatives, works only with the companies at the leading edge of the 'progressives', and boasted his group works in ways 'that pull the progressives, push the bulk and give the Luddites no oxygen'. Bourne then went on to ridicule others in the environment movement as either fixated on pointing to 'Nirvana but not how to get there' or being 'NGOs that name and shame, do demonstrations and in-your-face campaigns. They make few friends'.[8] WWF Australia claim that their expertise is in 'identifying political "log jams" on major national conservation issues', and then working closely with governments, industry and community groups to develop and implement 'science-based, economically viable solutions'.[9] In Sandman's terminology, WWF Australia is a 'wow, half a loaf' organisation.

Something fishy

A hallmark tactic of activist campaigns in the 1960s and 1970s was the use of consumer boycotts to punish recalcitrant companies. By the 1990s, however, the trend was more towards developing standards and accrediting retail products that passed muster. The theory was that an accredited product would be rewarded by consumers while the laggards would be under financial pressure to lift their game. One of the pioneering projects during the 1990s was the Forest Stewardship Council (FSC), which was established by a broad coalition of non-profit groups. Its aim was to shift timber production to sources designated as more sustainable and reduce the market share for forest products derived from the destruction of the world's great forests. Despite numerous problems, the FSC label had some impact, especially in Europe.

Fisheries were next. As Greenpeace in Europe stepped up its campaign against unstainable fisheries, Unilever, which supplied approximately 25 per cent of the European and US demand for frozen fish, began to feel the heat. The company's Birds Eye and Iglo brands in particular were vulnerable to consumer pressure.[10] Simon Bryceson, a consultant to the global PR firm B-M, advised Unilever that it should bypass Greenpeace and instead develop a partnership with the more 'conservative' WWF.[11] Unilever and WWF split the US$1 million start-up costs, and in 1997 the Marine Stewardship Council (MSC) was launched as a non-profit organisation, headquartered in London. For Unilever, accreditation offered the prospect that it could marginalise Greenpeace and reassure skittish customers. As a trial run, the MSC drafted principles and criteria for assessing what consti-tuted a 'sustainable' fishery. These were then tested against three small-scale fisheries, including the West Australian rock lobster fishery. All passed.

Following the trial accreditations, the MSC proclaimed to the world that a product that bore the MSC label would assure consumers 'that the product has not contributed to the environmental problem of overfishing'. However, instead of viewing itself as a tool for ensuring high environmental standards, the MSC wanted to position itself as being 'precisely in the middle' of the fisheries management prescriptions advocated by environmentalists and the fishing industry.[12] Once launched, the MSC needed some runs on the board. In the retail fish products market, the main game is in what is referred to as 'white fish'—large-volume fisheries that can supply quality, white flesh for products such as fish fingers. Having set itself a target of having ten fisheries accredited before it could launch a major promotional blitz, the MSC needed high-volume fisheries accredited. Having teetered on the brink of financial collapse on more than one occasion, the MSC also desperately needed fisheries accredited in order to generate sufficient revenue from licensing fees.

The New Zealand hoki, a fish with a long, silvery, tapering body that grows to well over a metre and can live for up to 25 years, was to be the first large-volume 'white fish' selected for MSC certification. The goggle-eyed hoki look sufficiently scary to ensure they are unlikely to ever feature in a full-colour WWF fundraising appeal. WWF had selected the New Zealand hoki fishery as one that would demonstrate the elegance of the MSC's arm's-length certification to deliver conservation outcomes via a corporate-friendly, but science-based, process. In 1999, WWF in Australia established a project to promote the MSC in the region, proclaiming that certified products met 'stringent sustainability guidelines'.[13] It had also landed a US$175 000 grant from the US-based David and Lucile Packard Foundation to facilitate its involvement in the process.

If WWF had a fairytale ending in mind, it wasn't to be. The hoki fishery relies on trawl nets, which can have a mouth opening

80 metres high and up to 400 metres long, big enough to swallow a skyscraper. Even though hoki are commonly found at depths of over 900 metres, New Zealand fur seals commonly become entangled when the nets are laid out or retrieved. Seabirds too, fall prey to the nets. The best estimates are that between 1989 and 1998, more than 5600 seals drowned in the industry's trawl nets. It was a major problem, with the population of the long-lived mammals having already collapsed to approximately five per cent of their original number. The fishery also killed more than 1100 seabirds annually, including albatross and petrels, which are internationally recognised respectively as a vulnerable threatened species and a threatened species. With their popula-tions already severely compromised, even the death of a few adult seabirds a year could prove devastating.

A coalition of fishing companies that owned the commercial quota for the hoki fishery formed the Hoki Fishery Management Company (HFMC) to apply for MSC accreditation. Part of the impetus for the HFMC's application was pressure from the German-based subsidiary of Unilever, Frozen Fish International, which bought supplied hoki to the European market. Accredi-tation held out the prospect that the NZ$300 million-a-year industry could rake in even more. The HFMC's application for certification was forwarded on to the Netherlands-based SGS Product and Process Certification, an MSC-approved consul-tancy. Despite finding that 'the medium to long term impacts of hoki fishing on the ecosystem or habitats are not well understood at this time', SGS recommended the fishery be accredited, subject to what it described as 'minor corrective actions'. The largest environment group in New Zealand, the Royal Forest and Bird Protection Society—which is commonly referred to as Forest and Bird—was horrified, and argued against rewarding an unsustainable fishery. Behind the scenes, WWF New Zealand was worried too. In an internal email, the group's then Chief Executive, Jo Breese, expressed her alarm to the head of WWF International, Claude Martin, that accreditation would end up:

> ... compromising MSC, WWF and of course the hoki fishery. There are some very sensitive issues, e.g. 1000 fur seals killed per year, by-catch of seabirds and maintaining the fish stock. These could potentially 'blow up' in the media and be very damaging internationally to WWF, MSC and SGS. Also that Green Groups [*sic*] in NZ have the international networks to make this look very bad for MSC. At this stage it appears likely that we will not be able to support the certification process and outcomes. If we are asked by the media we will be forced to publicly criticise the process and possibly the outcomes... Which will inevitably reflect badly on MSC.[14]

Her plea got her nowhere.

A little over a week later, the MSC announced the accreditation of the fishery at a level of 250 000 tonnes per year, with minor qualifications. The then CEO of the MSC was upbeat, extolling the hoki accreditation as an 'excellent example to other fisheries around the world'.[15] WWF New Zealand swallowed its pride, preferring to place its faith in promises of improved performance. In a joint media release with the fishing company and the MSC, the Washington D.C.-based head of WWF's Endangered Seas Program, Scott Burns, optimistically proclaimed his faith that the 'corrective actions' would be adequate to resolve the identified problems.[16] In a separate WWF statement, they were a little more cautious, stating only their 'general support for the decision', subject to undertaking steps to 'conserve seal populations'.[17] WWF, it seems, had a line for everyone. Against the din of applause from industry, government and WWF, the protests of Forest and Bird and other groups were drowned out.

Unilever quickly put the MSC's logo on its retail products and used the accreditation to introduce hoki into new European markets.[18] Other companies extolled the marketing edge MSC accreditation would give hoki over other whitefish in the all-important markets of Australia, Europe and the United States.[19] WWF Australia's Director of Conservation, Ray Nias, was ecstatic about the financial benefits that flowed to the company from the accreditation. 'The share price for the company', he gushed, 'sky rocketed because they gained access to markets in Europe'.[20] Forest and Bird thought the accreditation was so flawed that it decided to lodge an appeal. Eventually, the MSC-appointed panel agreed with Forest and Bird, concluding that there were 'several' aspects of the accreditation 'which would have justified a refusal of certification as at the date of the assessment'.[21] But instead of revoking the accreditation, the panel claimed that further tweaks would be sufficient to ensure that the fishery was in 'good shape'.

The hoki fishing industry, though, couldn't dodge ecological reality. The following year, the government bowed to scientific advice and cut the allowable catch of hoki to 220 000 tonnes. The following year, it was cut to 180 000 tonnes, but despite their best efforts, the industry could only catch less than three-quarters of that. In 2004, the allowable catch was slashed again, this time to 100 000 tonnes. As the fishery collapsed, fuelled in part by the legitimacy that went with the MSC label, the hope of a boom in export income vaporised. The cost to wildlife was staggering. One estimate was that in the first four years the fishery had been certified, approximately 3300 seals out of a total population of roughly 80 000 had been killed. In the same period, hundreds, possibly even thousands, of seabirds such as petrels and albatross were killed in the huge trawl nets, including some globally threatened species.

While WWF's primary mandate was to protect wildlife, in the five years after the accreditation, it remained publicly mute about the extraordinary impact of the hoki fishery on wildlife. Behind the scenes, WWF New Zealand participated in an Environmental Steering Group, established by HFMC, where it expressed its concerns that the 'corrective actions' were not being implemented and that not enough was being done to prevent seal deaths.[22] 'The first five years didn't go well', said Chris Howe for WWF New Zealand.[23] WWF's preference for quiet diplomacy was not only ineffective, but did nothing to alert the hoki-consuming public that they were being duped. It is even arguable that the MSC label on products in Australia containing hoki is contrary to the provisions of the Trade Practices Act, which bans misleading and deceptive conduct. While the Australian Competition and Consumer Commission (ACCC) allows eco-labelling schemes to make claims, this is only on the proviso that the 'scheme's stated environmental criteria are met'.[24]

In early 2006, the HFMC's proposal to extend certification for another five years, subject to only minor changes, was too much even for WWF. Jo Breese, CEO of WWF New Zealand, tentatively opposed recertification 'at this time', but optimistically held out the prospect that necessary changes would be 'achievable in the short term'.[25] Even so, the fishery was recertified, prompting WWF New Zealand to lodge an appeal. Despite being comprehensively rolled at every turn on the hoki fishery, WWF continues to be an MSC booster. In its 2006 annual report, WWF Australia brazenly states that it promotes 'fisheries products that meet the highest environmental standards and give consumers a way to make a positive environmental choice'. It is a sentiment WWF New Zealand echoes on its website. But, instead of WWF Australia informing its members of the collapse of the hoki fishery experiment, they proudly proclaimed that they were working with two fishing companies to have Australian mackerel icefish to be 'the first sub-Antarctic fishery' accredited by the MSC.[26]

While WWF proclaim the MSC a success, independent reviews presented to the MSC Board argue otherwise. One, commissioned by three US foundations, concluded that the MSC's claim to certify 'sustainable' fisheries 'in most cases is not justified', and fisheries 'that are not in compliance with the law can be, and have been, certified'.[27] If WWF had helped collapse the hoki fishery without even being funded by the fishing industry, what would happen when big bucks were on offer?

Kikori

In 1993, the US-based oil giant, Chevron, announced plans for a major oil development in the Kutubu rainforest in Papua New Guinea (PNG). When the US-based Rainforest Action Network raised concerns about the project, hundreds of letters from around the world poured into Chevron's head office. To blunt the criticisms, Chevron offered WWF United States a US$1 million per annum six-year agreement to establish a 'model integrated conservation and development project' (ICDP) for the Kikori River Basin. They couldn't resist. As part of the project, WWF helped establish what it touted as a model eco-forestry project, Kikori Pacific Ltd (KPL). The original concept was that timber from relatively low-impact selective logging operations could gain accreditation with the FSC and attract premium prices, especially in Australia. WWF hoped that landowners would sign up for eco-forestry rather than with the rapacious Malaysian logging companies.

It didn't turn out that way. When the project got under way in 1997, some landowner groups were already receiving funds from Chevron and just weren't interested in the project. Others had already signed over the rights to their forests to industrial logging companies. But having touted the project as a model, WWF were compelled to press on. The US-based MacArthur

Foundation, the US State Department, and the World Bank-affiliated International Finance Corporation all contributed funds. With the funds in the bank, KPL established a sawmill at Kikori and then began buying logs from a landowner company, Iviri Timbers. But soon afterwards, others involved in eco-forestry in PNG raised concerns about the operation. In early 2000, a joint WWF–World Bank report on PNG eco-forestry noted that the Kikori project was logging mangroves, which it referred to as 'fragile forests'. A later damning internal WWF report was blunter still. Iviri Timber, the report stated, 'sources its logs from mangroves. Under the PNG logging code of practice, it is illegal to log mangroves'. If the logging didn't comply with the logging code, there was no prospect of it gaining FSC accreditation. 'In this sense, KPL was doomed to failure from the beginning,' it stated.[28] If WWF's project was a PR boon for Chevron, it threatened to create a crisis for WWF. The report was ignored and the logging continued.

Finally, when Britain's Channel 4 television news broke the story in March 2001, WWF went into damage control, emulating the techniques used by corporate spin doctors. Initially, a WWF UK spokesman, Steve Howard, defended the operations as being in a legal 'grey area'.[29] 'There are very few things that are black and white in life', he said. WWF's UK Press Office distributed a WWF Position Statement, which gamely claimed that the logging project was a 'positive example' of sustainable development in the region. Initially, WWF claimed that, under the PNG code, logging of mangroves was only illegal for large-scale industrial operations, not community-based projects.[30] The story was then picked up with a major feature by a British journalist in the *Sydney Morning Herald*.[31] In a letter to the editor, the President of WWF Australia, the businessman-cum-environmental philanthropist, Robert Purves, argued that the statement in the WWF report that the logging was illegal was 'incorrect'. Purves echoed

WWF United Kingdom's briefing note claiming that the forestry Act 'applies to operations taking large volumes of timber, not to selective harvesting by landowners'.[32] An email from the Director of WWF US's Global Forest Program, Bruce Carbarle, sought to pin the supposed misunderstanding of the legality on the report's author, who he suggested 'incorrectly assumed' the code applied to small-scale projects. KPL, he claimed, was an 'economically viable and environmentally sustainable alternative' to the big-scale logging operations.[33]

WWF's spin may have been effective, but it was fundamentally flawed. That a project aiming for FSC accreditation would embrace standards *lower* than industrial-scale logging operations was a sad statement in itself. Nor did its tactic of trying to 'shoot the messenger' stand up to scrutiny. The consultant's report, which was based on interviews with numerous WWF staff in PNG, noted that 'not one person argued in favour of continuing to log mangroves … A number of WWF staff privately expressed concerns about the fact that the Iviri Timbers operation is illegal.' It also included a schedule of eight WWF staff, including the Operations Manager of KPL, who reviewed the report prior to completion. Nor was there much consolation for WWF in the forestry regulations. The 1996 PNG Logging Code of Practice, which was in force until amended in March 2000, was clear in specifying that mangroves could not be logged. At a minimum, the logging of mangroves prior to March 2000 was illegal. The revised code was equally explicit in excluding mangroves from logging, though it exempted small community-owned projects cutting less than 500 cubic metres. Even this was of little comfort to WWF, as the 1999 data on KPL revealed it had processed more than 700 cubic metres. WWF then claimed that the 500 cubic-metre threshold applied to each clan that supplied KPL. With 18 clans supplying KPL, WWF was astonishingly implying that a logging operation of up to 9000 cubic metres should be exempted from the code.

If the mangroves could not have been legally logged by industrial-scale projects in the first place, perversely the *only* threat to them came from a WWF-backed project touted as a 'solution'. Further, a separate report prepared by WWF and the World Bank identified PNG mangroves as being fragile ecosystems that should be excluded from logging. WWF United States's Bruce Carbarle had also claimed that KPL was not only legal, but an 'economically viable and environmentally sustainable alternative' to the big-scale logging operations.[34] As WWF's defences crumbled, it finally signalled a retreat, deciding that the logging of mangroves would end. If KPL were indeed legal, profitable and environmentally sustainable, why would they pull the plug?

There was one final ignominy for WWF in the Kikori debacle. In late October 2001, Channel 4 won a British Environment and Media Award for Best Television News & Current Affairs Coverage for a series of environmental reports, including their Kikori exposé. The awards, which were hosted by none other than WWF, were an example of where sponsoring a journalism award backfired. The only saving grace for WWF was that they maintained control over the awards' website, which discreetly omitted mentioning that one of the winning stories was on WWF's Kikori project.[35]

FiFuFo

As the campaign to end the logging of Tasmania's high-conservation forests gained traction ahead of the 2004 federal election, a senior WWF staffer sought to reassure Tasmanian wilderness photographer Rob Blakers that the group planned to work collaboratively with other groups. 'We don't want to get a reputation of being known as FiFuFo's', one WWF staffer said. FiFuFo, he explained, was the acronym for 'Fly In, Fuck Up, Fly Out'.[36] While Tasmanian environmental groups had been wary of WWF's new-found interest in the state's forests, the President of WWF Australia, Robert Purves, was prepared to stump up funds for projects. Purves had sold half the shares in his family's aged care company, of which he is chairman, and ploughed the $10 million proceeds into the Purves Environmental Fund. For Purves, making gains on major environmental issues comes down to a simple formula of collating the scientific evidence, compiling a blueprint brokered with the affected business interests, and taking the agreed 'workable solutions' to government for implementation.[37]

In Tasmania, WWF pledged faithfulness to ending land clearing, better biodiversity protection, and promoting the need to protect the Tarkine wilderness, Australia's largest rainforest wilderness. Purves funded the cost of the coffee table book *Tarkine*, featuring the work of many of Tasmania's best wilderness photographers.[38] WWF capitalised on its involvement in the issue with a direct mail fundraising plea too. 'An Ancient Forest Teeming With Life… Destined For Destruction', it proclaimed. The appeal stressed the importance of the Tarkine and railed against the logging of rainforests. Purves himself stated his opposition to the woodchipping of old-growth forests and their replacement with plantations. As the election grew closer, WWF decided that it should be the arbiter of what should be included in the package of proposals to go to federal and state governments. WWF staff flew in to Tasmania and commenced a series of secret negotiations with Forestry Tasmania, the Forest Industry Association of Tasmania and the Tasmanian and federal governments.

At a national forest industry conference in Melbourne, the then head of the National Association of Forest Industries (NAFI), Kate Carnell, told senior industry movers and shakers that 'public perception' was the industry's Achilles heel. As head of NAFI, an umbrella organisation for the state-based timber industry lobby groups, part of Carnell's job was to track the public standing of the timber industry across the country. Carnell's assessment of public opinion trends was gloomy, but she held out the prospect of 'developing a consensus between the leaders of our industry and the more moderate elements of the environmental debate'. For 'bridge-building' to work with 'moderate' groups, however, Carnell explained, it would require both parties to 'protect the ability of those with more reasonable opinions to find a place in the public debate and to win the ear of policy-makers'. According to Carnell, making modest concessions to groups such as WWF was a shrewd way of minimising the risk of continuing political instability. While hopeful at the prospect of negotiating a deal with WWF, she wondered if such a divide-and-conquer strategy was 'really realistic'. While praising WWF Program Leader–Resource Conservation, Michael Rae, and WWF for 'doing an absolutely stunning job' of attempting to negotiate with industry, Carnell fretted that they lacked the grassroots support to win the argument. 'The hard thing for industry', she complained, 'is working out who you do come up with the win-win outcomes with and whether you end up with an outcome that is then shot down by somebody else, even if the industry could stick together', which is exactly what happened.

The following week, WWF launched *A Blueprint for the Forest Industry and Vegetation Management in Tasmania*. Faced with a recalcitrant industry, WWF had opted to ditch most of the Tasmanian environment groups' proposals for new conservation reserves. All up, WWF earmarked more than half of the wet and dry forests in the Tarkine, and more than a third of the pure rainforests for logging. Other areas cherished by Tasmanian environmentalists—such as the Great Western Tiers, the Blue Tier, the Styx forests and Wielangta—were tossed the industry's way too. That many of the areas had been identified as being of World Heritage quality by state, national and international agencies mattered little. Despite the magnitude of concessions WWF brazenly claimed that their Blueprint 'relied on the best available science', even though they had undertaken no scientific review of the merits of protecting the areas it slated for logging. Where it had once objected to the woodchipping of native forests, WWF now supported proposals to feed them into a new pulp mill and a wood-fired power station. WWF even went so far as to defend the clearfelling of native forests. 'Despite the appearance of having a severe environmental impact, well-managed forestry is one of the more sustainable forms of human activity', WWF wrote. It was music to the logging industry's ears.

WWF's Blueprint was roundly criticised by environmentalists and scientists. Stung by the reaction, WWF attempted to defend its position. 'The idea the forest industry in Tasmania is embracing WWF is a very far-fetched fantasy indeed', said WWF's conservation director, Ray Nias.[39] When the bulk of the Tasmanian photographers whose work featured in WWF's book on the Tarkine wrote that they were 'deeply distressed' and urged the withdrawal of the Blueprint, WWF's senior communications officer, Andy Ridley, dismissed the protest and argued WWF's focus was the 'conservation of species' and that the logging of old-growth forests was 'not our argument'.[40] It was a claim in stark contrast with WWF's earlier fundraising appeal to supporters extolling the virtues of protecting old-growth forests from logging.

Several weeks out from the October 2004 election, with widespread speculation that the Howard Government might propose major extensions to Tasmania's forest reserves, WWF spent more than $71 000 from a $200 000 contribution from Purves on a series of half-page advertisements in national newspapers featuring an image of the now-extinct Tasmanian Tiger under the title 'Protecting Species in Tasmania: It's More than the Forests'.[41] 'Well-managed native forestry is a relatively low threat to animals and plants', it stated.

It was an extraordinary advertisement aimed at ensuring neither major political parties committed themselves to protecting what WWF considered too much of the state's forests. In the last week of the election, then Opposition Leader Mark Latham proposed a significant extension to the reserves and a major forest industry restructuring package. With Latham taking the high road, Howard opted for the low as champion of the timber industry. He made a personal appearance at a 3000-strong rally in Launceston's Albert Hall, in what could be regarded as the defining moment of the election campaign, and promised that protecting the forests would not cost any timber industry jobs.[42] But even with this commitment, Howard found the WWF package excessive, bowing just a little to public pressure by proposing that sections of the old-growth forests in the Styx Valley be protected. (After the election, Howard backtracked, halving the area of the Styx forests excluded from logging.)

Howard's win was greeted with jubilation in the logging industry. With federal funds pouring in to underwrite minor reforms, Forestry Tasmania and the logging industry were looking forward to good times. For their part, WWF has barely been seen in Tasmania since. In December 2006, Justice Shane Marshall in the Federal Court of Australia ruled that logging in the Wielangta forest—an area WWF had left open for logging—was in breach of the Environmental Protection and Biodiversity Conservation Act because of its impact on threatened species. In the wake of the court ruling WWF remained mute. There were no press releases or newspaper advertisements, just an embarrassed silence. Two years earlier Purves expressed his frustration at the continued controversy over Tasmanian forestry. Not with Gunns seemingly insatiable appetite for native forests. Nor with the refusal of the Tasmanian Labor Government to recognise the shift in local and national public opinion and negotiate an end to native forest logging, as their counterparts in Queensland and Western Australia have largely done. Instead, in a November 2004 speech to a business conference, Purves echoed the rhetoric of the logging industry and complained that environmental groups should 'stop holding intractable, extreme positions, as we have seen in Tasmania'.[43] In the eye of the FiFuFo, local advocates should simply defer to the out-of-town dealmakers.

Toxic defence

At the heart of the concern with corporate engagement is that not only is it ineffective and often counter-productive, but also that the independence of non-profit groups is seriously compromised. In the last decade, WWF in both Australia and New Zealand have attracted funding from a range of mining companies, including Alcoa, BHP, Placer Dome Asia-Pacific and Rio Tinto. Projects spanned everything from a $1.2 million 'partnership' with Rio Tinto over four years to work on frog conservation and a woodland conservation project funded by Alcoa.[44] In the world of corporate PR, soft-sell projects are viewed as bridge-builders to a long-term payoff on broader policy issues.

Across the Tasman in 2000, WWF New Zealand stitched up a $500 000 five-year deal, under which the Shell oil company sponsored a national newspaper campaign urging people to join the environmental group, and promoting an educational program for schools.[45] After the launch of the advertising campaign, leaked internal WWF documents revealed that, at a board meeting, the chairman of WWF New Zealand, Paul Bowe, flagged whether Shell New Zealand, 'due to their great commitment and contribution towards the WWF education programme, should have a place as a trustee'. Other documents revealed that Shell's close relationship with WWF New Zealand dated back to the controversy over the sentencing to death of nine Nigerian environmental activists, including author Ken Saro-Wiwa in November 1995.

With the Commonwealth Heads of Government Meeting scheduled for Auckland in November 1995, pressure increased on both Shell and the Nigerian government to ensure the Ogoni Nine were spared. But before the Commonwealth finalised a position on the issue, the Nigerian dictatorship had the nine executed. While the public outrage focused on Shell's close relationship with the seedy Nigerian military dictatorship, WWF New Zealand were so understanding that Shell penned them a thank you note. 'We very much appreciate your balanced and considered view on this issue…As you can imagine your approach is very welcome to us at the moment', Shell wrote. After the memo was revealed, WWF New Zealand's then Chief Executive, Jo Breese, defended the group's relationship with Shell. 'We are going to be able to have a better dialogue if we work with people from the inside than if we are always on the attack from the outside', she said.[46]

A few months later, in January 2001, WWF Australia teamed up with the major gold mining company, Placer Dome Asia-Pacific, to propose a scheme to accredit individual mines against a set of criteria, citing the Marine Stewardship Council as a successful model.[47] While Placer-Dome (later swallowed up by Barrick, one of the world's largest gold producers) was trying to help rustle up funding from other mining companies, WWF Australia was soon confronted with an awkward dilemma. When 100 000 cubic metres of cyanide-laced tailings spilled into the Danube River system on 1 February 2001 after a tailings dam collapsed at the Baia Mare mine in Romania, the global mining industry was soon reeling from demands for stricter regulation of cyanide use in mining. The disaster at the Baia Mare mine, which was managed and half-owned by the Perth-based Esmerelda Exploration, prompted a furious behind-the-scenes debate within the Minerals Council of Australia (MCA) as to whether it should distance itself from the company, which wasn't a member, or dismiss the controversy as a media beat-up. In the end, the MCA said nothing publicly. WWF Australia, too, remained mute.

In a frantic effort to short-circuit calls for legislative initiatives by the European Union, the International Council on Metals and the Environment (ICME)—the mining industry's global umbrella group—approached the United Nations Environment Project (UNEP) with a proposal that they jointly develop a voluntary code to cover cyanide management and tailings dam safety issues. UNEP agreed. At a May 2000 meeting in Paris of selected 'stakeholders', UNEP and ICME agreed that a voluntary code should be developed by the end of that year by a twelve-member Steering Committee, including a representative from WWF.[48]

Within WWF's international network, WWF Australia's Michael Rae had been designated as having carriage of mining issues. To fund the costs of developing the code, the cash-strapped UNEP turned cap-in-hand to the gold mining industry and cyanide producers, which eventually coughed up US$800 000. As the steering committee process ground on, one by one the key concerns of NGOs were jettisoned. 'There is no way to impose sanctions so this will be dropped at this point', the minutes noted.[49] As the code neared finalisation in December 2001, a coalition of NGOs sent a scathing letter to UNEP, arguing that it shouldn't endorse a code 'that fails to advance protection in a significant way and one that is riddled with gaps'.[50] A particularly egregious provision was for 'mixing zones', where regulatory standards could be exceeded between a point at which mine waste was dumped into a stream and a point downstream where compliance with pollution standards would cut in. (Placer Dome, for example, has a 140-kilometre-long mixing zone for its Porgera gold mine in Papua New Guinea. The Ok Tedi mine, once owned by BHP, has a 200-kilometre mixing zone). Fearing that UNEP would back away from the code, the mining industry responded with a letter of its own, claiming that 'we must act to gain incremental improvements'.[51] Alongside the names of executives from mining companies and cyanide producers was that of Michael Rae.

When the letter later leaked out, Rae explained he had 'some sympathy for' the issues flagged by the other NGOs, but he didn't object to the use of WWF's name torpedoing their concerns.[52] The cyanide lobby and WWF, though, had nothing to fear from a timid UNEP. In March 2002, the final code was released with acclamation from the industry, which now holds it aloft as an example of voluntary corporate responsibility and the model for future partnerships. (In 2006, Rae was appointed the CEO of the London-based Council for Responsible Jewellery Practices, a body charged with advancing the social and environmental credentials of the gold and diamond industry, and is a board member of the group overseeing the cyanide code.[53])

When, in November 2004, the Swiss-based mining and investment company Xstrata made a takeover bid for the uranium, copper and nickel mining company WMC, it added another element to the long-simmering debate over uranium. WMC, which owned the controversial Roxby Downs mine—later renamed Olympic Dam by the company—called in Andrew Parker and Sarah Cruickshank from the PR and lobbyshop, Parker & Partners (P&P), to help with their PR strategy. 'Essentially, WMC was a very conservative company that hated talking about uranium', Parker later told a PR conference.[54] But with WMC hoping to entice a rival bid from BHP-Billiton, the communications team agreed they needed to shift the debate away from the controversy over uranium and sell the positives. 'The media', said Cruickshank, a former ministerial adviser, was 'a largely ill-informed media who were much more focused on the traditional emotional issues around uranium'. The communications team, she said, feared that the takeover bid would be reported in the context of the association of 'risks', 'war-mongering overseas and nuclear stockpiles'. Instead, the WMC and the P&P team wanted to talk up the benefits of export earnings and local jobs. More than anything, though, it wanted to sell the idea that increasing concern about the greenhouse effect would mean a revival of nuclear power, which in turn would drive up the price of uranium. With a US$5 a pound increase in uranium prices touted as increasing the value of Roxby Downs by $1.6 billion, hyping the greenhouse credentials of nukes could help push up the value of the takeover bid and the share price. The strategy worked, with BHP-Billiton eventually offering $9.2 billion, trumping Xstrata's $8.5 billion bid. As part of its strategy, Parker said the communications team decided to contact people and groups 'that we would never have contemplated talking to before', including 'some green groups'. While WWF did not respond to requests for an interview, Parker subsequently confirmed in an interview with the author that the issue was discussed with WWF.[55]

What started as pro-nuclear hype for a takeover bid for WMC soon took on a life of its own, with key commentators and government officials up-beat about a dramatic expansion of Australia's nuclear industry. It was an illustration of what almost a decade earlier a Washington D.C. lobbyist for Philip Morris, John Scruggs, described the 'echo chamber effect' approach to advocacy, the repetition of a selected message by the most credible sources that surround a decision-maker: 'The more a particular view or piece of information "echoes" or resonates through this group, the greater its impact.' The more 'echoes' there were toward the 'target members', he noted, created 'enhanced credibility and influence of the essential message'. WWF Australia later added its voice to the echo chamber. No sooner had Greg Bourne taken up the reigns as CEO of WWF Australia than he endorsed an expansion of uranium mining in Australia, with the exceptions that it should not be in unspecified 'fragile and endangered ecosystems', that it should be used for 'peaceful purposes', the waste 'stored safely', and nuclear weapons proliferation avoided.[56] Bourne's caveats echoed the nuclear industry's key PR themes, that *it is feasible* to quarantine civilian nuclear power from weapons programs, and that waste *can* be stored safely somewhere. It was a speech that drew no comment at the time, but when Bourne repeated similar comments after Prime Minister John Howard talked up the need for a 'national debate' on expanding Australia's involvement in the nuclear fuel cycle, his views landed him on the front page of *The Australian*.[57]

For the uranium mining industry to expand with confidence, it craves bipartisan support from both Labor and the Liberal–National Party coalition. To gain that, they not only wanted to bury the Labor Party's 'three mines' policy, but also undermine the resolve of both the Queensland and the West Australian Labor governments' ban on uranium mining. Bourne's endorsement of nuclear power, though, involved turning a blind eye to WWF International's May 2003 policy, which dismissed nuclear power as a 'solution' to climate change and argued that massive subsidies would be required to facilitate nuclear power, thereby undercutting the potential for investment in renewable energy and efficiency programs. Large base-load projects, far from being flexible and encouraging energy savings, do the opposite. Compounding this, nuclear power proliferation increases the probability of both nuclear weapons proliferation and under-mining the United Nation's Nuclear Non-proliferation Treaty. With WWF's public pro-nuclear pronouncements unpopular among staff and some supporters, behind-the-scenes manoeu-vring was still on the cards. Several days after his splash in *The Australian*, Bourne winged his way to a meeting in London of WWF International's global energy taskforce. There, the *Australian* reported, he hoped to ensure that the option of nuclear power as a greenhouse 'solution' was kept open.[58] Bourne was rebuffed in London, leaving staff back in Australia to manage the embarrassment. In a flurry of media releases, WWF Australia disingenuously claimed that at no time had they supported nuclear power, and that discussion of an expansion of uranium mining was a 'dangerous distraction' from solving climate change. But if Bourne, who did not respond to requests for an interview, was constrained by pushing nukes by the organisation's anti-nuclear policy, Professor Tim Flannery, who had been drawn into WWF Australia's orbit by Purves, wasn't.

Since November 2002, Flannery has been a member of the Wentworth Group of Concerned Scientists, a group funded by the Purves Environmental Fund and 'convened' by WWF to research and propose environmental policy plans. Through his foundation, Purves underwrote Flannery's book, *The Weather Makers*. In it, Flannery synthesises the strengthening scientific evidence on the consequences of global warming. Turning to solutions, though, Flannery struggled, and, in seeming desperation, latched on to the nuclear nettle. He pointed to the May 2004 pro-nuclear proclamations of the proponent of the Gaia Hypothesis, James Lovelock, opining that environmental groups 'were shocked' and that 'Lovelock has a point'.[59] Flannery later explained his pro-nuclear evangelism as if cast as a heroic adventurer: 'Someone needs to come out and tell a few home truths.' Decades of anti-nuclear activism in Australia, he blithely claimed, 'was a failed policy'.[60]

It wasn't long before Prime Minister John Howard was approvingly citing both Lovelock and Flannery in support of his push for a massive expansion of Australia's nuclear industry.[61] However, there is no evidence that any anti-nuclear activists were 'shocked' at Lovelock's May 2004 claims, which were just the latest instalment in his decades-long support for nuclear power. Lovelock is so evangelical about nuclear power that, in 2001, he derided concerns about the safety of the technology as 'imaginary'. Even more bizarrely, he wrote that 'if permitted, I would happily store high-level waste on my own land and use the heat from it to warm my home'.[62] Nor are Lovelock's environmental credentials impeccable, having ridiculed scientific concerns over the thinning of the ozone layer.[63] In an article published after his book had been released, Flannery described Lovelock as a 'credible' voice on nuclear power as a 'solution' to greenhouse.[64] But in an interview with the author two months later, Flannery changed tack, describing Lovelock as 'way out on the extreme'.[65]

If Flannery's initial deification of Lovelock was based on limited research, it was taken at face value by others. Interviewing anti-nuclear activist Helen Caldicott, the ABC's '7.30 Report' host Kerry O'Brien deferred to Flannery's apparent authoritativeness: 'No-one can doubt Tim Flannery's scientific and environmental credentials. He says James Lovelock has a point on nuclear power. Flannery, too, is coming to see nuclear power as possibly a lesser of evils with regard to greenhouse in Australia.'[66] Flannery also flagged the prospect of developing a domestic nuclear power industry as an alternative to coal-fired power stations. It would 'a noble act', he wrote, and one that would result in 'less risk to human health than that posed by the current coal-based industry'.[67] Within six months he retreated on that position too. 'Here in Australia I believe nuclear power makes absolutely no sense because we have an embarrassing richness of renewable energy resources', he said.[68] However, he supported the expansion of uranium mining in Australia to help fuel what he saw as the inevitable and largely desirable expansion of nuclear power in China, the United States and parts of Europe. Flannery's research might have been flaky, but for the nuclear industry, desperate to marginalise the anit-nuclear movement, it was an example of an 'echo chamber' working at its best.[69]

·

In an address to business groups in late 2005, WWF Australia's President, Robert Purves, held his group up as a model and lambasted others that preferred more robust public advocacy. 'To be frank, if NGOs were subjected to the rigours of the corporate world, many simply wouldn't cut the mustard because they don't deliver on to [sic] their promise—i.e. better outcomes for the environment', he said.[70] It was an extraordinary claim, given the recent controversies WWF Australia has been embroiled in. As a large NGO that has long worked with corporations, WWF serves as a cautionary tale for those contemplating cuddling up with corporations. WWF's complicity in the collapse of the New Zealand hoki fishery, its solidarity with Shell rather than the Ogoni Nine, its role in the illegal logging of the Kikori mangroves in PNG, its pro-nuclear advocacy and its extraordinary campaign urging governments not to protect what it thought would be too much of Tasmania's forests illustrate the inherently political judgements it makes. The cost of long-term cuddling is a greater identification with corporations' policy agendas rather than with those advocating greater environmental protection and social justice.

It can also be argued that, instead of raising environmental standards, WWF have actively undermined them, such as through the misleading promotion of MSC-certified products to consumers. Sometimes WWF staff invoke the 'good cop, bad cop' analogy to defend their approach to cannibalising the campaigns that others have done the hard work on. However, it is a flawed analogy. First, cops that take funds from those they are investigating are usually imprisoned if caught and convicted. However, it is perfectly legal for non-profit groups to take funds from those they should be scrutinising. Second, for the 'good cop, bad cop' routine to work, it relies on the investigators sharing information and working to a common end, namely securing a prosecution and conviction for a breach of the law. WWF, on the other hand, embraces secrecy, disparages and undermines the work of the 'hard cops', and negotiates 'solutions' based on what is acceptable to the corporate suspects. These are not the sort of cops you'd want looking after the public interest.

EIGHT
GOVERNING WITH SPIN

In his 1989 report into corruption in Queensland, Tony Fitzgerald QC noted that a government media unit could be used:

> to control and manipulate the information obtained by the media. Although most Government-generated publicity will unavoidably and necessarily be politically advantageous, there is no legitimate justification for taxpayers' money to be spent on politically motivated propaganda.

If media units didn't result in citizens being better informed about government and departmental activities, Fitzgerald argued that 'their existence is a misuse of public funds, and likely to help misconduct to flourish'. To prevent their misuse, Fitzgerald flagged the possibility of introducing guidelines to govern their activities and the establishment of an all-party parliamentary committee to scrutinise the cost and operation of ministerial media staff and units. Such a committee, he suggested, could 'bring to the attention of Parliament any misrepresentation or misinformation emanating from the administration'.[1]

Traditionally, media discussion of government spin has focused on the tactical games played by ministers and their advisers to gain an upper hand in shaping media coverage. One of the progeny of the Fitzgerald Royal Commission into Corruption in Queensland was the Parliamentary Committee for Electoral and Administrative Review, which, in an April 1994 report, canvassed many of the common strategies used by the Bjelke-Peterson and Goss governments to tame the media. EARC listed common tactics as secrecy, the selective distribution of media releases, denying 'troublesome' journalists access to politicians or government agencies, selective 'leaks' and 'exclusives' to favoured journalists or media outlets.[2] The same tactics prevail today, and have been supplemented with a tight adherence to the centralised handling of media requests, a development that has been facilitated by the use of intranets to establish detailed tracking of media inquiries. The technology of media monitoring has also grown more powerful since Fitzgerald's days, and the media is more concentrated, leading to greater syndication of news stories. Not only are federal and state governments increasingly running big-spending, high-profile advertising campaigns, they are also running invisible PR campaigns that are more akin to propaganda designed to insulate government from political controversy and control public debate. When the PR industry was just getting going in Australia after the Second World War, the challenge for PR consultants was in persuading ministers to turn government information campaigns over to private consultants, which is not a problem today.

Spooky PR

Even though it was Asher Joel and George Fitzpatrick who established the first Australian PR consultancies in the aftermath of the Second World War, the company that made a big early impression was Eric White Associates (EWA). The company was founded in 1947 by Eric White, who had worked for three years as Public Relations Director for the Liberal Party of Australia. In mid-1959, White had grand plans to establish an office in London, but to make it viable he needed to snare a number of government contracts. His initial plan was to wrest the Common-wealth Government's Department of Trade contract for trade promotion in the United Kingdom from the grip of the incumbent London PR agency, F.J. Lyons & Co. White also had his eyes on the work of the department's in-house News and Information Bureau (NIB) offices in Europe and the United States, which aimed to lift Australia's media profile in key investment markets. Frustrated by departmental resistance to his plans, White went directly to Menzies, complaining that the 'commonwealth is not getting good value for its expenditure', and that the NIB should be privatised. 'Part of the problem, as I see it', White wrote, 'is that N.I.B. personnel overseas have no real incentive to work hard, produce creative ideas, or to extend and improve the propaganda issued from their offices.'[3] It is a PR company line that has echoed through the decades.

The then secretary of the Department of Interior, W.A. McClaren, dismissed the suggestion that the government should use the services of a private PR firm. 'The task of interpreting a nation demands full-time specialization, undivided loyalty and undivided responsibility. It would be unreasonable to expect these qualities in a commercial public relations firm serving more than one master', McClaren wrote.[4] Others, too, were less than impressed by White's claims. The Minister for Trade, John 'Black Jack' McEwen, scathingly informed Menzies of the department's unsatisfactory experience with articles sent from EWA in Australia for use in the United Kingdom. 'My officers advise me', McEwen wrote, 'that the firm's record of efficiency—and costs in relation to work done—has been anything but satisfactory. Much of their material had been rewritten in London.'[5] He also cautioned Menzies that 'all too frequently, in the view of my Department, commercial publicity people oversimplify the case for the use of commercial agencies by Governments'.[6] Frustrated with the lack of support on the UK front, in October 1959 White pitched a hare-brained proposal to help build EWA in the United States. This time, he proposed lobbying the US government to get funding from its overseas aid program for an Australian government trade promotion program in the United States. White made it clear that funding would be conditional on EWA being hired to run the program. Menzies informed White that his proposal could not be supported.[7] Behind the scenes, Menzies was blunt: 'As you know, I have no particular enthusiasm for him.'[8]

Despite these setbacks, by the end of the 1960s EWA had grown to have an impressive spread of offices in all Australian state capitals, and in Canberra, London, Wellington, Hong Kong, Malaysia and Singapore.[9] In 1964, it became the first publicly listed PR company in Australia, and, by early in the next decade, was ranked as the third-largest global PR company. In the late 1960s, though, EWA fretted that the poor standing of the PR industry was impeding its growth. 'Relationships with government have suffered slightly from the activities of a few who have labelled themselves public relations practitioners and publicly claimed an undue degree of influence on behalf of clients', EWA wrote in a review of PR in Australia.[10] What EWA didn't disclose, however, was that White's close relationship with the Australian federal government helped explain at least part of their global growth.

In 1968, EWA had established an office in Bangkok as a cover for the Australian Secret Intelligence Service (ASIS), the overseas equivalent of the Australian Security Intelligence Organisation (ASIO). The office continued to operate until 1975, when it was quietly shuttered after being assessed as providing little benefit. The existence of the spy operation remained a well-guarded secret until investigative journalists Brian Toohey and William Pinwell sought to disclose the covert operation in their 1989 book, *Oyster*. But Attorney-General Gareth Evans persuaded the High Court of Australia that EWA's name be deleted in a court-ordered pre-publication vetting.[11] Ultimately, Evans desire for ongoing secrecy mattered little. Shortly afterwards, Robert Haupt from the *Sydney Morning Herald* outed EWA's dirty little secret.[12] In the second edition of *Oyster*, Toohey and Pinwell noted that, in giving cover to ASIS, which 'routinely engage in deception, misrepresentation, bribery and lawbreaking', EWA had breached numerous provisions of the Public Relations Institute of Australia's (PRIA) Code of Ethics.[13] If running cover for spooks bothered PRIA, they said nothing publicly.

EWA also occasionally rated a mention in the files of ASIO over the company potentially working for foreign governments. In a March 1966 intercept report, ASIO's head office was informed that George Kerr from EWA had phoned Valentin Alexandrovich Profiriev to chase up a proposal made to the Soviet Trade Office. Profiriev though was non-committal.[14] The following year an unspecified 'political development' in relation to Nauru prompted ASIO to seek a background report on the legal and share structure of EWA.[15] In 1970, ASIO recorded that they had been informed that EWA had been retained by the Embassy of the United Arab Republic 'to disseminate pro-Arab and anti-Israel propaganda in Australia'. The file note recorded that a representative from the Jewish Board of Deputies in Sydney had phoned White directly to ask whether this was the case and that 'White denied this was so'. Obviously the Jewish lobby group weren't persuaded by White and had passed the information along to ASIO.[16]

EWA's global reach led to the company becoming an affiliate of the giant US PR company, Hill & Knowlton, which finally took over the company in January 1974. Subsequently, Australian staff were posted to Indonesia to work on the account with the

Indonesian government's National Development Information Office.[17] In the years since EWA set up shop, the breadth of government PR programs has grown dramatically.

Originally the programs aimed at overseas audiences were selling Australia as a desirable place to live, holiday or invest. Domestic programs—aside from military propaganda campaigns—tended to be more passive information programs. In an era of much lower expectations of being informed about how government decisions were made or being involved in decision-making, the PR function within government agencies tended to be quite distant from their own management. These days, however, PR campaigns are more closely tied to the strategic purposes of the government and its departments. Government PR campaigns are gravitating more towards the covert selling of controversial policies and restoring tarnished reputations than providing citizens with free and easy access to information on government activities.

Lounge room patrol

'More than 20,000 people enter Australia every day by sea and air. This is the front line against drug runners, illegal migrants and potential terrorists', the narrator warned in the opening show of Channel Seven's 'Border Security' in October 2004. 'You'll witness the detective work, the conflict and compassion that goes into Border Security', the introduction concluded. The series promised 'fly-on-the-wall footage' gained from 'access to all areas' at airports and ocean patrols of the Australian Customs Service, the Australian Quarantine Service and the beleaguered Department of Immigration and Multicultural and Indigenous Affairs (DIMIA). For Channel Seven, there was a lot riding on the series, as it sought to win the ratings war with its long-dominant rival, Channel Nine. Good ratings would divert a river of advertising cash to flow into the company's coffers. There was a lot riding on the success of the program for the Howard Government, too.

At the height of the October 2001 election campaign, Howard played the tough man routine on immigration, and the terms 'border protection' and 'border security' became part of the political lexicon. 'We decide who comes to our country and under what circumstances', was the punchline he used in his campaign launch and a last-minute flurry of election-day advertisements. Having stoked anxiety about the arrival by boat of a few thousand asylum seekers before the election, Howard needed to reassure voters afterwards that his policy was firm but fair. If the 'Border Security' television series is about 'watching human nature at its worst',[18] as series producer Lyndal Marks described it, it is also about government propaganda at its most flagrant.

The program had its origins with Cream TV, a New Zealand television company that produced 'Border Patrol', a series on the New Zealand Customs Service that was first screened in 2002. The Nine Network rebroadcast the series in Australia later that year with modest ratings results, spurring interest in a local spin-off. Channel Seven, Nine and Cream TV all pitched proposals to the Australian Customs Service. 'There were a lot of people, including the Prime Minister, who were very interested in seeing whether this became a reality', Customs Service Director of Corporate Communications, Simon Latimer, later said.[19] Customs communications staff had to get approval for the concept for the program and an accompanying 14-page contract from their own CEO, their minister, the prime minister's office, the Government Communications Unit within the Department of Prime Minister and Cabinet, and finally the Ministerial Committee on Government Communications.

The deciding factor in Seven's favour was that it offered Customs a veto over what aired. 'The key clause is one which grants the Commonwealth agencies involved in the project the right of veto over the vision shot by Seven. Each episode can only be broadcast after written approval from the relevant agencies featured in the stories', Customs Media Manager, Matt Wardell later told a PR conference. 'Without the veto power, no show... For us it was crucial. It was the thing that got it over the line [with the government]', Latimer added.[20]

The initial four-program pilot series rated over one million viewers per week in its 9.30 p.m. Wednesday timeslot, sufficiently well to get the go-ahead for a second season. The second series in 2005 did even better, rating more than 1.3 million viewers per week, making it one of Seven's biggest successes for the year. In 2006, the program was bumped up to the prime-time 7.30 p.m. slot, a move that saw its ratings correspondingly leap up to more than two million. (By way of comparison, the commercial current affairs programs 'A Current Affair' and '60 Minutes' rate approximately 1.5 million and 1.6 million viewers per week respectively, and the ABC's 7 p.m. news rates around the one million viewers' mark.) For the Customs Service, there were numerous benefits from the program, including improved staff morale and easier recruitment of new staff.[21] 'We are getting a huge return for a limited spend', Wardell said. The government, too, had a potent communications weapon with which to shape public debate on immigration and refugee policy. One of the biggest beneficiaries of the program, though, is DIMIA. Not surprisingly for a government-controlled program, there are no hard-case stories of the treatment of traumatised asylum seekers in the network of immigration prisons in Villawood, Baxter, Christmas Island or Nauru, and no images of women and children behind razor wire or embarrassing interviews with the dozens of people wrongly deported from the country.

For government PR representatives assembled at the Sydney PR conference, Latimer posed the question of 'whether something

like this could work for you'. Some have decided it can. The
Royal Australian Navy spent 15 months helping a Western
Australian film Company, Electric Pictures, produce six episodes
of *Submariners*. For the RAN, the benefit was clear: the Collins
Class submarines had long been a source of controversy for the
Navy, with major budget overruns and problems with opera-
tional effectiveness due to propellers that generated excessive
noise.[22] State government agencies are getting in on the act, too.
In late 2005, the ABC screened 'Real Life Water Rats', a four-part
series on the Tasmanian Police's Marine Division and State
Security Unit.

Does it matter if government agencies are facilitating documentary programs? After all, isn't it obvious to viewers that the
program has been produced with the cooperation of the
government agencies involved? Even though government advertising campaigns have been the subject of parliamentary scrutiny,
the largely invisible role of the government in primetime television
'reality' television hasn't. In the 18-month-long gestation period
between the Australian Customs Service receiving the three
pitches for the program in 2002 and the completion of more
than six months of filming for the pilot program in 2004, the
series escaped mention in agency annual reports. Even though
government agency PR people involved in the programs insist
that they are not propaganda, the reality is that there is a co-
dependent relationship. The access granted by Customs in return
for veto over content has proved an advertising boon for Channel
Seven. Latimer himself explained to PR industry colleagues that
'we are making the show because they want to sell bucket loads
of advertising'. For the government and the agencies involved,
the program works far better than an advertising campaign in
selling reassurance. The success of 'Border Security' on an issue
as politically controversial as immigration policy also confers a
substantial benefit to the government in helping marginalise

dissenting points of view in the lower-rating news and current affairs programs. (Kristin Austin, from the Sydney office of the PR firm Ruder Finn, explained at one industry gathering that a rule of thumb used by her company was that 'each negative story requires six or seven positive stories to negate people's misgivings'.[23]) With 'Border Patrol', the federal government was building up a substantial buffer of good news stories. For all the criticisms government members have directed at the Australian Broadcasting Corporation, the national broadcaster has at least a series of checks and balances to allow objections over bias to be heard. There are none with programs such as 'Border Security'.

Getting the gig with the G-G

The speed with which a crisis can overwhelm a government agency can be a godsend for PR companies. An agency that plays Scrooge with its PR budget one day can dig deep the next. When John Howard appointed Dr Peter Hollingworth as Governor-General in June 2001, the expectation was that Hollingworth wouldn't be in the news anywhere near as much as his predecessor, Sir William Deane. It was not to be.

In December 2001, the Supreme Court of Queensland awarded $834 000 in exemplary damages against the Brisbane Diocese of the Anglican Church of Queensland for failing to protect a 12-year-old girl attending Toowoomba Preparatory School a decade earlier. The girl had been sexually abused over a seven-month period by a 39-year-old teacher, Kevin Guy. Guy was charged in November 1990, but committed suicide the day before he was scheduled to appear in court the following month. In a suicide note, he wrote that he 'was in love with so many girls', and included the names of 20 students. Several months before Guy's suicide, Hollingworth had been appointed Archbishop of Brisbane, which included responsibility for the

Toowoomba school. Following Guy's death, Hollingworth had decided that only the parents of the 20 girls on Guy's suicide note should be informed that their daughters may have been molested. This was despite the fact that at the time, police had received two complaints against Guy, one of which was from a girl who wasn't on his list.

For almost two weeks after the court decision, Hollingworth opted to say nothing publicly. As the anger of the parents grew, Hollingworth finally issued a two-page media release, in which he sought to explain his reasons for not informing all parents of Guy's sexual abuse of students. 'I accepted it was imperative that insurance coverage not be jeopardized', he wrote.[24] Hollingworth's explanation succeeded in infuriating the parents and their supporters. Despite the intervening Christmas break, the pressure on Hollingworth grew. With his grip of the vice-regal office slipping, Hollingworth and his staff discussed how they could defuse the growing crisis. 'The judgment was made that 'Australian Story' was useful for that', Hollingworth's Official Secretary, Peter Bonsey, later said of the Governor-General's decision to offer an exclusive television interview to the soft-focus ABC television program.[25] The weekend before the ABC program aired, the *Sydney Morning Herald* had reported that in 1995, a woman had told Hollingworth that as a 14-year-old in the 1950s, she had been abused by a priest at a church boarding house. He had rejected her request that the priest should not be allowed to continue as a minister. Just hours before 'Australian Story' was set to go to air, Hollingworth was re-interviewed about the claim. 'I believe she was more than 14 and I also understand that many years later in adult life, a relationship resumed', he said.[26] In the eyes of the public, it came across as blaming the victim, and that, for all the earlier controversy, Hollingworth just didn't grasp how to sensitively resolve the concerns of those who had been molested and their families.

Earlier that day, Bonsey had been asked at a Senate Estimates committee whether the Governor-General would be hiring additional public relations support beyond his existing media adviser. It was, he stated, 'certainly something which is in our minds'.[27] Deborah Hollingworth, the Governor-General's eldest daughter and a Melbourne-based lawyer, had recommended that Mike Smith, the former editor of *The Age* and founder of his own PR firm, Inside Public Relations, be employed to help Hollingworth. 'It was unusual, probably unprecedented for a Governor-General to engage an external public relations consultant for an issue like this', Smith later observed.[28] Based on a verbal agreement, Smith was offered $1000 a week retainer, with time to be charged at $250 an hour plus expenses. The week after Hollingworth's 'Australian Story' debacle, the investigative 'Sunday' program broadcast more allegations. Smith was called up to Canberra to craft a response to quarantine the fallout from the issues raised.[29] 'The strategy', Inside Public Relations stated on their website, was 'to produce a point by point rebuttal of all the allegations against him. The previous strategy was to say less than more.'[30] Part of Smith's role was to produce a detailed rebuttal to the claims against Hollingworth and script a speech to the nation.

It had all the standard elements of PR crisis management—an expression of sympathy for the victims, contrition for his errors of judgement, and a comprehensive response to the allegations that had been made to date. However, central to the strategy was maintaining control of his message by avoiding live interviews where he could be asked more probing questions. 'Originally I was supposed to be invisible, just a backroom adviser helping with the statements and giving him general advice', Smith later said. However, only two days into the job, Smith was photographed leaving Hollingworth's Melbourne office building. While embarrassing, Hollingworth had no option other than to ride out the flurry of media interest.[31] Hollingworth's fourteen-page statement gave the appearance of being addressed to the public, but in Smith's assessment it was addressed to the only person who could decide whether Hollingworth stayed or went: John Howard. Smith believes that Howard had encouraged 'or insisted' that Hollingworth confront the allegations.[32] Bonsey later confirmed that Smith was also advising Deborah Hollingworth on how she could help manage the crisis.[33] It was, Bonsey explained, 'media activity for the Governor-General, possibly to some extent through the medium of the Governor-Generals' daughter'.[34] The possibility that public funds had been used to advise Deborah Hollingworth prompted Senator John Faulkner to query the appropriateness of the expenditure in a Senate Estimates committee hearing. (Smith and the Governor-General's office later insisted that any advice to Deborah Hollingworth was provided on a pro bono basis separate from the contract with the Governor-General.[35])

Smith's three-week consultancy, which came to just over $14 800, ultimately made little difference to Hollingworth, who became a lame duck Governor-General.[36] Ray and Faulkner's questioning of Bonsey also had the effect that when the crisis surrounding Hollingworth re-emerged later in the year, Smith wasn't called in. 'If I had been brought in my re-engagement would have simply added another layer of political difficulty for Hollingworth', he said. Apart from which, he wasn't sure that he could have made any difference to the fate of Hollingworth, who resigned in May 2003. For the federal government, the utility of hiring PR consultants relied on them being publicly invisible. While it was corporations that pioneered the third-party technique to advance or defend their interests, governments were also keen to embrace the use of proxies to invisibly shape public opinion on contentious issues.

Nuclear spin

Finding a state government willing to accept radioactive waste from across the country was always going to be a tough job. By 2002, the federal government had resigned itself to the politically messy job of establishing a nuclear waste dump on Commonwealth land, but against the wishes of the South Australian Government. The proposed dump was opposed by the state government and opposition, as well as Aboriginal groups, environmentalists and a majority of the public.

In October 2002, armed with results from a market research survey confirming strong opposition to the proposal, the Minister for Science, Peter McGauran, and the Commonwealth Department of Education, Science and Training (DEST) felt the need to call in a PR company. The manager of the Communications Branch of DEST, Lorraine White, wrote to a number of PR companies, inviting them to tender for a $220 000 contract to help ease opposition to the government's announcement on where exactly the low-level nuclear waste dump would be located. White's twelve-page brief and the accompanying nine-page communications strategy outlined that it expected the 'use of the minister and other agreed "willing experts" to provide facts about site selection issues in media interviews and radio talk-back programs and other media outlets'.[37]

Hill & Knowlton pitched for the contract. In its presentation, it boasted 'we have unparalleled international experience in nuclear waste management', listing work that the company's consultants had done in France, Canada, the Czech Republic and the United States.[38] Rod Nockles, the General Manager and Melbourne-based head of the Hill & Knowlton's team, concluded that 'it would be impossible to turn around the current level of opposition and achieve majority support' for the dump.[39] The most that could be hoped for was to 'achieve reluctant acceptance of the decision—in other words, to reduce the degree of active opposition'. Nockles suggested:

> people will be more receptive to information provided by independent experts than by government. To this end we propose to marshal and empower a group of respected independent experts—academics, scientists, environmental risk managers, and practitioners of nuclear medicine—who are willing to advocate publicly on behalf of the Commonwealth in addition to [personal information deleted].[40]

The experts—who they suggested be primarily sourced from within South Australia—would serve as a 'talent pool' for the media and talkback radio in particular, and would be crucial in 'winning the talkback war' when the final dump location was announced. 'The key to ensuring balanced treatment is to strategically deploy our panel of experts in support of the ministers, particularly in the first 24–48 hours following the announcement, to add credible reassurances to the community and to tackle head on myths and misinformation', they suggested.[41] What Hill & Knowlton had in mind was a pincer movement that relied not only on using purportedly independent experts but dampening down the possibility that talkback would even be receptive to critical views on the waste dump. The PR company proposed to 'separately brief key talkback radio presenters and producers in advance of the announcement and ensure that they are issued daily rebuttals of claims made by opponents of the repository'.[42] The committee reviewing the bids liked Hill & Knowlton's scheme, and they got the contract.

Despite touting the experts as 'independent', the reality was they would be trained, briefed and funded by DEST to support the waste dump. For their efforts, members of the panel would be offered 'an honorarium on an hourly and daily basis'.[43] In later correspondence, an attachment to one email listed both potential 'panel members' and friendly 'media/commentators', though all names were deleted before public release.[44] According to the documents, DEST contracted an unnamed science commentator who '... would facilitate discussion of the issue on radio (in her usual science commentary broadcasts)...'[45] The DEST Annual Report lists a contract for the 'engagement of science communicator to arrange expert panel discussion on radio' on the 'national radioactive waste repository'.[46]

Running concurrently with Hill & Knowlton's contract, the government department had also initiated an $80 000 market research project to track public opinion. Soon after the initial results were in, DEST's Director of Radioactive Waste Management Section, Dr Caroline Perkins, quietly sought legal advice on whether it would be possible to terminate Hill & Knowlton's contract. When the *Adelaide Advertiser* revealed the PR campaign's proposal for the panel of scientists, Hill & Knowlton's Bill Royce suspected they were being set up to take a fall. 'Is there any way that we can verify whether the news of the panel was "placed" with the Advertiser by the Minister's office or a Departmental source? Neither we nor [deleted] have spoken to anyone about this', he asked in an email to DEST staff.[47] There was no email response from the departmental officers. Two days later, the Deputy Secretary of DEST, Grahame Cook, dispatched a letter to the PR company, informing them that their services were no longer required. 'Recent qualitative research indicates that there is not a case for an intensive media campaign', he wrote.[48] In response, Royce conceded that there was little point continuing, as debate about the role of the PR company 'would shift attention away from the substance of the debate and instead focus on the tactics, techniques and forms of communication used by the Commonwealth'.[49]

Just as it became a liability for Hollingworth once it was known that Mike Smith was working for him, Hill & Knowlton's contract evaporated once their role in selling a nuclear waste dump was known. The best chance for PR companies working on government contracts is if they manage to stay out of the limelight. But even then, there are no guarantees. Just as many corporate executives are bedazzled by the reputation of PR professionals as all-powerful fixers, government agencies often have unrealistic expectations of what they can deliver, too.

Playing information gatekeeper

Biotechnology Australia (BA), a government agency established in 1999 to help soften public opposition to the new technology by fostering debate on genetic engineering and its uses, was another that decided it needed to call on the expensive services of PR consultants. Shortly after BA was established, it sought bids from government-accredited PR companies to run a $1.2 million-dollar public awareness campaign slated to run over eighteen months. The Ministerial Committee on Government Communications (MCGC) reviewed the proposal, but some members of the government committee were nervous. Senator Chris Ellison cautioned that in some instances the government could get better value for money from hiring in-house staff than hiring 'expensive private firms'. A member of Prime Minister John Howard's staff, Tony Nutt, prophetically warned that the agency's management of the contract would need to be very good to ensure value for money.[50] Despite these concerns, the contract was awarded to Turnbull Porter Novelli (TPN).

Overseeing the campaign was a working group that spanned BA's 'partner' agencies from the government sciences agency, CSIRO, the Australian and New Zealand Food Authority (ANZFA), and the Interim Office of the Gene Technology Regulator. TPN churned out an impressive strategy document that ran for over a hundred pages, and for the first six months, the big-budget campaign ran smoothly. By August 2000, however, working group members were growing alarmed. A website developed by TPN was summarised by the working group as 'disastrously bad. Unprofessionally managed. Has made us very vulnerable to criticism'.[51] Others worried that the quality of advice 'had progressively declined'. Working group members were disturbed to find that staff who had been nominated to work on the account in the initial plans 'seemed to be no longer working on the account'. CSIRO thought TPN had had little effect in gaining substantial positive media coverage on biotechnology, while ANZFA expressed concern over TPN's 'high billing rates for management'.[52] Just over nine months into the contract, a divisional head of BA suggested that having a private PR firm 'was not considered appropriate in the political climate to progress certain aspects' of the agreed strategy.[53] After discussion with TPN, $466 000 was slashed from the budget, with the intent that the company refocus on the areas where it was considered it could offer something the government agencies lacked—high-level strategic advice and rural communication activities. Not long afterwards, the contract was left to lapse. Another raft of government agencies had discovered that the ability of a PR company to conjure up campaign-winning publicity can be illusory.

If hiring external PR consultants can be problematic for government agencies, there have been spectacular hiccups bringing high-flying PR consultants in-house too. In May 2003, a Senate committee was told that DEST had signed a contract with PR consulting company Staunton Consulting to work as the public affairs consultant for the CSIRO, the Australian government-funded scientific research agency. At a time when major staff cuts were in the air, the generosity of Staunton's contract also fuelled controversy. Donna Staunton's company was paid $22 000 a month for a four-day work week, in addition to travel and expenses. Staunton's background working for the Tobacco Institute of Australia, with a further four years doing PR for the world's largest private tobacco company, Philip Morris, raised eyebrows too. In 1994, she told a Senate committee that 'I do not believe that cigarette smoking is an addiction, based on any reasonable definition'.[54] Staunton had also been a director of the Melbourne-based free-market think tank, the Institute of Public Affairs, which was a long-time critic of the science behind the Kyoto Protocol on achieving cuts to greenhouse gas emissions.

In the wake of public controversy over Staunton's consultancy deal, the CSIRO moved to make an in-house appointment and, after spending $100 000 on a head-hunting company, Staunton was appointed as the Executive Director of Communications of CSIRO. Soon after joining the agency, Staunton drafted a communications policy, which was ratified by the board, preventing staff from commenting to the media unless they first got permission from senior agency executives. It was a policy that reflected the conventional PR mindset of centralising control and staying 'on message'. But attempting to control what scientists could say about their work undercut one of the central tenets of good science, which relies on improving knowledge by subjecting research to open debate. Not surprisingly, the CSIRO policy was greeted with hostility by staff and derision by science journalists.[55]

Even though many in the PR industry insist that a major role of PR people is as a friendly facilitator of journalists' inquiries, Staunton opted to play punitive gatekeeper. For eleven months, she maintained a bizarre ban on granting *Australasian Science* journalist Peter Pockley any interviews with CSIRO staff because he had written articles that were critical of some aspects of CSIRO. After widespread protests by journalists and scientists, Staunton and CSIRO's Chief Executive, Geoff Garret, grudgingly relented. In mid-July 2006, shortly after Staunton had tendered her resignation, CSIRO finally did a backflip on its policy on public comments.[56] While Staunton's tenure at CSIRO was characterised as playing information gatekeeper, other government agencies have gone in the other direction of soliciting advice from stakeholders on how to perform their statutory obligations.

Stakeholder logging

Bill Manning was an unlikely whistleblower. After working for 32 years with the government forestry agency, Forestry Tasmania, and its predecessor, and then with the logging practices regulator, the Forest Practices Board (FPB), there wasn't much he didn't know about the Tasmanian logging industry. After being sidelined when he refused to turn a blind eye to some illegal logging activities, Manning sought to blow the whistle by writing to the then Tasmanian Attorney-General, Peter Patmore. Nothing happened.

After media reports circulated, such as on Channel Nine's 'Sunday' program, that he had sought to blow the whistle, he was subpoenaed to appear before a Senate inquiry into plantation forests. After Senator Kerry O'Brien unsuccessfully attempted to prevent him giving his evidence in public session, Manning finally appeared before the committee in Canberra.[57] O'Brien's nervousness about the impact of what Manning would say about the Tasmanian government was well justified. In opening what was to be more than two hours of evidence, Manning launched a blistering attack on the mismanagement of the state's forests. FPB, he stated, was 'a rubber stamp to be used by industry and government' and then 'doubly abused as the mouthpiece for defending the most appalling forest practices'. The forestry industry, Manning explained, had become:

> so woefully negligent in its practices that it has been forced
> to be exempted from all other state environmental, planning

and land management legislation for the simple reason that were it to be judged by the legislation that other Tasmanians have to abide by, it would be found to be comprehensively in breach of Tasmanian law.[58]

The federal government's Regional Forest Agreement (RFA), Manning argued, had simply weakened the Forest Practices Code and led to the 'corruption of forest management in Tasmania such that there is no enforcement of this weakened code of forest practice'. He added that the RFA had led to the 'decimation' of vital habitat of Tasmanian endangered species, and had also created 'a culture within the Tasmanian forestry industry of bullying, cronyism, secrecy and lies'. Manning's evidence was a devastating blow to the Tasmanian government's claims that its system of forestry management was 'world's best practice'. It also created a crisis of legitimacy for the FPB.

The following year, the FPB, which was later rebadged and reorganised as the Forest Practices Authority (FPA), turned to the PR consultant, Katherine Teh-White, who runs her own Melbourne-based consultancy company, Futureye. The FPA, Futureye explained on its website, had been 'widely recognised as a best practice example of the contemporary regulatory theory of "co-regulation"'. The only concession to the nature of the problem was that public controversy 'had led to calls for higher levels of independence and transparency in forest regulation'.[59] Documents obtained by the author under the Freedom of Information Act reveal that Teh-White's pitch to the FPA board in February 2004 was far blunter, stating that the agency was seen as 'ineffective, corrupt and controlled by friends of the forest industry'. While the board wanted to be seen as an independent and tough regulator, and therefore ease pressure on the forest industry for more substantial reforms, it was constrained by a lack of funding, a reliance on companies self-policing their own logging operations, and its own timid approach to enforcement. Futureye noted that the board didn't have provision for substantial fines nor did it 'often prosecute breaches of the Code unless they are "serious"'.

In the eyes of the Tasmanian public, both the code and the board were toothless tigers. In a September 2004 proposal to develop a communications plan, Futureye's Vickie Burkinshaw, who had worked as the PR person for the Body Shop in Australia, suggested that the board needed a 'pro-active media relations strategy'.[60] For $29 000, she proposed Futureye would conduct half a dozen interviews with selected stakeholders, run a one-day workshop, and spend a week preparing a communications plan. The pitch proposed that one-day media training workshops would cost $3500 for Teh-White and $3000 for Burkinshaw. In case the FPB thought the cost of the workshops was a bit steep, Futureye noted that after six workshops, they would throw in another one for 'free'. Even though the organisation's crisis originated from the criticism of an internal whistleblower and a wide range of individuals and groups, the consultants determined that only those who would 'want to be involved in a Community Advisory Panel and directly negotiate with senior managers, ministerial advisers or Ministers' would be canvassed for their views. It was an extraordinary decision designed to marginalise the bulk of those who were most critical of the agency, and did little to address the underlying issues that created the crisis in the first place. Nonetheless, the FPB liked the proposal and signed up for the initial workshop, interviews with eight selected stakeholders, and a one-and-a-half day workshop for its newly-appointed directors. Which stakeholders were consulted remains a mystery, as the FPA refuses to disclose details. But The Wilderness Society, perhaps the single most persistent critic of the agency, wasn't one that Futureye and the board were interested in talking to.

In a summary of the December 2005 workshop with the board members, Futureye suggested that the highest priority issues to address included 'self-regulation—conflict of interest and cynicism of system' and 'breaches compliance with code'. Those consulted in the review felt that there should be strict enforcement of any breaches of the code. 'They believe the regulator is pro-forestry', Futureye noted, and that the agency was 'viewed as spin doctors and misleading the public'. To help rectify this, the consultants suggested that they needed to acknowledge their prior sins to indicate that 'you are clearly taking into account past (eg Manning allegations)'. They also suggested that an immediate priority was to set about building a positive relationship with the media and 'hear their concerns'. In their eyes, media that were more receptive to the FPA would help reduce the chances of community 'outrage'. The logging industry, though, still clearly didn't understand that the role of a regulator should be to enforce their standards. Futureeye noted that forest industry representatives thought of the code 'not as a cage within which it should sit, but a set of guidelines some of which are more serious than others'. Instead, the logging industry wanted there to be plenty of flexibility when it came to enforcing code standards, proposing that there should be some provisions that were deemed standards that they were 'able to collaborate on'.

One of the PR advisers on the restructuring of the FPA was former Tasmanian correspondent for *The Australian*, Bruce Montgomery. After eighteen months pushing the government and industry to make substantial concessions, he resigned in frustration to return to journalism: 'Where I deluded myself was that the industry would be flexible and that they would change.'[61] If the industry were inflexible, it was an issue that the agency would have to confront if it were to avoid a repeat of the crisis that led to Futureye's consultancy. Instead, the agency acquiesced to the intransigent logging industry, agreeing to consider which elements of the code were to be in the regulatory 'cage' to be enforced, and which were to be subject to 'collaboration'.

Despite an expensive consultancy, little had changed. Nor did those outside the authority see that the PR contract had much impact. 'I can't tell the difference', said The Wilderness Society's Tasmanian Campaign Coordinator, Geoff Law.[62] Even one of the stakeholders who provided confidential input into the review is uncertain if it made any significant difference. 'It is true that they are easier to talk with but has it made any difference on the ground yet? Not that I can see', said the Tasmanian Conservation Trust's Alistair Graham.[63]

The backlash

The growing appetite of governments for PR, though, is generating a political backlash. Opposition political parties around Australia have embraced an anti-spin campaign message as part of their advertising. In New South Wales, the leader of the Liberal Party launched billboard ads in mid-2006 that stated 'Nurses, not spin doctors'. In the August 2006 Queensland election, the Liberal Party ran a billboard advertising campaign, 'Funding for Real Nurses and Doctors, Not Spin Doctors'. With the rapid growth and ever-escalating cost of government 'information' campaigns, questions have been raised about just where the boundary lines are between what constitutes the legitimate provision of information to citizens and what is designed to deliver a partisan political advantage to the incumbent government. In the wake of a series of adverse public opinion polls in an election year, in 2007 John Howard's government stepped up its advertising programs on everything from its controversial industrial relations policies to its tarnished credentials on handling global warming. A little over a decade earlier, Howard as Leader of the Opposition had complained in a statement that Prime Minister Paul Keating was 'beginning an unprecedented propaganda blitz using taxpayers' money on advertising promoting government policies'.[64] Howard however, is on track to spend $2 billion since becoming Prime Minister.

A Senate committee canvassed the issue of what is legimate provision of information and what is political canvassing, but the discussion centred on visible and expensive advertising campaigns, not the invisible lower-budget media-management campaigns.[65] For example, the committee's report noted that the cost of the advertising campaign promoting the government's radical industrial relations changes was in the order of $55 million, which it reviewed in some detail. However, the far smaller contract awarded to the Sydney-based PR firms Jackson Wells Morris for an issues management strategy escaped scrutiny entirely. For its work in 2006, the Department of Employment and Workplace Relations forked out more than $451 000.[66] What exactly they did, the government have not disclosed.

Even though state governments' interest in advertising campaigns seems to be growing, perhaps their most pervasive but largely invisible role is through the influence of the central government communications units. As Tony Fitzgerald rightly worried, government media units can abuse their power. In one bizarre case, Lindsay Tuffin, the editor of the feisty Tasmanian online news and discussion site, TasmanianTimes.com, was on the receiving end of an email from the then head of the Tasmanian Government Communications Unit, Ken Jeffreys, threatening legal action unless an English translation of a damning article on Tasmanian forestry issues in the French newspaper *Le Figaro* were removed.[67] Aside from adding an excerpt from Hansard on the site, Tuffin ignored the threat. Sure enough, Jeffreys was all bluff and no writ. But it begs the question of whether such a censorious approach is more common but just invisible. Or perhaps this threatening approach is reserved only for those viewed as potentially vulnerable to legal action. To date, there has been little investigation of what the state-based government communications units do, even though it is arguable they have even greater potential to shape media coverage than their federal counterparts, simply because of the thinner ranks of political reporters at a state level.

•

As governments at every level spend more on PR and are increasingly embracing the use of covert PR strategies aimed at shaping what we think rather than simply providing factual information, there is a far greater need for scrutiny. In comparison to the corporate sector, government PR is subject to more parliamentary scrutiny, and records are potentially accessible through state and federal freedom of information acts. More effective and efficient FOI laws would go some way to helping facilitate this. But perhaps the biggest single hurdle is to create greater awareness among citizens, journalists and politicians that government PR has gone far beyond the peddling of soft promotional features, which characterised what was done in Eric White's era, or the routine spoiling tactics of ministers and minders identified in the post-Fitzgerald era in Queensland.

NINE
IT TAKES TWO TO TANGO

Under a large canvas tent erected in the backyard of the Canberra house where the late Australian historian Manning Clark had lived, Bill Rowlings stepped up to the podium to offer his thoughts on the impact of the PR industry on the media. After eighteen years in journalism, mostly with Rupert Murdoch's News Limited newspapers, and another eighteen years in PR, including with Hill & Knowlton and as co-author of a PR textbook, Rowlings was in a good position to judge their relative strengths. 'I think the spinners are winning and I think they are winning hands down', he said.[1] In the world of PR, an unwritten rule is to avoid publicly discussing how PR runs rings around journalists. Far from bragging, though, Rowlings was venting his frustration at the inadequacies of a media that had become too dependent on PR and too easily outmanoeuvred.

At the heart of the notion of the media as the 'fourth estate' is a dogged editorial independence from government and commercial influence. The media, we are often reminded, play a vital role in ensuring citizens can be well informed and play an active role in a modern democracy. But as media companies have grown into massive corporations, the tension between independence and the demands of owners and shareholders have sharpened. To insulate the editorial side from commercial considerations, the better media outlets have insisted on a strict firewall between the news and advertising divisions. The funding of advertising-free public broadcasters was another idea embraced to ensure that vital public interest journalism could thrive. But in the face of declining audiences, managers are under pressure to relentlessly deliver solid profits relative to both other commercial media companies and other sectors of the economy. Public broadcasters are under increasing pressure from politicians resentful of a journalism they see as too independent of political control. Both commercial and public broadcasters are expected to continually do more with less. Media companies with diversified business interests are under pressure to cross-promote or protect the business and political interests of their parent companies. While citizens expect journalists to be independent gatekeepers filtering out puff and digging for the real story, advertisers, shareholders and ministers judge the performance of the media quite differently.

In the shadow zone between journalists under pressure to produce to tight deadlines and editors with a large news and entertainment 'hole' to fill, the PR industry plies its trade. Its aim is to insert advertising and advocacy material for their clients in the guise of news. There has always been an uneasy relationship between PR and journalism that could be characterised as sibling rivalry. The role of independent watchdog the public expects of journalists is what is so often feared by those in PR. While there are no hard statistics about the relative size of the two professions, all agree that the PR industry is growing rapidly while journalists—and especially those that have the time to spend more than a day on a story—are thinning. Indeed, many PR professionals complain that the ranks of journalists are so thin that it is hard to elbow their way past others in the PR industry to sell their client's story.

'I think the consumer is in fact being disadvantaged by an under-resourced media and a highly resourced propaganda industry,' said Jim McNamara, the General Manager of Research with the Sydney-based media monitoring and content analysis company, CARMA International (Asia Pacific).[2] In 1994, McNamara documented a high level of PR-derived content in the media in research for his PhD thesis.[3] The year before, Clara Zawawi, then Assistant Professor in Public Relations at Bond University, sampled 192 stories from the *Sydney Morning Herald*, *The Australian* and the *Gold Coast Bulletin* to test the level of reliance on PR material. She calculated that almost two-thirds of the stories appearing in *The Australian* and the *Sydney Morning Herald*, and just over half in the *Gold Coast Bulletin* were PR-derived, and in the business pages it was more than 83 per cent.[4] She also observed that those driving the PR agenda tended to be favourably covered in the stories they generated.

If there is a high degree of dependence on PR in general news reporting, what of investigative reporting? After all, investigative journalism trades on the stereotype of heroic crusaders outsmarting the forces of spin. Gary Hughes, who has worked as a journalist for most of the last thirty years, including more than a decade as an investigative reporter at *The Age*, has a sobering assessment on the impact of PR on investigative journalism. 'The "feeding" of mainstream media investigative journalists has made many of them lazy and steadily eroded investigative skills. In some organisations, the definition of being an investigative journalist is simply cultivating a long list of public relations contacts', he told a freelance journalists conference in May 2000.[5] The 'feeding', he said, can range from 'sanctioned leaks' from ministers or government agencies to high-profile journalists at strategically important media outlets pre-empting a damaging story. A media dependent on PR often relies on concealing from the audience the origin of what is dressed up as 'news'.

Faking it

Jonathan Raymond, a former ABC TV producer and veteran PR industry executive, who is now Director of the Melbourne-based company Medialink Productions, agrees that there is 'something of a symbiotic relationship' between journalism and PR.[6] Medialink Productions is one of Australia's largest producers of video news releases (VNRs), pre-packaged news stories developed by a PR company for a client and delivered direct to the newsroom. The use of VNRs without disclosure on the origin of the material is a perfect illustration of the cohabitation of journalism and PR. There are no hard figures on the scale of the industry in Australia, but guesstimates are that there are somewhere between 100 and 200 VNRs distributed each year. VNRs come either as a ready-to-screen 'story', complete with a 'reporter' from a PR company presenting the 'story', or as what is referred to in the trade as 'B-roll'—a tape comprising interviews with experts or company spokespeople, along with graphics, background footage and story briefing notes. From what is often a 15-minute-long B-roll package of raw elements of a story, a television station can splice and dice the content as they choose. Whether TV stations add in a 'stand up' of one of their reporters talking to camera, to add a veneer of independent authenticity to a pre-scripted story, or they are broadcast in their entirety, VNRs confer a powerful benefit to their sponsors.

When broadcast unedited, VNRs are unadulterated PR dressed up as independent journalism. Secrecy on the source of the interviews or footage enables VNR sponsors to launder their PR story as news, boosting its credibility in the eyes of viewers and bypassing the sceptical filters most people apply to advertising.

VNRs are a way for companies and government agencies not only to help set the news agenda, but to actually write the 'news'. For media outlets, the attraction of VNRs is being able to save time and costs, fill the news bulletin, and create the appearance of independent journalism. The use of undisclosed VNRs is little more than the deception of audiences and regulators.

Raymond scoffs at the suggestion that Australian news networks don't routinely use the 50 to 60 VNRs a year that his company produces. He recounts the tale of a former television reporter he hired to work for him in a PR capacity:

> When he crossed to the 'dark side' he said to me 'Oh, you know, we never used them'. We just fell about laughing and then showed him [tapes of] several VNRs that he had in fact been the reporter on and had done the stand up for and suddenly [he said] 'Oh, but that was a good story'.[7]

Raymond also dismisses the suggestion that VNRs are used without the knowledge of station management. 'It is not the case. We are dealing with the chiefs of staff', he said.[8] When a VNR is distributed via satellite, the PR company or agency distributes a media release notifying the media outlet of the story and the date, time and coordinates of the satellite or the news station, such as Sky TV, from which it is available. To ensure maximum reach of the VNR the company will phone newsrooms to follow up on their email or fax pitch. To catch the VNR, the news station outlet has to decide to record the transmission off the satellite feed. Nor can the station credibly claim they didn't know where the material came from, as the producer and sponsor are also identified in the video frames prior to the actual VNR or B-roll.

VNRs can cost as much as $20 000 to produce and distribute, depending on the location and complexity of the story, but they can be far more cost-effective than advertising. Most VNRs are commissioned by major companies wanting a soft-sell promotion for a product, or a government agency wanting to get its message out. Some Medialink Productions clients have included Australia Post pushing newly minted stamps, Masterfoods selling reassurance in the wake of the recall of Mars Bars, or the Melbourne City Council spruiking that the Commonwealth Games were ready to roll. The Sydney-based company VnR, the other main producer of VNRs in Australia, also boasts that it achieves national coverage for clients. In a testimonial on its website, Jacqueline Wilson, a senior consultant with the PR firm Hill & Knowlton, was effusive: 'The client was very pleased with the VnR and the extensive National TV coverage. In fact Prime TV covered the story solely from the VnR which is great as the client can see the value in producing the VnR'.[9] In June 2005, Medialink Productions produced a VNR on the results of a clinical trial of an obesity drug, which they claimed 'ran on 38 television news bulletins around the nation—seen by more than 7 MILLION people'[10] (emphasis in original).

For drugs that haven't even been approved by regulators, there can be multiple benefits from a VNR with an up-beat tale about a new pill. A media profile can help recruit participants in a clinical trial and boost both corporate profile and investor interest. As with most PR tricks, VNRs promoting drugs work to a formula. A 'PR Toolbox' column in the global PR trade publication *PR Week* suggested including 'a personal' story. 'A news station doesn't want to appear as if it is promoting a product', but 'someone who has a personal story to tell...will be viewed as a Good Samaritan who wants to help others...not merely as a spokesperson'.[11] The specialist healthcare PR company, Palin Communications, which works for global giants such as GlaxoSmithKline, cautions that VNRs shouldn't be too overt: 'Keep the branding subtle and focus on the news rather than the product'.[12]

For a few thousand dollars extra, a client can have the sound track from a VNR repackaged as an audio news release (ANR) for distribution to radio stations. While VNRs are most commonly distributed via satellite, ANRs are produced and distributed differently. Medialink Productions, for instance, loads the clips onto a dedicated 1-800 number and dispatches an alert to radio stations. All a radio station producer has to do then is dial the number and record the 'interview' as it is automatically replayed. 'A series of different audio grabs are provided on the Medialink ANR so the broadcaster can re-use your story in successive bulletins throughout the day whilst varying the interview content each time,' the company explains. Medialink suggests that the benefits of using ANRs are that they not only provide radio newsrooms with access to otherwise 'hard to catch' people, but also ensure 'your spokesperson does not get flustered or confused on the phone or in a press conference'.[13]

In conventional journalism, a critical role of journalists is being able to ask well-researched questions and, based on the responses, determine what is most relevant to include in a story. The use of VNRs and ANRs removes journalists from the interviewing role and instead puts PR professionals in control of what questions are asked and which answers are used. The easier it becomes for media outlets to fill their news slots with free VNRs and ANRs, the more budgets for travel and journalists research time will be trimmed to match, undermining the ability of the journalists to invest time independently researching and preparing stories. The use of VNRs and ANRs also reinforces the trend of news organisations seeing their role as delivering advertising to potential consumers rather than independently informing them as citizens.

With the rise of broadband connections, the VNR companies are adapting, too. ANRs can now be sent out via an email alert with an embedded MP3 audio file. 'We recently got huge results for a client [doing this]', Raymond said. 'We put it out at 5am and it was nationally across all radio stations at 5.30am because the grabs are there, it is in the newsroom first thing in the morning and controlling that electronic morning media agenda'.[14]

The rise of online news has seen Medialink develop a new system for direct notification and delivery of sponsored multimedia 'stories' for 'direct placement on the websites of television stations', and posting to clients' video and audio podcasts on the Internet through Yahoo! and Google.[15] Nor are VNRs produced by Australian companies the only ones to grace our televisions screens. In its 2003 Annual Report, Medialink Worldwide, the global affiliate of Raymond's company, boasted that it generated:

> thousands of broadcast news airings worldwide reaching billions of viewers, listeners and readers on media as diverse as *CNN*, *The New York Times*, *ABC*, *Sky News*, *The Washington Post*, *BBC*, *Bloomberg Radio*, *AOL*, *Yahoo!* and *China Central Television*, the national television station of the People's Republic of China.[16]

Occasionally a station will identify externally supplied footage with an on-screen tag such as 'corporate video', but most go undisclosed.

As VNRs are not readily accessible to individuals, viewers are not to know whether what they watched in a news bulletin was real news or fake news. If viewers are to be informed that a broad-caster is using a corporate or government-supplied VNR, one of either the VNR producers or the broadcasters must label the vision. Technically, it would be a simple matter to caption footage with 'this video was supplied by Corporation X'. But neither media outlets nor PR companies are likely to volunteer to do that. On-air disclosure of who sponsored a 'news' item would inevitably curtail the use of VNRs, as viewers would discover how much of what they view was unadulterated PR. 'You'd be having a lot of captions on a lot of news', Raymond observed.[17] For their part, media outlets are wary of openly talking about the use of VNR footage without attribution. Despite this, VNR producers argue that all stations use material from VNRs, with only a fraction of the broadcast stories disclosing the origin. VNR producers have powerful evidence on the use of VNRs in the form of detailed tracking data identifying which stations used which part of a VNR. 'We wouldn't keep paying for video news releases if no one was using them...they [journalists] can talk about them as disparagingly as they like but we can show them the graphs that demonstrate how widely they are used', Martin Palin said.[18]

In the United States, the Government Accountability Office (GAO) has ruled that, to avoid breaching a legislative ban on covert government propaganda, federal agencies funding VNRs must disclose their sponsorship to viewers. More recently, the US Federal Communications Commission, which licences news corporations' right to use the public airwaves for radio and television broadcasts, has begun an investigation into the undisclosed use of VNRs.

In Australia, some companies and government agencies have bypassed their reliance on short segments in VNRs and ANRs. For four years until 2003, the CSIRO produced and distributed an entire national science radio program, 'The Sci Files'.[19] The monthly program was distributed via CD to approximately 250 radio stations. Up until 2003, CSIRO also produced the 'Australia Advances' program for free-to-air television stations, which it was estimated gained 75 TV spots a week, reaching four to five million viewers.[20] These days, the program—now into its sixteenth series—screens on cable television stations and is available over the web.[21] Of course, many of the stories on CSIRO's work—from widgets to wildlife—could be the topic of legitimate stories if produced by television stations themselves. But, despite its high public standing, CSIRO is not a neutral player in major public policy debates, such as genetic engineering, where it has direct commercial interests in biotechnology patents, and in attracting funding from commercial partners.[22]

CSIRO's Gene Technology Information Program, which was established in 1998 and ran until 2003, was one that took advantage of the CSIRO's PR operations to produce radio interviews with scientists for 'The Sci Files' and six video clips 'about gene technology research'. The six video clips were funded by Biotechnology Australia (BA), a federal government agency created to address public concerns about biotechnology. In other segments in the television series, the conflict between CSIRO's roles as an agency involved in a controversy and a supplier of 'news' was blatant. In March 1995, CSIRO established a research station on a small island in South Australia to test the effects of calicivirus as a method of controlling rabbit populations. After only six months the virus escaped from the island and spread through rabbit populations across mainland Australia, leading to widespread media coverage reporting the failure of CSIRO's quarantine standards. CSIRO, on the other hand, were keen to look at the upside. 'And as the rabbits disappeared, the barren landscape flourished once again', one of their TV clips ran.[23]

While passing off VNR and programs that originated from the PR industry helps media companies boost profits by keeping costs down, the main commercial game is in dominating broadcast markets and capturing a lion's share of advertising. And to do that, some media companies have gone all out to nobble their commercial rivals.

Media spinners

Peter Johnston, from the Melbourne suburb of East Malvern, was so concerned about the state of radio broadcasting in regional

Australia that he began writing letters to media outlets, regulators and state and federal politicians, demanding a parliamentary inquiry into what he claimed were falling standards in the sector. So too did Peter Townsend. Both Johnston's and Townsend's letters claimed that DMG Radio—which was 75 per cent owned by the UK-based *Daily Mail* Group company—was undermining local radio programming. With the spectacular success of Pauline Hanson's One Nation Party tapping into the deep disaffection within regional Australia fresh in the minds of politicians, the Minister for Communications, Senator Richard Alston, opted for caution. In early September 2000, he directed the relevant House of Representatives committee to conduct a 'broad-ranging' inquiry into the 'adequacy of radio services in non-metropolitan Australia'.[24]

Both the letters and the inquiry set off alarm bells for DMG Radio. Earlier that year, it had won a bidding war for a new FM radio frequency when it paid $155 million, which it used to launch its Nova FM station.[25] At the time, media commentators considered that the company had paid way too much and would struggle to attract enough advertising revenue to make a profit. No sooner had the station been launched than critical letters began to trickle into the offices of politicians. Facing the prospect that the inquiry would recommend changes that could undermine its business plans, DMG hired a private investigator to uncover who was behind the campaign against it. As for 'Peter Johnston' of 207 Darling Road, East Malvern, DMG's investigator could find no trace. 'No one by that name lives or works at that address', DMG later wrote in its submission to the inquiry. DMG reported similar problems in tracing 'Peter Townsend' and 'John "Long John" Chapman'. A University of Melbourne linguist, Dr Laura Tollfree, reviewed the letters and concluded they all probably originated from the one author.[26] The letters, DMG suggested, 'appear to be nothing more than a prank or hoax orchestrated by one of our major competitors'.

While the campaign was intended to be invisible, traces were accidentally left behind. The mobile phone number left with the *Australian Financial Review* for the bona fides of the author of one letter to the editor tracked back to Ken Davis, a director of the PR firm Turnbull Porter Novelli (TPN). On another, there was a computer code 'KEN'. Davis's clients included Austereo, which owned the MMM and 2DAY FM stations, Nova's rival stations.[27] Another client was Austereo's parent company, Village Roadshow. As the first public hearings of the inquiry got under way, the *Sydney Morning Herald* reported that Davis was behind the bogus letter-writing campaign. TPN Chairman, Noel Turnbull, announced that the company had severed its relationship with Davis. 'He acted privately in conjunction with third parties unconnected with us or any of our clients. His actions were in no way authorised by the company or any of our clients', Turnbull said.[28] DMG, though, weren't prepared to let the matter end there.

In December 2000, they launched legal action in the Federal Court, alleging Davis, Turnbull Porter Novelli (TPN), Austereo and its executive chairman, Peter Harvie, had engaged false and misleading conduct in contravention of the provisions of the Trade Practices Act. DMG's action also alleged that the company had been defamed. At a preliminary hearing in May 2001, evidence that undermined Austereo's denial came to light. Harvie admitted that, three years earlier, Davis had been hired by him to organise a campaign in favour of more community radio station licences being issued, a move that was aimed at soaking up the available new broadcast spectrum with non-commercial stations that would pose little threat to Austereo's existing advertising income. In August 2001, a month before the case was scheduled to go to full trial, Austereo and Turnbull Porter Novelli settled the case and issued a statement explaining that DMG had received 'a substantial payment in respect of damages and costs'.[29] As part of the settlement, DMG accepted that Davis had acted alone in running the deceptive letter-writing campaign. Aside from revealing the depth commercial media companies would plumb in order to undermine their rivals, the case also set a precedent of PR companies being sued for breaching the provisions of the Trade Practices Act.

Covert campaigns against rivals of the Austereo variety might be rare, but most major media companies employ spin doctors to help advance their own business interests and reassure investors. It would be a stretch to argue that the lack of reporting on PR is attributable to media companies' own use of PR, but it is certainly true that reporters wouldn't have too far to travel if they wanted somewhere to start. One area where the conflict between companies is intense is in the battle that goes on between media players over broadcast rights to sport. The mammoth legal action initiated by Kerry Stokes's Channel Seven network against News Limited and 21 other companies over his unsuccessful bid for the pay TV rights for the National Rugby League shed light on some of the behind-the-scenes media massaging that goes on. As part of News Limited's defence, its legal counsel, Noel Hutley SC, turned to internal documents authored by Seven's PR consultant, Tim Allerton, and its in-house PR adviser, Simon Francis. Allerton had been employed by Stokes's private company, Australian Capital Equities, on an $8000 per month retainer to promote a favourable media profile for the Seven Network by cultivating senior journalists.[30] Hutley also tabled a 23 November 2000 email written by Francis during the period when Seven was finalising its bid: 'we have... been careful not to have our fingerprints on any [media] story in the past 10 days'. In another email several months earlier, Francis mentioned how material had been 'seeded' with a number of senior newspaper journalists, whom he described as the 'usual suspects'.[31]

Where media companies have paid vast sums for multi-year deals on the exclusive broadcast rights for sport, they have a major financial interest in protecting the credibility of sport in times of crisis. When, in 1999, the first media reports of corrupt match-fixing of international cricket matches began to emerge, the International Cricket Council (ICC) feared it could severely damage the commercial future of the game. To help defuse the crisis, the ICC turned to Porter Novelli in Australia (PN) and its UK counterpart, Countrywide Porter Novelli. Even though the initial crisis subsided, the story was bubbling away below the surface. In May 2000, the crisis erupted once more when the captain of the South African cricket team, Hansie Cronje, admitted accepting bribes to throw games. Other big-name cricket stars were soon drawn into the controversy, including one of Australia's leading cricketers, Mark Waugh. As one Porter Novelli document described it, the ICC, which was 'viewed by many as a weak and ineffective governing body', was faced with saving international cricket 'from collapse'.[32]

As with much in PR, one common element in developing an issues management plan is to have a game plan of how media coverage is likely to unfold. Often an 'audit' of past media coverage and the identification of key themes and journalists can be used as a crude predictor of likely future coverage. Specialist media monitoring tools also allow a detailed analysis of past stories on a particular topic, even down to a 'favourability' rating against keywords, media outlets or themes selected by the client and trends over time. For journalists, the first port of call for background research is often a quick scan of recent newspaper clippings to identify key themes and potential interviewees. For this reason, most news coverage follows predictable themes and a relatively narrow set of commentators. This pattern often breaks down when a crisis erupts, but the PR advisers still need to know with as much precision as possible how the media are likely to report the story. 'We occasionally do confidential journalist surveys where, if there is say a problem with very unfavourable coverage a high-level client might sometimes ask us to say "can you, confidentially, anonymously interview a series of journalists and ask them their perspective"', said Jim McNamara, from the Sydney-based media analysis company, CARMA Asia Pacific.[33] In the world of PR, a little strategic courting of the most influential journalists can help set the parameters of how a story is reported. Why would journalists discuss how they might report a story with those on the 'dark side'? It is here that PR companies benefit immensely from having former journalists on their staff. Journalists are usually more than happy to give their opinions on topics of interest, especially to friends and former colleagues. Such surveys are often seen as no different from answering a market research survey.

For the ICC, Porter Novelli undertook a series of interviews with leading cricket journalists 'regarding prevailing views, identify misconceptions, and understand information requirements'.[34] With journalists' assistance in pinpointing the key information targets, Porter Novelli could confidently set about developing the objectives of a five-month-long plan to contain the crisis and rebuild the credibility of the game. Central to its plan was the necessity to 'divert media attention from corruption issue to more positive ICC initiatives'.[35] For while the ICC knew that it couldn't bury the corruption issue entirely, it was sufficiently confident that a series of proposals could gain a substantial share of media space and help overcome the view that the ICC was a toothless tiger. But as so often occurs in a crisis, spin doctors have to cope with plans to control the flow of information that go awry. It had been intended that when Mark Waugh was interviewed by the ICC-appointed Anti-Corruption Unit (ACU) in February 2001, it would occur without the knowledge of the media. The details of the hearing leaked out anyway. In a bid to reassert control over the media, Channel Nine—the national television network that holds the exclusive rights to broadcast cricket on free-to-air television—was granted exclusive rights to film the ICC Board meeting. 'In return, approved film is used as pool footage for other networks', a Porter Novelli document stated.[36]

The following day, the ICC convened another press conference, this time to announce three new initiatives in an attempt to 'turn media attention away from match fixing'. It was a move that had limited success. In response to calls from journalists for access to the captains of the national cricket teams, PN and the ICC made a limited concession. Instead of a free-wheeling media conference, Porter Novelli and the ICC granted exclusive interviews to an unspecified media outlet with the 'captains following approved scripts'.[37] Ahead of the release of the ACU's final report into match-fixing in May 2001, the ICC negotiated an agreement with the BBC's 'Panorama' program that would allow them to film an exclusive feature program on the ICC's anti-corruption efforts. This was 'used as a preliminary positioning piece prior to release of ACU report', Porter Novelli later wrote.[38] Ultimately the match-fixing crisis receded and the PR company was pleased to note that the standing of the ICC in the eyes of sports journalists had been enhanced. Part of the success of the campaign was the ability of the PR company to have journalists themselves pinpoint ways in which the scandal could be addressed. As with so many aspects of PR, the conduct of media audits is largely invisible as, having volunteered to participate in them, journalists are unlikely to write critically about them.

A substantial part of the success of the PR industry is attributable to its ability to recruit journalists, who bring their extensive personal networks of contacts to bear for the benefit of a client. Why is it such a common career move for journalists to migrate to the world of PR? The most common explanation given for what is often described as 'crossing to the dark side' is money. It is certainly true that PR pays far better than journalism, commonly a premium of more than 30 per cent, but this is too neat and simplistic an explanation. It smacks of little brother hacks pointing an accusing finger at big brother flacks. It pretends all the fault is with PR, and conveniently absolves media companies of any responsibility. Most journalists' work is largely reactive, usually shaped as a response to the events of the day. Few know when they turn up for work what stories they will be filing later on that day. Fewer still have the luxury of spending more than a day preparing a story. After years of the daily grind, combined with the constant stress of working to tight deadlines, the challenge and stimulation recedes. After working for eighteen years as the Tasmanian correspondent for *The Australian*, Bruce Montgomery was headhunted by Tasmanian Premier Paul Lennon to be a PR fixer on forestry issues in Tasmania. 'Journalists spend most of their lives observing and never really making any positive contribution as I see it … I thought there was a prospect of specialising in one subject for once instead of trying to cover everything that moved', he said.[39]

Becoming jaded with the daily journalistic treadmill is one thing, but an equally common frustration is with the quality of middle and upper management in media companies, the constant restructurings and budget cuts, and the shift to more product-driven 'news'. On top of that are the stories that are considered out of bounds lest they offend editors or owners. For those journalists who don't aspire to join middle management, there are limited opportunities for career advancement. In comparison, the world of PR looks attractive. Most work on an account for a PR company's client is often pre-planned and relatively controlled. In PR, there are also a myriad of specialist areas that are expanding as the PR industry grows. As initiators of stories, former journalists who turn to PR feel they have far more impact getting issues onto the public agenda than they ever did while working in the media.

Cash for ... ?

Another venue for the increasingly intimate dance between corporate PR professionals and journalists is at the ever-proliferating number of corporate-sponsored journalism prizes. Sir William Gaston Walkley, the founder of Ampol Petroleum, instituted the Walkley Awards for journalism in 1956 out of appreciation for 'the media's support for his oil exploration efforts'.[40] Following his death, the awards were hosted by the Australian Journalists Association and its successor, the Media, Entertainment and Arts Alliance, and are now the premier Australian journalism awards. These days, the awards ceremony is televised nationally and the number of prizes on offer has grown from five to 33. The proliferation of award categories in part reflects the proliferation of sponsors, some of which are broadly part of the media industry but also included are major corporations such as Telstra and the financial services company CommSec.

Where the Walkley Awards emerged as peer acknowledgement of high professional standards in the journalistic profession, companies and industry associations have been busy creating their own awards. The most lucrative are those associated with the drug industry. Medicines Australia, the peak drug industry lobby group, sponsors the annual National Press Club of Australia Excellence in Health Journalism Awards, with Qantas, the National Australia Bank and the drug company Pfizer as co-sponsors. The awards themselves are organised under the aegis of the National Press Club in Canberra, a body whose members comprise journalists, lobbyists, political advisers and PR professionals. The Club itself, which operates from a dowdy clubhouse a stone's throw away from Parliament House, is best known for its weekly televised National Press Club luncheon. Four of the five Medicines Australia awards are for $1000 and a certificate. The grand prize, though, is Health Journalist of the Year, which has an all-expenses-paid 'study tour' to Washington D.C. Co-ordinating the event for the NPC is Jon Gaul, a long-time Canberra lobbyist and Liberal Party campaign strategist, who heads up the PR and lobbying company, Gavin Anderson. As with most journalism awards, a small pot of money and the lure of professional prestige lures a significant field of high-profile contenders. The night before the awards are announced, all those who have applied for an award are invited to a cocktail function 'to meet, mingle and network' with the sponsors of the awards, judges, press club directors and 'VIP guests'.

Why do companies, such as those in the drug industry, fork out tens of thousands of dollars sponsoring journalism awards? Are Medicines Australia simply wasting their members' money? Or is the payoff far bigger than the investment? Paul Cross, from the Canberra PR firm Parker & Partners, who organises the event for Medicines Australia, dismisses the idea that awards influence media coverage. 'If you look at who has won the awards they are not advocates for the industry, that's for sure', he said.[41] Indeed, the awards have featured some of the big names of Australian medical journalism such as ABC Radio National's Health Reporter, Norman Swan. Cross, who worked as a political adviser to both Paul Wooldridge and Kay Patterson when they were ministers for health, insists that the industry sponsorship is an example of disinterested philanthropy rather than self-serving cultivation of a strategically important network. It is, he said, like 'sponsoring a sporting team or a local community group'. The problem is that it isn't. If Medicines Australia were sponsoring an award for sports journalism or motoring writers, Cross would have more of an argument. But sponsors of sporting teams establish measures to evaluate media exposure so that they can do a cost-benefit analysis on their investment and determine whether it is worth continuing with the sponsorship. It is inconceivable that an industry association for drug companies, which has a deeply entrenched marketing culture that seeks to measure and evaluate everything with a high degree of precision, hasn't established benchmarks against which to judge the benefits that flow from their generosity to journalists.

'I think it is all about access', says Peter Mansfield, from the drug industry watchdog group, Healthy Skepticism.[42] Mansfield believes that while the quality of medical journalism in Australia is high by international standards, drug industry awards are likely to subtly shape the content of coverage over time:

> If you have accepted an award from industry or have accepted hospitality from Medicines Australia you would be in a difficult position if you had a story that might lead you to criticise patient groups or doctors for receiving drug company money or hospitality because it then becomes hypocrisy.

Medicines Australia are pleased that an increasing number of journalists are submitting material for the awards, but it is a cause of dismay for respected medical journalist, Melissa Sweet. After working as an Australian Associated Press journalist for four years, Sweet spent a year as a healthcare consultant in the Sydney office of Hill & Knowlton before returning to journalism. 'I can't believe that journalists don't think there is a problem with these awards', she said. The creation of corporate-sponsored journalism prizes, she believes, suits the interests of all those involved. Journalists get recognition among their peers, it looks good on a CV, and may even help impress a manager at the time of a performance and pay review. Media outlets, too, love their journalists winning awards as it enables them to boastfully dress up as news what is really brand-enhancing marketing.

Sometimes, the submission of a story for an award originates with editors, not the individual journalists. 'It suits everyone . . . it suits the individual journalist, it suits the company, it suits the media brand but ethically it is indefensible', Sweet said.[43]

The National Press Club awards are by no means the only one, even for health journalists. Eli Lilly, which manufactured hormone replacement therapy drugs, established an award for 'excellence in journalism in the field of menopause', which later morphed into an award for women's health journalism. Kellogg's had an award for nutrition reporting.[44] Aventis—a drug company that makes drugs for the bone-thinning condition, osteoporosis—sponsored an international osteoporosis media award, Upjohn sponsored a medical award, and the giant drug company Pfizer sponsored an Australian Medical Association rural media award. In 2001, Pfizer instituted a $10 000 cash prize for medical and health research journalism as one of the Australian Museum Eureka Prizes. The museum's Manager of Strategic Initiatives, Roger Muller, defended the inclusion of Pfizer's media affairs manager, Craig Regan, as one of the judges. 'Judging panels are chosen by sponsors. An increasing number of sponsors have representatives on the judging panel', he said.[45]

The Clinical Oncological Society of Australia hosts the rather bizarrely titled Luminous Award Australia for 'enlightened, intel-ligent, inspiring cancer reporting', courtesy of sponsorship from the drug company, Eli Lilly. The winner gets a cash prize of $5000, a commemorative plaque and a 'congratulatory letter to the winner's editor'. Nominees are also entered into the Inter-national Luminous Award, with the winner landing a one-week trip to Boston, London, New York, Paris or Sydney, 'to be enlight-ened by the work of a leading oncologist or cancer researcher'. The winner also has a €10 000 scholarship in their name to help a journalism student. Journalism prizes, especially covering the more lucrative industry areas can be good for the bank balance, frequent flyer points and ego. Others take a different approach to subsidising journalists' careers.

Over the last 15 years, Citigroup, a huge global financial services company, has sponsored its Journalism Awards For Excellence.[46] The prize for the winning business journalist is a ten-day study tour to the Columbia Graduate School of Journalism in New York. The Minerals Council of Australia—the peak body representing the largest mining companies—runs an annual 'journalist fellowship program' over four days, in conjunction with its annual workshop in Canberra. The 'invitation only' program—which is organised in conjunction with the Department of the Senate and the Department of Industry, Tourism and Resources—aims to provide an 'intensive, high profile, professional development opportunity' to 'experience public policy development' in Canberra.[47] In 2006, the half dozen journalists who took the trip came from ABC regional radio stations in the Northern Territory and Western Australia, and from newspapers in New South Wales Hunter Valley and Ballarat. But scour the media all you like and you won't find a single report on what is involved in the program, even though it has been running for four years.

Does it matter that companies and industry groups are putting up cash to celebrate the efforts of journalists on topics near and dear to their interests? Is accepting corporate money laundered via an award compatible with the independence the public expects? Or is the defence of the awards as lame as the line trotted out by doctors, that accepting drug company gifts doesn't affect their prescribing patterns? Central to the success of PR activities is masking a self-serving activity behind an apparently civic-spirited project. In the absence of evidence that justifies scepticism, the expectation is that activities should be taken at face value. In the world of journalism awards, the sceptics are heavily outnumbered. However, nearly all PR programs are the result of a carefully thought plan to achieve strategic objectives. One internal tobacco industry PR document illustrates how a harmless-looking art award had little to do with supporting budding artists, but was all about building bridges to key audiences—politicians and bureaucrats.

In 1997, a Philip Morris Corporate Affairs Plan reviewed the company's PR activities in Asia, including its sponsorship of the Asian Art Award. The sponsorship of the award, they approvingly noted 'provides Corporate Affairs and management with direct access to senior government officials in each country and [has] given us strong relationships at the ASEAN Secretariat'.[48] While many in the media dismiss the suggestion that corporate-sponsored trips influence coverage, a British American Tobacco (BAT) internal memo revealed its confidence in the practice. In 1994, BAT's Corporate Communications division pondered whether it could sponsor a visit to BAT's London head office for South American editors and journalists. They noted in frustration that some media organisations refused corporate-sponsored trips for journalists, and would only cover the costs themselves if they were convinced it was 'not just a junket or a pure publicity exercise'. 'In this respect, freelancers can be a better bet as they are more open to having their trip paid for, and they are less likely to "bite the hands that feed them" as they will want to safeguard their place on any future trips', they candidly wrote.[49] Other approaches to courting journalists are more blatant.

In June 2005, the Korean car company Hyundai was showing off its new Sonata sedan for the benefit of Australian motoring journalists. At the event, the company's local boss, Bong Gou Lee, announced a special offer: 'Half price for journalists, tonight only.' A *Sydney Morning Herald* journalist, Tony Davis, reported that several journalists identified the models and colours and provided their credit card numbers. The one-night-only deal would have saved the journalists more than $17 000 on a brand new, below-cost car. Once Davis began making inquiries, the offer was withdrawn and Hyundai spokesman Richard Power claimed the offer was a joke. However, one journalist told Davis 'there's no way people joke about things like that and take names and colours...I bought one. Plenty of people did'.[50] Nor has the Australian Government had any reservations about having a leading newspaper columnist do a little ministerial ghostwriting on the side.

In February 2007, a parliamentary committee reviewing government expenditures was informed that Christopher Pearson, a columnist on national politics and foreign affairs in the *Weekend Australian* and a board member of SBS, had been employed indirectly by the Department of Foreign Affairs and Trade on five occasions in 2004 and 2005 as a speechwriter. The department paid Spherion Recruitment Solutions, also known as Verrossity, $11 364 for Pearson's assistance on everything from 'input into a terrorism white paper' to a speech for the Minister for Foreign Affairs and Trade, Alexander Downer, for an evangelical Christian gathering and another on the environment. At the committee hearing Senator Robert Ray quipped that 'not only have we got the snout in the trough; we have all the trotters as well'.[51]

•

In the grand scheme of things, does it really matter if the worlds of journalism and PR are closely intertwined? There are some within the PR industry who wish journalists would cut the criticism of spin doctors and learn to accept their co-dependency. Others wish journalists would do a better job of exposing the sloppy practices all too often on display in both the media and PR industries. But the core issue is whether journalists and media companies can assert their independence from a growing PR industry that seeks to tame independent voices in a debate. It is unlikely that the corporate side of media companies and broadcasters will stop hiring PR companies and consultants to run campaigns to advance their business interests. At best, they are most likely to encourage reporting on PR campaigns run by others when it suits their strategic interests. At the editorial level, there are greater prospects of editors and journalists asserting the central importance of independence from PR. In this, journalists could look to the vibrant debate within the medical profession on how ensuring credibility in the eyes of those they aim to serve requires disentangling themselves from the influence of PR.

In the realm of journalism, some good places to start would be in ending the use of VNRs and ANRs, and putting an end to the culture of freebies, such as the corporate sponsorship of journalism prizes. An additional step would be to increase reporting on the intertwining industries of PR and marketing, and the myriad ways they seek to influence independent voices in a democracy. The less reliance journalists have on government and corporate orchestrated 'exclusives', leaks and handouts, the better the prospects are that journalism will fulfil its public function of being an independent check on those who wield power in our society, and as a vehicle to provide information, not advertising, to citizens.

TEN
SPINBUSTERS

Harold Burson, the 86-year-old founder of Burson-Marsteller (B-M), one of the world's largest PR firms, expressed his irritation when asked in 2005 about the company's work in the 1970s promoting foreign investment in Argentina at the time of the military dictatorship's 'dirty war'. 'Had I known that I would still be defending our work in Argentina after 30 years, I wouldn't have accepted the military government as a client,' he told a reporter for the German magazine, *Der Spiegel*.[1] What irritated Burson was not that his company helped prop up a military dictatorship, but that citizens and journalists wouldn't let him forget it. And it is doubtful that, if B-M were offered the opportunity to work for a brutal military dictatorship now, the account would be turned down. In 1993, long after helping out the Argentinean dictatorship, B-M signed up for a US$5 million account to help buff the image of the Indonesian military dictatorship on East Timor and the environment. The massacre of dozens of people attending a funeral in the Santa Cruz Cemetery in Dili in 1991 and the ongoing controversy over rampant rainforest logging did little to deter B-M then.[2] Of course, there is no provision in any of the industry's various codes of ethics preventing anyone in the PR industry from working for odious clients, let alone require them to publicly disclose that they are. Forty years ago, though, the Public Relations Institute of Australia (PRIA) at least aspired to a higher standard. Tucked away in the 1962 edition of PRIA's code of ethics was a provision, long-since jettisoned, stating that members 'shall refrain from associating with any questionable enterprise'.[3]

Public scepticism about much of corporate and government PR is well justified. Campaigns designed and implemented by PR professionals have dressed up self-serving commercial marketing as philanthropy, fuelled think tanks to run campaigns their clients aren't prepared to own up to, and created corporate front groups to counter critics or commercial rivals. Others aim to quietly court and co-opt potential critics as a way of starving important public debates of oxygen. Above all, much high-level PR is about eroding the independence of thought and action of key individuals, organisations and professions so that they no longer pose a threat to the interests of PR professionals' clients or employers. While many in the industry proclaim that modern PR is about designing 'win-win solutions', the reality is that in contests over public policy there are nearly always losers. A partial win for a tobacco company, after all, results in others losing their lives.

There are those within the PR industry who insist that the days of being in the business of propaganda are long gone. However, the closer PR practitioners gravitate to the heart of corporate and government decision-making—a role that its most senior practitioners crave—the more inevitable it is that their role is *primarily* propaganda. Increasingly, the role of PR is to ensure that those who can afford their expensive services—predominantly corporate and government agencies—dominate debate over critical public policy issues. Some in PR hear of dubious practices within the industry, but feel powerless to do anything about it. Either they have little faith in the industry's code of ethics or they fear making

a complaint will adversely affect their career. Others—especially
those at the more harmless end of the industry—feel unfairly
maligned by criticism of the industry, or dispute that there is
much to worry about. Sometimes, this comes from people in the
industry who have little or no knowledge of what goes on in other
companies, or—such is the level of secrecy in PR—sometimes
even within their own company. They believe, or perhaps want
to believe, that if the accusations directed against PR don't square
with their experience, then it doesn't happen anywhere; however,
internal PR industry surveys point to a substantial problem.

An ethics survey of 1700 PR professionals in 2000 by *PR
Week* revealed one-quarter admitted they had lied in their job,
and 39 per cent disclosed they had exaggerated in their job.[4]
Sixty-two per cent of those surveyed felt they had been compromised in their job by being told lies by clients or prevented from
finding out the full story. Just over half revealed they had refused
to work on an account or project because of ethical concerns,
and almost one in five had resigned a job because of ethical
concerns. More than half of those surveyed supported stricter
ethical standards within the industry. A year later, a survey of
PR Week Asia yielded similar results.[5] An August 2005 survey
commissioned by the Public Relations Society of America (PRSA)
asked members of the public, corporate CEOs and Congressional staffers whether they agreed that PR practitioners 'sometimes
take advantage of the media to present misleading information
that is favourable to their clients'.[6] Eighty-five per cent of both
the public and congressional staffers agreed with that statement,
while 67 per cent of the corporate executives agreed.

Spinner, heal thyself?

Is there any realistic prospect that the PR industry can reform
itself? In a submission to the Australian Broadcasting Authority's

inquiry into the 'cash for comment' affair, PRIA's then national president, Lelde McCoy, explained that the organisation's 'principal aim is to achieve adherence to the highest standards of ethical practice and professional competence'. The submission went on to state that the code of ethics requires members to 'deal fairly and honestly with the communication media and with the general public, as well as with clients and other stakeholder groups'. It sounds reassuring, but it begs the question that if the 50-year-old PRIA has always placed such great weight on ethical standards, why is the reputation of the industry so low? Is PRIA's code of ethics really as strict as claimed? Or are the PR industry's blues inherent in its secretive self-regulatory system itself?

PR is not a regulated profession that requires practitioners to meet accredited standards and submit to the jurisdiction of a professional body. Regulated professions, such as medicine, are designated by the government and given the power to sanction members for misbehaviour, including disbarring them from continuing to practice. But legal advice to the institute is that any public censure of a member opens the body up to being sued for defamation and damages. Former PRIA National President Jim McNamara believes this is the single biggest factor limiting the effective enforcement of the code. An attempt in 2000 by PRIA to have the federal government designate PR as a regulated profession was rebuffed. In the absence of effective sanctions, a member subject to an ethics complaint can simply resign and remove themselves from the jurisdiction of PRIA. Without the legal insulation that goes with being a regulated profession, McNamara describes the code as a 'toothless tiger and it frustrates the hell out of everyone who has been involved in the process'. He recounted that, when President of PRIA:

> we were going to throw the book at a couple of people in my
> term and then the lawyers came in and said, 'fine but have

you got your house in your own name'...And you go 'Oh,
hang on a minute'. You know PRIA is important but I'm not
going to lose my house over this.[7]

Even if the code were effective and enforced, PRIA represents
only about one-quarter of the estimated 10 000 PR professionals
in Australia.

As with much in the Australian PR industry, the code of
ethics developed by PRIA is largely derived from the code adopted
by the Public Relations Society of America (PRSA). In October
2000, following extensive consultations within the industry, PRSA
adopted a revised version of its Code of Ethics. 'Emphasis on
enforcement of the Code has been eliminated', they proudly
reported.[8] Abandoning any pretence of self-regulation, PRSA
stated that their Board of Directors would only consider expelling
a member if they had already been 'sanctioned by a government
agency or convicted in a court of law of an action that is in
violation of this code'. In effect, PRSA outsourced any investigation, prosecution or determination of ethical breaches to public
agencies with very limited jurisdiction over the PR industry. Why
did they adopt such a timid approach? Back in October 1999,
O'Dwyer's PR Services Report noted a twelve-page report by
Seattle-based PR counsellor Bob Frause, who was then chair of
PRSA's Board of Ethics and Professional Standards. 'Pure and
simple, our entire committee is frustrated, powerless and unable
to do justice to the spirit of the PRSA code... The once dominant
belief that the PRSA's ethics code had meaning and was strictly
enforced is now defunct', the report bluntly stated.[9] 'A recurring
issue...and frequently discussed in the media concerns a
member's obligation to identify clients and front groups', the
report said. 'It is absolutely imperative that the Society address
the frequent criticism that PR practitioners are party to misleading
and deceptive practices with front groups.'[10]

The committee also identified a litany of other problems, including limited powers to gather documents, the destruction of documents, and outright denials by members that they were involved in unethical behaviour. The lack of disclosure surrounding what complaints were actually made and what action was taken, the committee complained, deprived the code of any educational benefits to other practitioners. The one explicit improvement to the code PRSA did make was to include specific examples of what would constitute unacceptable practice. In a section titled 'Disclosure of Information', the PRSA code states: 'Front groups: A member implements "grassroots" campaigns or letter-writing campaigns to legislators on behalf of undisclosed interest groups.'[11]

In Australia, the PRIA's code of ethics is less emphatic. The fact that PRIA might only receive a few complaints a year is hardly evidence that there aren't significant problems. Even though PRIA's code of ethics obliquely hints at the benefits of transparency, it certainly doesn't require companies to reveal their client list. In the absence of this information, it is rare that a member of the public will ever know who was behind what campaign. Indeed the people most likely to know about and have access to the evidence of a breach of the code of ethics are other PR insiders. Not surprisingly, few bother. Complainants from within the industry also risk being the subject of a commercial backlash.

A close reading of PRIA's manual for handling ethics complaints, issued in August 2003, reveals PRIA is fearful of possible legal consequences for itself and wants to keep all but the most serious ethics breaches secret. Aside from the prospect that a member could be expelled, the next most serious punishment is a maximum fine of $10 000, which in the world of PR is small potatoes. PRIA have embraced the idea of naming and shaming those fined, but only via a notice in the public notices section of a major newspaper. The more common but less serious reprimands are tucked away in text of PRIA's annual report to members. All lesser offences—such as those for which a warning was issued or a member censured or deprived of some rights—would remain hidden from view of even most PRIA members. Instead, warnings are only recorded in the minutes of PRIA Board, the Ethics Committee, and the state PRIA branch from which the offender operates. Nor is there any guarantee that PRIA members will find out about such findings, as the Board may, at its discretion, only publicise general details of the offence, without the name of the offender, in the membership journal or website. As a result, only a tiny fraction of breaches of the code of ethics would ever see the light of day.

In the absence of disclosure, there is limited public pressure for better performance, no deterrent effect and little educational value for PR professionals, especially for the three-quarters of the profession who aren't PRIA members. McNamara, for one, wants to see changes made, such as the inclusion of people from outside the profession on the panel, and the ethics committee decision to be binding, not merely a recommendation to the board. Even the flawed complaints procedure developed by Medicines Australia, the peak drug industry lobbying group, puts PRIA's complaints process to shame. At least Medicines Australia disclose some details of all the complaints made, the rationale for their determination, the details of any sanctions, and the outcome of any appeal. On top of that, the details of the complaints are made publicly available on a website. An important difference between the two industry sectors is that the drug industry was subject to sufficient public scrutiny and risked the imposition of tougher regulatory standards unless they initiated changes themselves. However, there are rumblings within the broader PR industry from some who aren't PRIA members.

Two Australian PR practitioners and bloggers, Trevor Cook from the Sydney-based PR firm Jackson Wells Morris and Paull Young from the sports PR agency BAM Media, have launched an anti-astroturfing campaign. The aim is to get PR agencies to adopt a policy against using front groups, and to display the campaign logo on their website. Cook wrote an opening salvo in the campaign that was uncharacteristically blunt for a PR practitioner:

> Astroturfing is evil. Astroturfing is always unethical and usually illegal. It corrodes democracy which relies on transparency. It is usually undertaken by people who are afraid, or lack the skills, to engage in open and honest public debates.[12]

So far, though, the disquiet is confined to the periphery of the industry.

In response to Cook and Young's stirring, PRIA's President Annabelle Warren issued a stern media release urging anyone to 'report any instances of suspected astro-turfing in order that the appropriate action can be taken'.[13] It was a statement that sat uncomfortably with PRIA's scathing dismissal of Senator Christine Milne's complaint relating to Tony Harrison's Tasmanians for a Better Future campaign. However, the case did prompt PRIA to issue a guidance note in mid-2007 interpreting the code of ethics provision stating members must 'be prepared to identify the source of funding' for a campaign. In its wisdom, PRIA determined details of funding only need to be disclosed where it is a legal requirement to do so, such as under electoral laws. Where disclosure is not a legal requirement, such as in Tasmania, PRIA advises that all a practitioner needs to do is to provide journalists with contact details of the client. Sheila O'Sullivan, the head of PRIA's College of Fellows, which handles ethics complaints, accepts PRIA's standards are weaker than those developed in the United States. 'One might describe the Australian situation as being much less transparent than the American one,' she said.[14] But just because we currently don't have US-style standards of transparency, doesn't mean we shouldn't.

If the self-regulatory system is weak for the Australian PR industry, it is virtually non-existent for lobbyists of which there are somewhere between 500 and 1000. In the United States, pre-Second World War fear of Nazi propaganda agents led to the passage of the Foreign Agents Registration Act of 1938 (FARA). Under this legislation, all agents or lobbyists for foreign governments, individuals and corporations are required to register with the US Department of Justice. For each quarter, it compiles reports listing current registrants, the amount they were paid, and why they were hired. Lobbying scandals in the 1990s led the US Congress to pass the Lobbying Disclosure Act of 1995, which requires lobbyists to register with the Clerk of the House of Representatives and the Secretary of the US Senate and House, and report each quarter on the clients they worked for, the agencies lobbied and the approximate amount paid for their services. From both these sources, Australian citizens can discover some of what Australian companies are up to in the United States.

In the first six months of 2005, a BHP-Billiton subsidiary paid the law/lobbying firm Akin Gump Strauss Hauer & Feld US$220 000 to lobby the Environmental Protection Agency to get an air permit and favourable provisions in legislation for its proposed Cabrillo Port liquefied natural gas plant in Southern California, a proposal opposed by local environmental groups. (Ultimately BHP-Billiton's lobbying efforts came to nought when, in mid-2007, the Californian government rejected the proposal.) Rupert Murdoch's News Corporation's in-house lobbying team spent approximately US$1.4 million in the first six months of 2005 on a range of bills before Congress. From 1998 through to 2000, the Electricity Supply Association of Australia hired Tom Watson from Watson & Renner to keep a watchful eye on global climate change developments. In a bid to fight off legislative moves in the United States aimed at cracking down on music file-swapping websites, Sharman Networks spent big on its US lobbying operation. Sharman ran the music file-swapping website Napster, which the Federal Court of Australia found to have violated copyright restrictions. In 2004, the Australian Bankers' Association was keen to ensure favourable outcomes on issues from proposed new accounting standards, corporate governance regulations and anti-money-laundering measures. In 2000, Telstra hired The Wexler Group, as it was then known, to keep an eye on telecommunications issues before switching its account to Ogilvy Public Relations Worldwide. We also know from these records that AWB hired the Washington D.C. law and lobby shop, Piper Rudnick, to lobby on 'policies and investigations with regard to international trade matters'.[15] Why should Australian citizens and shareholders be able to find out what lobbying Australian companies and government agencies are doing in the United States but not know what they are doing here? Clearly, if companies such as Telstra, News Corporation and the Australian Bankers Association can live with basic regulation and disclosure of their US lobbying activities, they can handle it here, too. Isn't it time for a little more 'internationally competitive' disclosure?

In the wake of the 1983 Coombe-Ivanov 'affair', in which ASIO raised concerns that the former national secretary of the Australian Labor Party, David Coombe, was being cultivated by the Soviet diplomat, Valery Ivanov, the newly elected Hawke Government felt compelled to increase the level of disclosure involving lobbyists. In September 1983, the then Special Minister of State, Kim Beazley, released a discussion paper outlining options for regulating lobbyists. Lobbying, the discussion paper noted, had been derided as 'a parasitical growth on the business of government', representing 'clients who are not known to the general public'.[16] It went on to suggest that:

> it is an important democratic principle that voters, the Parliament and individual members and Senators have a right to know who is seeking to exert influence, and on behalf of whom. This seems especially desirable in the case of lobbyists who act for foreign governments or other overseas interests.

The department suggested that the disclosure net would be confined to professional lobbyists who worked for many clients, but exclude those who worked as in-house lobbyists for other groups such as trade associations, companies, community groups and unions. Rather than emulate the US system, the Department of State paper proposed a more limited option under which only the name of the lobbyist and their client would be included in a list that would be published annually, but with public access at other times 'on request'. The professional lobbyists preferred a self-regulatory code, even though there was no organisation representing lobbyists that could have crafted one. Nor were they keen on a requirement to disclose the names of clients, claiming it was commercially sensitive information. After a public comment period, the original proposal was watered down even further in favour of a register that would be only available to ministers and senior departmental officials. The public and media, Beazley timidly decided, had no role in scrutinising the affairs of lobbyists.[17]

The code came into force in 1984, but was largely ignored. In November 1996, as the Howard Government's first parliamentary year wound down, the then Minister for Administrative Services, David Jull, was asked in the House of Representatives question time about the operation of the code. Jull told the house that the code 'was a toothless tiger and its provisions were really unenforceable'.[18] Jull pointed out that in 1993, 1994 and 1995, on only eight occasions did ministers or officials request information from the register. 'There has also been quite a bit of criticism that the register was not available for public scrutiny and that the scheme was an unnecessary hindrance to the business sector', he said. Instead of instituting a tougher, publicly accessible version of the code, Jull announced that it had been scrapped altogether. He suggested that a revised Ministerial Code of Conduct to be released the following year would include 'additional guidelines for ministers to observe when dealing with lobbyists'.

The idea of a public register of federal lobbyists sank from view until, in March 2004, the federal Labor member for Fremantle, Carmen Lawrence, breathed life back into the idea following a trip to Canada.[19] There, the parliament had instituted a tough disclosure regime just before Australia's was scrapped. It was a proposal embraced by the then Leader of the Opposition, Mark Latham, who committed a future Labor government to reinstitute a regulation-based disclosure system. The lobbyists were divided. Gavin Anderson & Company's chief executive, Ian Smith, said he could 'see no compelling reason' for a register, but would comply with a 'reasonable scheme'. Andrew Parker, of Parker & Partners, could see no problem with a 'reasonable scheme'. Other lobbyists spoke to the *Australian Financial Review* on condition of keeping their anonymity: 'I think our clients would have a big problem with their competitors knowing exactly what they were doing', one said.[20]

Following Latham's electoral defeat, the prospect of regulating lobbyists receded once more, only to re-emerge in the wake of public hearings by the Corruption and Crime Commission (CCC) of Western Australia in early 2007. The CCC investigation revealed the lobbying prowess of former West Australian Premier, Brian Burke, and his partner, Julian Grill. It also laid bare the network of ministers willing to provide the lobbyists with inside information and take advice that would benefit the lobbyists' clients. As the controversy raged, the Western Australian Labor Government pushed through legislation requiring the registration of all professional lobbyists. In response to criticism of the Leader of the Federal Opposition, Kevin Rudd, for meeting with Burke on three occasions, Labor's promise to introduce a national register for lobbyists was dusted off once more. Nervous Canberra lobbyists, fearful of a regulatory scheme requiring comprehensive disclosure of campaign work for clients, began discussions to form a peak body to advocate the need for a weaker self-regulatory system. One of those involved in the discussions was Andrew Parker, the managing director of the PR and lobbying firm, Parker & Partners.

In an opinion column on the fallout from the Burke scandal, Parker wrote that 'transparency is the best antiseptic'.[21] But the nascent lobbyists group wants a weak antiseptic at best. Instead of aiming for the level of disclosure mandated in Canada or the United States, Parker confirmed their preference is for the far weaker UK standards.[22] Instead of requiring a description of the work they have been commissioned to do and the amount to be spent on the campaign, a lobby company would only reveal who worked for them, the name of clients and a total figure earned from lobbying from all their clients. Not surprisingly, what a lobbyist considers as transparency amounts to opaqueness for everyone else.

The fear in the hearts of some lobbyists that public debate could ruin some of the campaigns is well founded. In mid-2005, the non-profit Philippine Center for Investigative Journalism used lobbying data obtained in the United States to reveal that President Gloria Macapagal-Arroyo had entered into a $75 000 per month contract for lobbying services with Venable, a Washington D.C. law firm.[23] The contract specified that Venable's work would include 'securing grants' to help achieve amendments to the Constitution of the Republic of the Philippines to pare back restrictions on the foreign ownership of land and the media. In the ensuing controversy, the previously secret contract was cancelled.[24] It was an example of democracy in action, of an informed citizenry deciding what the government should be doing in their name and with their funds.

If the prospect for better disclosure and standards originating from within the PR and lobbying professions appears forlorn, should we pin our hopes on corporations voluntarily divulging what they are up to? Corporate social responsibility (CSR) reports may seem like an appealing vehicle for ensuring greater transparency and accountability, but they are pretty unimpressive. Strip away all the gloss and it is clear that the potential for 'corporate social responsibility' has been crippled by the combination of voluntary standards and the lack of any sanctions for deceptive reporting. As well, such social reporting has been subject to comparatively little scrutiny by journalists or NGOs. At its core, voluntary CSR is asking the public to tolerate the corporate irresponsibility of the laggards so that those pushed to make some concessions can reap the profits. Of course, if companies really believed in CSR they would be arguing for mandatory standards to lift the performance of *all* companies.[25] CSR also relies on endless pressure from the media and NGOs, forces that many companies actively seek to nobble, co-opt or control. There is also a broader challenge for NGOs: the more they are drawn down the alleyways of a company-by-company struggle, the less likely they will have the resources to advance broad industry or corporate-wide change. At best, CSR has become another management tool used by companies to standardise assessment of their business's performance and tweak aspects at a pace that suits them. At worst, CSR has become a vehicle by which companies pretend to be virtuous while secretly stalling the very change their stakeholders demand of them. And on the way through, the words 'transparency' and 'accountability' have been debased and appropriated to describe secrecy and evasiveness. Australian social researcher Hugh Mackay neatly ridiculed the corporate misuse of CSR. 'Nothing diminishes virtue like trying to draw other people's attention to it. You're a good corporate citizen? Get on with it, then, don't brag about it,' he said in a speech to a non-profit disability group. 'If we are doing the right thing for a commercial advantage, we've missed the point of good corporate citizenship. Ethics is not a business tool.'[26]

The Melbourne think tank, the Institute of Public Affairs, is no fan of CSR either. Its gripe is that it doesn't want companies taking other activist groups seriously at all. The IPA argue that non-profit groups should be transparent and accountable, while—as so often with culture war warriors—seeking an exemption themselves. Nor do they want individual supporters of advocacy groups they disagree with to be able to claim a tax deduction on contributions. Not surprisingly, the IPA prefers a system where disclosure of sponsors is optional, an approach that suits both corporate donors and their proxies. The IPA and some other think tanks defend the lack of disclosure on the grounds that it is a peripheral issue. 'Why always look for the motives? Why not look at the ideas?' asked the Executive Director of the Centre for Independent Studies, Greg Lindsay.[27] Of course, there is an element of truth to the argument that disclosure of funding doesn't, and shouldn't, negate an idea. After all, funding only enables an idea to be amplified. But knowing the origin of funding helps explain why some campaigns feature prominently in a think tank's agenda when others are ignored. If Gunns, ExxonMobil and Monsanto fund an IPA project that advocates stripping The Wilderness Society and Greenpeace of tax-deductible status, we are better able to understand why that agenda is being advanced. And it begs the question of why Gunns and Monsanto, who aren't known for being shy, don't run the campaign themselves. If corporations want arm's-length cut-outs for their attack campaigns, why should journalists and citizens focus on the dummy and ignore the ventriloquist?

As the most prolific provider of free opinion columns by a think tank to newspapers around the country, the IPA routinely avoid disclosing actual or potential conflicts of interest. More perplexing, though, is how infrequently major media outlets require them to disclosure any details of relevant sponsors before publication. As a result, readers are routinely deceived as to who is refuelling the battle tank. A simple first step for journalists would be to get into the habit of asking think tanks to disclose actual and potential conflicts of interests. Those publications that publish a steady stream of free opinion columns should adopt a simple standard—no disclosure, no free space. When publications require disclosure, outfits such as the IPA have been willing to reveal relevant funders.[28] Keeping funding sources secret from the public also means that, at least for companies listed on the stock exchange, shareholders are kept in the dark too. If corporate executives want to support a think tank, they should do it out of their own generous packages rather than secretly lifting funds out of shareholders' pockets. Even if participation in public policy debates has the support of shareholders, companies should be honest enough to run the campaigns in their own name.

It would be relatively simple to make disclosure of corporate contributions to groups such as political parties, think tanks and advocacy groups mandatory rather than leave it to the whim of executives. While Exxon is a corporate dinosaur when it comes to its policy on climate change, at least in the United States it voluntarily discloses the annual amount of funding it gives to think tanks and advocacy groups, and the purpose of the grant.[29] (They don't disclose similar data in Australia and did not respond to a request for an interview by the author on the topic.) Despite strong public expectations that companies should be meeting higher standards of accountability and transparency, recent changes to electoral laws have expanded the zone of secrecy available to companies making donations to political parties.[30] Where a company had to disclose donations greater than $1500 in total, the threshold has been lifted to only those greater than $10 000.

The second strand to the disclosure net should be to make it mandatory for the amount and purpose of corporate contributions to all non-profit groups to be included in their annual reports. At present, many companies, especially through their glossy colour CSR reports, proudly outline the various feel-good projects they fund, but say nothing about their funding of more controversial activities. If companies are required to disclose both income and liabilities in their financial statements, it doesn't seem too much to ask that they disclose the grants they want to boast about alongside those they'd rather hide. Of course, non-profit groups—think tanks included—should disclose their specific sources of funding too.

As a general rule, government PR campaigns are far more vulnerable to scrutiny from journalists, opposition and minor party politicians and citizens. Government agencies tend to be far more porous and leave more of a paper trail for the inquisitive to follow. There are annual reports, estimates committee hearings, answers to questions buried in *Hansard*, submissions made to government inquiries, and archives and documents tabled in response to parliamentary motions. Often there are sufficient leads that can be followed using the Freedom of Information (FOI) legislation. Where the Fitzgerald inquiry found that well-functioning FOI laws were an essential element in preventing the abuse of government power, it is a view out of favour with the federal and some state governments. In 2005, the Treasurer and prime ministerial wannabe, Peter Costello, disingenuously claimed that FOI legislation was 'particularly to allow citizens to know what the Government knew about them... And to allow citizens to correct information that the Government has wrongly held about them'.[31] In fact, the legislation was intended to allow citizens to scrutinise both what was recorded about them *and* what the government was doing with their money. The Secretary of the Treasury, Dr Ken Henry, went further than Costello and claimed that 'I'm satisfied, having reviewed a number of them [FOI requests], that by and large they have been motivated by a desire to either embarrass the Government and Treasurer, or the department'.[32]

The FOI legislation explicitly states that a government 'agency's or minister's belief as to what his or her reasons for seeking access' is irrelevant in determining the right of access to a document. Like his predecessors, Costello has issued what are referred to as 'conclusive certificates'—in effect exemption edicts—to prevent potentially embarrassing documents becoming public. In particular, Costello defended the right of the Treasury to reject an application by *The Australian* on the grounds that public release could 'create or fan ill-informed criticism', 'confuse and mislead the public', 'create confusion and unnecessary debate' and 'encourage ill-informed speculation'. Emboldened by this stonewalling of relatively harmless information, in March 2006 high-level officials from a number of government agencies were briefed on using 'conclusive certificates' to stymie other potentially embarrassing FOI applications.[33] In September 2006, the High Court rejected a legal challenge by *The Australian*, and co-funded by a number of other media companies, against Costello's use of a 'conclusive certificate'.[34]

Despite *The Australian*, the *Sydney Morning Herald* and Channel Seven having FOI editors tasked to dig out documents, FOI is still a tool that is sparingly used by journalists.[35] Well before the adverse High Court decision, journalists were dismissing FOI

as being too hard to use when what it seems they meant is that
it is too hard for *them*. There are a range of reasons journalists
find FOI hard, but many of them are to do with the lack of
support, training, time and budgets within media organisations.[36]
But it is far less troublesome to write an article playing the 'we
are a victim of government stonewalling' card than writing that
'management are stingy bastards'. As media organisations become
addicted to a diet of fast, easy and cheaply produced news, FOI
is a tool for those few remaining slow news practitioners. Certainly
there is a need for the overhaul of FOI laws to make it easier and
cheaper to access documents that are sought in the public interest.
But there is a risk that journalists' willingness to proclaim FOI a
lost cause will become a self-fulfilling prophecy. The more that
well-paid journalists at big-budget media organisations proclaim
FOI as being too hard, the more likely it is that citizens, opposition
politicians and non-profit groups will come to think that, with
a fraction of the resources of the big media outlets, it is way
beyond them too. While the Howard Government has steadily
made it harder to access information, FOI requests to local and
state government agencies are often successful. There are grounds
for optimism, though. In May 2007, a coalition of major private
and public Australian media organisations launched Australia's
Right to Know to identify and lobby for legislative changes,
including to FOI laws. Despite the lack of broader community
representation in the coalition, it is the first sign that major
publishers may help organise the necessary rebellion to make
FOI laws more effectively serve the public interest.

Which estate?

Is there any prospect that journalists and the media can become
more effective spinbusters? Several media organisations appear
to sense, perhaps from their own extensive market research, that

the public expects the media to get behind the spin served up by the PR industry and government. A glossy insert distributed in February 2005 promoting subscriptions for the Fairfax-owned *Australian Financial Review* stated: 'Every day the AFR goes beyond the spin to bring you a unique blend of financial analysis and insight.'[37] On the website of *The Australian*, the paper's Editor-in-Chief, Chris Mitchell, states: 'we seek to take our readers beyond the "spin" of the political, business and sport press release machinery.'[38] It is a reassuring message, but what news outlets are doing now is little different from what they have always done. Even though news outlets are seeking to market themselves as spinbusters, it is hard to see how such claims are justified. Despite Australian news outlets having numerous specialist reporters and columns on everything from astrology to yachting, there is not one specialist writer on the PR and lobbying industry. (The only program that could lay any claim to the mantle is the ABC's 15-minute weekly TV program, 'Media Watch'.)

There is legitimacy to the claim by PR practitioners that much of the content of news publications invisibly originates from PR practitioners. But it also creates an opportunity to make the PR industry more visible. If PR companies won't disclose who their clients are, journalists can. The single most important step individual journalists can take is to identify the name of any PR company and their client involved in a story. It takes only a few words, but over time it helps makes the scale of the PR industry become more visible, and it enables savvy citizens and journalists to reverse engineer a PR company's client list.

A good place to start the disentanglement of journalism and PR would be with ending the use of video news releases (VNRs) and audio news releases (ANRs), which are routinely packaged up as independently produced news. As both radio and televisions stations are regulated by their licences, it would be a relatively straightforward step to make a condition of the broadcaster's licence that any use of VNRs or ANRs must be disclosed to the audience. If undisclosed use constituted a breach of the licence, it wouldn't take long for news directors to decide that their news value was negligible. Through full disclosure, viewers and listeners would discover how much of their 'news' was advertising in disguise, and they would likely change channels to get real news elsewhere. But as citizens' news sources shift from print to TV to the Internet, PR is exploring new frontiers in covertly subsidising the media. Companies whose staple was once VNRs and ANRs are now shifting to the provision of videos and webgraphics for websites willing to use freebie material in order to help PR companies' clients advance their agendas. Added to this is the increasing use of product placement in programs, and programs that PR companies pay to have placed on cable channels.

In the wake of the 'cash for comment' controversy, where commercial radio broadcasters had secret agreements with major companies, Fairfax promulgated a new code of ethics which stated that reporters would not accept subsidised travel. It was a good step towards curtailing the culture of freebies, but there is resistance from within the industry. In 2002, the then finance editor for the Nine Network, Michael Pascoe, derided the Fairfax ban on freebie travel as representing a 'new Puritanism'.[39] Just as doctors dismiss the suggestion that free gifts, dinners or trips affect their prescribing decisions, journalists want to believe they, too, are inoculated from being affected by freebies. Medical journalist Melissa Sweet is one who believes that journalists should wean themselves off sponsored prizes: 'If you want to have awards fine, but you could have them without sponsorship. You might not get the cash and the fancy dinner but they would have credibility and status.'[40]

Central to much of the effectiveness of PR is a reliance on delivering the 'right' message through a credible authority figure, journalists deferring to the so-called experts' apparent credentials and uncritically reporting what they say. In politics, the ability of government officials and politicians to be reported simply because they said something prompted veteran *Washington Post* defence reporter Walter Pincus to suggest that a new element of 'courage' was needed in political reporting:

> Journalistic courage should include the refusal to publish in a newspaper, or carry on a TV or radio news show, any statements made by the President or any other government official that are designed solely as a public relations tool, offering no new or valuable information to the public.[41]

If the ranks of conventional media are thinning at a time when the need for spinbusting is growing, what hope is there? Is it conceivable that citizen journalism and non-profit media groups can become powerful spinbusters? The emergence of blogs, text-searchable online databases and wikis have provided new tools that facilitate citizens, especially those with broadband and high-speed cable connections, to research and publish original material on topics of interest to them. Citizen journalism is surging ahead, often in conjunction with the emergence of non-profit media and other groups. As much more primary source data becomes available online, citizen journalists have a number of advantages over mainstream journalists. First, they usually aren't working to a pressing deadline, so can spend time to dig out data tucked away in various nooks and crannies. Second, they research a topic because they are interested in it, not because they have been directed by an editor to become an instant expert on a topic they know relatively little about. Third, they don't have to conform to an editorial line or avoid offending the business or political sensibilities of proprietors, advertisers or editors. As the global PR firm GolinHarris observed in an overview of the emerging economic and media landscape, 'If a company feels wronged by a newspaper or TV station, it can always threaten to pull its ads. Try that with a blog.'[42]

It is not that citizen journalism will replace mainstream journalism, but it has the potential to play an important supplementary role. A little understood aspect of the power of blogging is the potential reach, once a blog has been deemed sufficiently newsworthy to be included in the indexes of news stories, such as Google News. In this way, a blogger can easily reach a specialist global audience. The size of the audience matters less than who is in it. Another emerging interconnection is between blogs, news outlets and wikis. Wikis are an entirely different beast to blogs in that they allow registered users, or in some cases anyone at all, to create or edit an article in an online database. Where blog postings are the work of an individual, a wiki article is a collective work. It seems counter-intuitive that such an open system could work well, but they generally do. The strength of wikis is in synthesising material on a particular topic, with citizen editors refining and updating earlier drafts. For a number of technical reasons, wiki pages tend to float to the top of Google and other search engine rankings. SourceWatch, a wiki on the PR industry I edit for the US-based non-profit group, the Center for Media and Democracy, is based on the principle that anyone can add to or edit content as long as material is fair, accurate and referenced. Increasingly, bloggers link to wikis as a way for readers to get more detailed information on a topic or contribute in a more meaningful way than simply posting a personal comment. It is not that wikis or the better blogs are perfect: they aren't. The point is that their weaknesses are different ones to those of the mainstream media.

The combination of these factors means that the traditional gate-keeping role of journalists is breaking down. While some journalists fear that this could enable propaganda to flourish more easily, it is an unnecessarily protective approach to the ability of discerning audiences to spot the difference between spin and substance. Perhaps more important than all of these factors is a willingness of citizen journalists to collaborate and openly acknowledge the contributions of others. This is in stark contrast to the brand-centric approach of many mainstream media outlets where, all too often, important stories will sink without trace because a story originated with a rival media outlet. Or, alternatively, the attribution will extend only as far as 'as reported in the media'. It is as if intelligent readers don't notice the curious double standard where unattributed use of another's work is deemed a grievous offence for students but a routine practice in the media.

Indeed, it seems that small non-profit groups are doing more to facilitate citizen research and journalism than are the mainstream media. There are now an increasing number of text-searchable online databases that allow anyone to access various collections of internal industry documents. The largest is the seven million documents totalling over 40 million pages from the tobacco industry that have been organised by the University of California, San Francisco. Yet major media outlets have been slow to embrace the possibility of publishing text-searchable databases of primary source documents, such as the documents they obtain under freedom of information searches. Some media outlets, primarily in the United States, have at least taken to including links on their website to government reports, announcements or, occasionally, a leaked document.

One area where we can see how spinbusting might evolve is in the response to pervasive PR, marketing and lobbying influence of the drug industry. Over recent years, medical journal editors have adopted tougher standards, requiring authors to comply with stricter standards of disclosure of financial interests. They have also moved to end the practice of doctors signing articles ghostwritten by drug company sponsors. The editors have also encouraged a vibrant discussion on disease-mongering, drug company PR, medical ethics and the impact of drug company promotions on prescribing practices. Numerous academic papers have explored the impact of drug company funding and gifts on doctors' prescribing patterns. The previously invisible role of drug company PR and lobbying has been dragged into the open for debate, and often picked up in the mainstream media.

In recognition that soft media coverage of pre-masticated drug industry PR can be a major driver of drug usage, a group of health researchers based at the University of Newcastle established the Media Doctor website. The researchers score media coverage against a set of key criteria they consider central to good medical reporting. Stories are then scored against a five-star scale before being posted to the website. Over time, the performance data of individual media outlets can be tracked. While the project runs on a tiny budget, the idea has spread, with projects modelled on it now established in Canada and the United States.

The Adelaide-based group, Healthy Skepticism, analyses and critiques drug industry marketing aimed at doctors. Like the US-based group, No Free Lunch, one of the practical measures they advocate is that doctors don't agree to see drug company sales representatives. It is a trend that has growing momentum, with major US medical schools adopting a policy that places a ban on accepting gifts from drug companies or seeing sales reps. On a different tack entirely, the Center for Public Integrity, a Washington D.C.-based non-profit investigative journalism group, has trawled through US lobbying disclosure reports to build a searchable database on pharma lobbying and political campaign contributions.[43] Another group has launched a website, using the same software the tobacco industry archives are based on, for internal drug industry documents from various court cases in the United States.[44] Within SourceWatch, there are a set of pages on everything from links to the best academic articles on direct-to-consumer advertising, profiles on drug company-funded patient groups and PR techniques such as video news releases.

•

The examples of PR campaigns reviewed in this book are just a tiny fraction of those run. Every day, we are exposed, nearly always invisibly, to the handiwork of the PR industry. Some campaigns only come to light because of a public slip-up, or a document dug out in a legal action, or because a company has irritated a commercial rival. Numerous PR campaigns escape investigation to the detriment of democracy. In part, this is because so many whose roles are to act independently are courted and co-opted. Once co-opted, voices that could otherwise have been independent participants in public debate fall silent or, worse still, become spinboosters. This is why the most effective spinbusters are likely to emerge from the ranks of citizens determined to end the era of invisible spin.

WHISTLEBLOWERS

There are many who work in companies and government agencies keen to help the public get behind the spin but are under the mistaken impression that whistleblowers always suffer persecution. However, with a few sensible precautions, people can safely ensure important information is made public. For more information *see* <www.sourcewatch.org/index.php?title=Freedom_of_Information/A_Brief_Guide_To_Safe_Leaking>.

If you have documents, tips or even suggestions for potentially productive Freedom of Information searches, please feel free to email me at <bob@sourcewatch.org>, or you could post a copy of any documents to me at:

P.O. Box 228
South Hobart, 7004
Tasmania, Australia.

ACKNOWLEDGEMENTS

This book, which has been evolving over the past decade, wouldn't have been possible without the love, support, encouragement and constructive feedback of Fran Murray. Thank you, too, to our four-year-old daughter, Isla, for her exuberance, humour, inquisitiveness and office-floor artwork. Special thanks to Mark Burton, Marie-Louise Fitzpatrick, Vanessa Morris and Marina Ligeros for helping out with childcare when various deadlines loomed.

When I started on the first draft of the book I had the privilege of spending a few weeks ensconced at the South Durras house of Geoff Bartram and Sarah Lachlan. Writing a book alone is hard, but I always got a boost from regular phone conversations with my New Zealand friend and colleague, Nicky Hager, as we both laboured with our respective manuscripts.

My colleagues John Stauber and Sheldon Rampton deserve special mention for their pioneering efforts in writing *Toxic Sludge is Good For You*, launching *PR Watch*, and founding and sustaining the Center for Media and Democracy in Madison, Wisconsin. John and Sheldon's persistence, humour, encouragement, support and technical know-how have done more for spinbusting than just about anyone else. More recently I have had the pleasure of working with other CMD staff including Diane Farsetta, Anne Landman, Judith Siers-Poisson, Patricia Barden, Sari Williams, Conor Kenny, Jonathan Rosenblum and Laura Miller. Thanks also to David Miller, Andy Rowell and Eveline Lubbers from the UK-based Spinwatch for sharing information.

There have been many people who agreed to be interviewed for this book, for which I am deeply appreciative. My sincere apologies to those whose views I couldn't include due to space or other constraints. There have been many people who have assisted in one way or another with this book including: Clare Henderson, Larry O'Loughlin, Andrew Nette, Miriam Lyons, Glenn Ellis, Ray Moynihan, Annabel Stafford, David Margan, Andrew Dodd, Angela Savage, Nick Fahey, David Pope, Stafford Sanders, Simon Chapman, Barry Weeber, Peter Bostock, Nick Housego, Michael Cebon and Sholto Macpherson. For those my book-fogged brain hasn't remembered, my sincere apologies.

Thanks to the Freedom of Information officers at Telstra and the Forest Practices Authority in Tasmania for their prompt handling of my inquiries. I dream of the day that I can write that about all the government agencies I submit Freedom of Information applications to. I also appreciate the assistance provided by the staff at the National Archives of Australia and National Library of Australia.

A special thanks to Klaus Mueller and Brian Walters for providing legal assistance way above and beyond my miniscule budget in what became a protracted appeal before the Victorian Civil and Administrative Tribunal over documents held by Victoria Police relating to the Coode Island fires and eco-terrorism.

Thank you to the staff at Allen & Unwin for their professionalism and assistance: Elizabeth Weiss, Joanne Holliman and Pedro Almeida. Thanks also to David McKnight and an anonymous reviewer for taking the time to provide invaluable advice on the draft manuscript.

Finally, the proposal for this book was selected in 2005 for the Iremonger Award for Writing on Public Issues organised by Allen & Unwin. I never had the pleasure of meeting John Iremonger, but I hope the book does justice to his spirit and to the faith of the judges.

NOTES

1 Invisible PR

1   D. Welch, 'Powers of Persuasion', *History Today*, vol. 49, no. 8, 1 August 1999, pp. 24–26.
2   *ibid.*
3   E. Bernays, *Propaganda*, Liveright, New York, 1930, p. 9.
4   R. Manvell and H. Fraenkel, *Doctor Goebbels*, Mentor, London, 1968 (2nd edition), p. 185.
5   Jane Johnston and Clara Zawawi's description of Joel's impression of MacArthur's operation is based on an interview they did with him in 1995: 'He saw how news was suppressed and manufactured for journalists, news photographers and broadcasters. Most importantly, he learned that public relations was not just about getting publicity. Rather, public relations was often based in *not* getting publicity.' *See* J. Johnston and C. Zawawi, *Public Relations: Theory and Practice*, Allen & Unwin, Sydney, 2000, p. 25.
6   J. Handfield, 'Training for Public Relations' in T.J. Dwyer, *The Australian Public Relations Handbook*, Ruskin Publishing, Melbourne, December 1961, p. 212
7   'Do we have a story for you!: As advertising struggles, PR steps into the breach', *The Economist*, 19 January 2006, cited at <www.economist.com/business/displayStory.cfm?story_id=5418124>, accessed December 2006.
8   T. Muzi Falconi, 'Who's Afraid of Big Bad PR?', Global Alliance, 28 February 2005, cited at <www.globalpr.org/knowledge/features/falconi_contatti.pdf>, accessed December 2006.
9   D. Francis, 'The world needs more spin', *National Post* (Canada), 11 August 2006, p. FP7.
10 J.E. Grunig and T. Hunt, *Managing Public Relations*, Holt Rinehart and Winston, Austin, 1984, p. 13.
11 R. Manveil, *Dr Goebbels: His Life and Death*, Simon & Schuster, New York, 1960.
12 P. Lazar, interview with author, 28 July 1998.
13 D. Francis, 'The world needs more spin', *National Post* (Canada), 11 August 2006.
14 *Minivan News*, 'Police Presented with Flowers on Anniversary of Evan's Death', 19 September 2006, cited at <www.minivannews.com/news/news.php?id=2447>, accessed December 2006.
15 J. Macken, 'Logging money talks loudly in battle for Tasmanians' vote', *Australian Financial Review*, 3 March 2006.

16 T. Harrison, 'Tasmanians for a Better Future Campaign', Public Relations Institute of Australia 2006 Golden Target Awards and State Awards for Excellence, undated (c. June 2006), p. 6.

17 *ibid.*, p. 9.

18 'Tony Harrison', cited at <http://web.archive.org/web/20060821053159/ http://cctas.com.au/team/list/th.html>, accessed March 2006.

19 ABC Online, 'Tas business people get behind majority government', 27 February 2006, cited at <www.abc.net.au/news/newsitems/200602/ s1579641.htm>, accessed January 2007; ABC Online, 'Tasmania guesses at election ad backers', 28 February 2006, cited at <www.abc.net.au/news/ newsitems/200602/s1579762.htm>, accessed January 2007; T. Jeanes, 'Mystery group funds Tas election ad campaign', 'PM', ABC Radio National, 28 February 2006, cited at <www.abc.net.au/pm/content/2006/ s1580712.htm>, accessed January 2007; S. Neales, 'Mystery of the majority push', *The Mercury*, 1 March 2006, cited at <www.themercury.news.com.au/ common/story_page/0,5936,18308237%5E3462,00.html>, accessed May 2006; J. Macken, 'Logging money talks loudly in battle for Tasmanians' votes', *Australian Financial Review*, 3 March 2006; M. Denholm, 'Mystery adverts have Greens seeing red', *The Australian*, 3 March 2006, NSW country edition, p. 8.

20 S. Neales, 'Mystery of the majority push', *The Mercury*, 1 March 2006.

21 J. Macken, 'Logging money talks loudly in battle for Tasmanians' votes', *Australian Financial Review*, 3 March 2006.

22 C. Milne, Electoral and Referendum Amendment (Electoral Integrity and Other Measures) Bill 2006: In Committee, Senate *Hansard*, 20 June 2006, cited at <http://parlinfoweb.aph.gov.au/piweb/TranslateWIPILink.aspx? Folder=HANSARDS&Criteria=DOC_DATE:2006-06- 20%3BSEQ_NUM:102%3B>, accessed May 2007.

23 J. Mahoney, 'PRIA Ethics: Decision', email to C. Milne, 8 May 2006.

24 J. Mahoney, 'PRIA: Request for statement of reasons', email to C. Milne, 9 August 2006.

25 C. Milne, Electoral and Referendum Amendment (Electoral Integrity and Other Measures) Bill 2006: In Committee, Senate *Hansard*, 20 June 2006, cited at <http://parlinfoweb.aph.gov.au/piweb/TranslateWIPILink.aspx? Folder=HANSARDS&Criteria=DOC_DATE:2006-06-20%3BSEQ_ NUM:102%3B>, accessed May 2007.

26 Public Relations Institute of Australia, 'Best of the best celebrated at the PRIA Gala Dinner', 5 September 2006, cited at <www.pria.com.au/ prianews/id/118>, accessed November 2006.

27 M. Denholm, 'Trapped pair a PR minefield', *The Australian*, 29 June 2006.

28 Anvil Mining, 'Advice on rebel activity in village of Kilwa, DRC', media release, 15 October 2005.

29 Anvil Mining, 'Report for Quarter ended December 31, 2004', news release, 28 January 2005, p. 4.

30 S. Neighbour, 'The Kilwa Incident', 'Four Corners', ABC TV, 6 June 2005, cited at <www.abc.net.au/4corners/content/2005/s1384238.htm>, accessed November 2006.

31 Anvil Mining, 'Anvil Mining Limited Response to Television Report of June 6, 2005', media release, 7 June 2005.

32 Anvil Mining, 'Anvil Confirms Denial of Unfounded Allegations', media release, 21 June 2005.

33 Anvil Mining, 'Anvil Confirms That Allegations Are Unfounded', media release, 23 August 2005.

34 F. Shiel, 'No basis to massacre claim, Perth miner says', *The Age*, 25 August 2005, cited at <www.theage.com.au/news/national/no-basis-to-massacre-claim-perth-miner-says/2005/08/24/1124562921675.html>, accessed November 2006.

35 B. Burton, 'Australian Mining Firm Worms Out of Congo Massacre Charges', *Inter-Press Service*, 31 August 2005, cited at <http://ipsnews.net/sendnews.asp?idnews=30076>, accessed November 2006.

36 M. Priest, 'Anvil clarifies massacre involvement', *Australian Financial Review*, 15 July 2005.

37 'Project Green Board Paper for 15 February 2001 James Hardie Industries Limited Meeting of Board of Directors', cited at <www.cabinet.nsw.gov.au/__data/assets/pdf_file/355/K.pdf>, accessed December 2006.

38 James Hardie Industries, 'James Hardie Resolves Its Asbestos Liability Favourably for Claimants and Shareholders', media release, 16 February 2001.

39 Jackson Report, Special Commission of Inquiry into the Medical Research and Compensation Foundation, New South Wales Government, pp. 358–59.

40 James Hardie Industries, 'Shareholders well-served by award-winning Investor Relations team', media release, 7 December 2003, cited at <www.ir.jameshardie.com.au/jh/shareholder_services/hardienews/december_2003/article_7_december_2003.jsp>, accessed March 2007.

41 Gavin Anderson & Company, 'Public Relations Strategy', July (approx.) 2002. *See also* C. Jackson, 'Leaker pulls the plug on AVCC's secret leaks strategy', *The Canberra Times*, 20 August 2002; *and* D. Illing and J. Richardson, 'VC lobby puts faith in spinners', *The Australian*, 14 August 2002.

42 R. Cameron, 'Public Relations Ethics' in 'Preface' to Thos J. Dwyer (ed.), *The Australian Public Relations Handbook: A guide to the principles and practice of Public Relations in Australia*, Ruskin Publishing, Melbourne, December 1961, p. 77.

43 I. Robertson, 'Community relations—government approvals are not everything', Proceedings of Public Affairs in Minerals and Energy Conference, 19 March 1996.

44 P. Lazar, interview with author, July 1998.

45 G. Freeman, 'IFAW axes Shandwick to bring PR in-house', *PR Week*, 22 September 2000, cited at <www.prweek.com/news/news_story.cfm?ID=110847&site=1>.

46 P. Sandman, 'AWB Oil-for-Food controversy', email to Jill Gillingham, 7 December 2005; *and* F. Shugg, Executive Assistant to Jill Gillingham, 'AWB, Email to Peter Sandman', 13 December 2005. Documents tendered to the Australian Government's Oil-For Food Inquiry, cited at <http://203.94.171.34/offi/exhibits.htm>.

47 P. Sandman, interview with author, December 2005.

48 B. Herskovitz, 'The Agency Business: Keeping confidential relationships from leaking to the media', *PR Week*, 10 January 2005, cited at <www.prweek.com/uk/search/article/231867/>, accessed November 2006.

49 J. Frank, 'PR won't gain respect with secret contracts', *PR Week*, 21 March 2005, cited at <www.prweek.com/uk/search/article/236647/>, accessed November 2006.

50 G. Allen, 'The Future of Public Affairs', 2005 National Public Affairs Convention, 7 September 2005.

51 A. Little, 'A green corporate image—more than a logo', Green Marketing Conference, Hotel Intercontinental, 25 and 26 June 1990, (unpublished) p. 12–13.

52 John Clemenger Pty Ltd, 'What Every Corporate Communicator Should Know About His Hostile Audience', June 1975. The report cited US survey data in which the standing of business collapsed from a high of 75 per cent in 1968 to just 25 per cent in 1972. Similar trends were observed in Australia.

53 In 1984, the National Social Science Survey asked respondents whether they agreed that big business has too much power; 62 per cent agreed. The Australian Election Study asked the same question in 1987 (51 per cent agreed); 1990 (62 per cent agreed); 1993 (62 per cent agreed); 1996 (65 per cent agreed); 1998 (71 per cent agreed); and 2001 (72 per cent agreed). In 2003, the Australian Survey of Social Attitudes asked a slightly different question: whether big business should have more or less power. Only six per cent of over 4000 respondents wanted more or a lot more power in the hand of big business, while a third settled for the same amount of power.

54 M. Western and B. Tranter, 'Are Post-materialists Engaged Citizens?' in S. Wilson, G. Meagher, R. Gibson, D. Denemark and M. Western, *Australian Social Attitudes: The First Report*, University of New South Wales Press, Sydney 2005, p. 96.

55 Grey Worldwide, 'Connecting with the Solo Generation: Eye on Australia 2005'. *See also* S. Lloyd, 'Heroes rise again', *BRW*, 5–11 May 2005. A few years earlier Sweeney Research's 2002 'Eye on Australia' report found that 57 per cent of those surveyed did not trust big corporations, while 60 per cent agreed that most big corporations have no morals or ethics; 83 per cent believe corporate Australia is greedy, while 66 per cent believe it is heartless.

56 Edelman, '"A Person Like Me" Now Most Credible Spokesperson for Companies; Trust in Employees Significantly Higher Than in CEOs, Edelman Trust Barometer Finds', media release, 23 January 2006, cited at <www.edelman.com/image/insights/content/FullSupplement_final.pdf>, accessed November 2006.

57 Dr C. Steiner and Ms L. Black, *Australian PR Professionals in Corporate Strategic Planning: Educational implications*, RMIT Business, Melbourne, November 1999, p. 7.

58 L. McCoy, 'Cynicism in the Ranks: Are PR practitioners fighting an uphill battle in a hostile communications environment?', Proceedings of PRISM Summit, Sydney, June 2004.

59 D. Welch, 'Powers of Persuasion', *History Today*, vol. 49, no. 8, 1 August 1999, pp. 24–26.

2 Food fights

1   T. Abbot, 'Concerns raised over obesity in Australia', doorstop interview, 3 February 2006, cited at <www.health.gov.au/internet/ministers/

publishing.nsf/Content/health-mediarel-yr2006-ta-abbsp030206a.htm>, accessed July 2006.

2   M. Metherell, 'Labor to junk food ads on children's TV', *Sydney Morning Herald*, 17 June 2004, cited at <www.smh.com.au/articles/2004/06/16/1087244980469.html?from=storylhs>, accessed January 2007.

3   S. Canning, 'PM echoes food giants' ad ban fight', *The Weekend Australian*, 19 June 2004, p. 3.

4   Australian Association of National Advertisers, 'Issues Management', cited at <www.aana.com.au/6_issues_management/Login.asp>, accessed July 2006.

5   P. Bush, Presentation to Obesity Forum, Parliament House, Canberra, 2 December 2005.

6   Professional Public Relations, 'What's On Your Plate—Nutrition Education Program', Submission to the 1993 Golden Target Awards.

7   M. Sheehan, 'Super Size Me: A comparative analysis of response to crises by McDonald's America and McDonald's Australia', in C. Galloway and K. Kwanesh-Aidoo (eds), *Public Relations Issues and Crisis Management: Asia, Australia and New Zealand*, Thomson, Melbourne, 2005, pp. 67–79.

8   *Crisis Manager Newsletter*, 'Just a Thought', 1 July 2004, cited at <www.bernsteincrisismanagement.com/nl/crisismgr040701.html#jat>, accessed January 2007.

9   S. Dabkowski, 'Spitting chips, McDonald's fights back', *The Age*, 14 June 2004, cited at <www.theage.com.au/articles/2004/06/13/1087065034025.html?oneclick=true>, accessed January 2007.

10 'Mr Big Mac To Be Grilled By McLibel Two', media release, 1 May 1996, cited at <www.mcspotlight.org/media/press/press_rel01may96.html>, accessed May 2007.

11 McDonald's Corporation, 'Ronald McDonald House', Submission to Public Relations Society of America 1981 Silver Anvil Awards, p. 1.

12 Professional Public Relations, 'McHappy Day Post Mortem', May/June 1991, p. 3.

13 In 1999 the Public Relations Institute of Australia adopted a policy that using advertising value equivalents was inappropriate and unethical way to measure the value of a public relations campaign. *See* Public Relations Institute of Australia, 'PR Industry calls for marketing to reject unethical measurement', media release, 22 August 2006, cited at <www.pria.com.au/prianews/id/54>, accessed November 2006; *and* J. Macnamara, *The Serious Practical & Ethical Flaws in Using Advertising Value Equivalents to Measure PR*, CARMA International (Asia Pacific) Pty Ltd, June 2005, cited at <www.pria.com.au/sb/modules/prianews/attachments/54/AVEs%20Discussion%20Paper.pdf>, accessed November 2006.

14 M. Skelsey, 'Disease victim planned a party', *Daily Telegraph-Mirror*, 24 April 1992.

15 P. Meadows, 'Memo: Cooling Towers & Legionnaires Disease', 14 July 1992.

16 Public Relations Institute of Australia, 'Hypothetical', *Proceedings of Public Relations Industry of Australia and New Zealand Vox Pop Conference*, Sydney, November 1995.

17 K. Meagher, 'McDonald's and Legionella—Crisis Management', 1993 Golden Target Awards Outstanding External Communication of the Year, Professional Public Relations, p. 2.

18 'As of yesterday there are no water-cooled air-conditioning units operating in any of McDonald's 317 restaurants', the advertisement stated. *See* McDonald's Australia, 'As of yesterday', advertisement, 19 August 1992.

19 Public Relations Institute of Australia, 'Hypothetical', *Proceedings of Public Relations Industry of Australia and New Zealand Vox Pop Conference*, Sydney, November 1995.

20 Grace Dearborn, 'Consulting Service Report', 6 May 1992.

21 D. Margan, *A Current Affair*, March 2001.

22 G. Russo, *A Current Affair*, March 2001.

23 McDonald's Australia, 'Highly Confidential: 60 Minutes Strategy', undated, 1995.

24 P. Lazar, interview with author, 28 July 1998.

25 Four years later, it was revealed that after McDonald's committed over $170 000 as sponsorship for 'recorded spots' on 2UE's breakfast program for 1999, the station's program director, John Brennan, wrote a memo to John Laws and Alan Jones stating, 'It is obviously imperative that no derogatory comments about McDonald's are made by any broadcaster on the station. Any such comment would see an immediate cancellation of the contract.' *See* B. Lagan, 'No Grilling, please, it's McDonald's', *Sydney Morning Herald*, 22 July 1999, p. 1.

26 P. Lazar, interview with author, 28 July 1998.

27 Mothers Opposing Pollution, 'MOP Column', *Women's Environment News*, August 1994, p. 2.

28 Mothers Opposing Pollution, petition, undated.

29 Mothers Opposing Pollution, 'Thousands sign petition against plastic milk bottles', *MOP News*, undated, p. 2.

30 *Sunshine Coast Daily*, 'Mums seek switch to milk cartons', 22 May 1995.

31 Mothers Opposing Pollution, 'Public uproar over plastic milk bottle dumping scandal in SA', *Women's Environment News*, April 1994, p. 3.

32 B. Atkinson, 'Mothers Opposing Pollution', Legislative Council *Hansard*, 4 May 1994, pp. 57–58.

33 *ibid.*

34 Mothers Opposing Pollution, 'Worldwide warning to women about cancer link to plastic milk bottles', press release, 6 December 1994.

35 A. Taylor, 'Milk in plastic safe, say experts', *The Evening Post*, 8 December 1994.

36 A. Taylor, 'Toxic milk lobbyists' motives questioned', *The Evening Post*, 10 December 1994; 'Toxic milk warnings prompts questions', *The Southland Times*, 10 December 1994.

37 B. Williams, 'Question over business links: greenie in carton war', *The Courier Mail*, 10 February 1995, p. 1.

38 *ibid.*

39 J. Rundle, Mothers Opposing Pollution, letter to politicians, 7 August 1995. The National Food Authority was the predecessor of the current food regulator, the Australia New Zealand Food Authority.

40 Ogilvy & Mather Public Relations New York, 'Nutritional and Flavour Advantages of Milk in Paper Packaging', submission to the Public Relations Society of America 1984 Silver Anvil Awards, p. 1.

41 J.E. Davey, 'The Society of Plastics Industry Inc vs the Paperboard Packaging Council Inc, Civil Action no 84-3122', 30 August 1985.

42 J. Rundle, 'An application to vary the Australian Food Standards Code to require milk packaging to properly protect the vitamins in milk against light damage', Mothers Opposing Pollution, September 1995.

43 J. Lewis, National Food Authority, letter to J. Rundle, 2 November 1995.

44 J. Rundle, Mothers Opposing Pollution, letter to National Food Authority, 21 November 1995, pp. 4–5.

45 Association of Liquidpaperboard Carton Manufacturers, 'Kids lead supermarket protest', media release, 21 November 1995.

46 National Food Authority, 'Information Summary: protection of the vitamin content of milk from photodegradation', January 1996.

47 G. van Rijswijk, 'Submission to the National Food Authority on protection of milk vitamin content from photodegradation', Association of Liquidpaperboard Carton Manufacturers, March 1996, p. 6.

48 National Food Authority, 'Summary of Public Comment', attachment 2.

49 Prepac Australasia Ltd, letter to Market Milk Federation of Australia Inc., 1 May 1996.

50 J. Lewis, 'Note for file A288 photodegradation of milk vitamin content', National Food Authority, 1 August 1996.

51 J. Rundle, Mothers Opposing Pollution, letter to National Food Authority, 2 August 1996, p 3.

52 J. Lewis, Australia New Zealand Food Authority, letter to J. Rundle, 7 August 1996.

53 Federal Court of Australia, '1839/99 Kirella Pty Ltd v Hooper (includes corrigendum dated 31 December 1999 [1999] FCA 1839', 23 December 1999, cited at <www.austlii.edu.au//cgi-bin/disp.pl/au/cases/cth/ federal_ct/1999/1839.html>.

54 Westfield Holdings, 'Statement to Media in relation to the *Sydney Morning Herald* article of 18 December 1999'.

55 D. MacFarlane, 'Westfield boss sorry for "spying" on rivals', *The Australian*, 4 February 2000.

56 *ibid.*

57 RWE Company Announcements, 'Westfield says legal action resolved', 9 July 2004.

58 S. Glew, interview with author, 21 September 2006.

59 'Towering Inferno', In The Know, *The Australian*, 18 March 2004.

60 A. Davies, 'Public relations, private interests', *Sydney Morning Herald*, 16 December 2000.

61 D. Johnston, 'Mall or nothing for Lowy's US rivals', *The Daily Telegraph*, 25 August 2001.

62 M. Vellinga, 'Setback for Lent Ranch project', *Sacramento Bee*, 8 June 2002, p. A1; L. Kalb, 'Community groups seek a united effort; Summit sparks call for residents to work together for change', *Sacramento Bee*, 24 August 2006.

63 D. Johnston, 'Lowy plays hardball in the US—Shopping mall world is survival of the fittest', *The Courier Mail*, 23 September 2002.

64 G. Maddaus, 'Chang rallies against plan for racetrack', *Pasadena Star-News*, 22 March 2006; *see also* Arcadia First! at <http://arcadiafirst.org/>.

65 C. Harris, 'Mall Owner Battles Renton Plan It Sees Development as Threat to SouthCenter', *Seattle Post-Intelligencer*, 14 July 2006, p. D1.

66 C. Harris, 'Supporters Come In For The Landing: Ground Broken On
    Retail Developments: SouthCenter Mall Owner Contesting Project', *Seattle
    Post-Intelligencer*, 16 August 2006, p. C1.
67 'Renton 1, Westfield Group 0', *Seattle Post-Intelligencer*, 7 September 2006, p. C2.

3 Pushing drugs

1   P.E. Langton, G.J. Hankey and J.W. Eikelboom, 'Editorial: Cardiovascular
    safety of rofecoxib (Vioxx): lessons learned and unanswered questions',
    Medical Journal of Australia, 26 October 2004, cited at <www.mja.com.au/
    public/issues/181_10_151104/lan10728_fm.html>, accessed August 2006.
2   P. Mansfield, interview with author, August 2006.
3   G. Hastings, E. Devlin and S. Anderson, *Dealing in Drugs: An Analysis of
    the Pharmaceutical Industry's Marketing Documents*, memorandum by the
    University of Stirling, Appendix 33, House of Commons Health Select
    Committee, cited at <www.publications.parliament.uk/pa/cm200405/
    cmselect/cmhealth/42/42we39.htm>, accessed January 2007. The consultants
    were precluded from mentioning the names of specific companies.
4   *ibid.*
5   R. Coulthart, 'The doctors' gravy train', 'Sunday', 5 August 2001, cited at
    <http://sunday.ninemsn.com.au/sunday/cover_stories/transcript_896.asp>,
    accessed January 2007.
6   Allens Arthur Robinson, 'Submission to Australian Competition and
    Consumer Commission', 5 August 2003, p. 1.
7   R. Napier, Chair, AMA Therapeutics Committee, letter to G. Samuel,
    1 August 2003.
8   Allens Arthur Robinson, 'Submission to Australian Competition and
    Consumer Commission', 1 September 2003, p. 2.
9   B. Burton, 'Drug companies succeed in keeping payments to doctors secret',
    British Medical Journal, vol. 327, 29 November 2003, p. 1248, cited at
    <http://bmj.bmjjournals.com/cgi/content/full/327/7426/1248-a>, accessed
    January 2007.
10 C. Oddie and E. Marsh, Allens Arthur Robinson for Medicines Australia,
    'Memo re Bronwyn Davis, Assistant Director, Adjudication Branch,
    Australian Competition and Consumer Commission', 15 March 2006, p. 2,
    cited at <www.accc.gov.au/content/trimFile.phtml?trimFileName=D06+
    15852.pdf&trimFileTitle=D06+15852.pdf&trimFileFromVersionId=758872>,
    accessed August 2006.
11 *ibid*, p. 7.
12 *ibid*, p. 8.
13 C. Oddie and E. Marsh, Allens Arthur Anderson for Medicines Australia,
    'Medicines Australia—application for revocation and substitution', email to
    Australian Competition and Consumer Commission, 7 April 2006.
14 Australian Competition and Consumer Commission, Determination:
    Medicines Australia Inc Code of Conduct 15th Edition, 26 July 2006, p. 63.
15 *ibid.*, p. 64.
16 Australian Medical Association, 'ACCC Falls for Media Beat-Up On
    Pharmaceutical Education', media release, 22 July 2006, cited at
    <www.ama.com.au/web.nsf/doc/WEEN-6S3CAY>, accessed March 2007.

17 R. Moynihan, 'Roche defends buying lavish meals for doctors at Sydney's restaurants', *British Medical Journal*, vol. 333, no. 169, 22 July 2006, cited at <bmj.bmjjournals.com/cgi/content/full/333/7560/169?>, accessed January 2007; R. Moynihan, 'Drug giant forks out $65K for doctors' meals', *The Australian*, 21 July 2006, cited at <www.news.com.au/story/ 0,10117,19857708-2,00.html>, accessed January 2007.

18 Heather Ferguson, 'AMA views erode trust in doctors', *Australian Doctor*, 4 October 2006, cited at <www.australiandoctor.com.au/news/ 62/0c045862.asp>, accessed March 2007.

19 J. Kerr, 'Tougher code on freebies a "kneejerk"', *The Australian*, 28 July 2006, cited at <www.theaustralian.news.com.au/story/0,20867,19937156- 23289,00.html>, accessed January 2007.

20 A letter sent by the Australian Competition and Consumer Commission's General Manager Adjudication Branch, S. Gregson, to Medicines Australia's legal adviser, F. Crosbie, from Allens Arthur Robinson, three days before Moynihan's story broke, responded to a complaint from the drug industry body about a lack of procedural fairness. In the letter Gregson sets out that the ACCC informed Medicines Australia about the proposed change on 7 June 2006 and subsequently received submissions from the drug industry body on 14 and 13 July and 28 June, and 6 and 13 July 2006.

21 Australian Competition & Consumer Commission, Applications for Revocation and Substitution: Medicines Australia Inc. Code of Conduct 15th Edition, 26 July 2006, p. 64. The ACCC notes receiving a submission from the AMA on 6 July 2006, one month after Medicines Australia had been informed about the proposed condition.

22 P. Cross, interview with author, July 2006.

23 J. Young, Medicines Australia memorandum, 3 August 2006, p. 2. *See also* A. Stafford, 'Drug firms fight move to reveal spending on doctors', *The Age*, 17 August 2006, cited at <www.theage.com.au/news/national /drug-firms-fight-move-to-reveal-spending-on-doctors/2006/08/16/ 1155407888833.html>, accessed August 2006.

24 A. Stafford, 'Backlash over doctor entertainment feared', *The Age*, 14 November 2006, cited at <www.theage.com.au/news/national/backlash- over-doctor-entertainment-feared/2006/11/13/1163266481632.html>, accessed December 2006.

25 P. Mansfield, interview with author, September 2006.

26 B. Curtis, comments at 3rd Annual Pharma Marketing Congress, Sydney, 18–19 May 2005.

27 L. Allen, 'Push to stop drug ads loophole', *Australian Financial Review*, 4 April 2005.

28 F. Mills, *Patient Groups and the Global Pharmaceutical Industry: The growing importance of working directly with the consumer*, Urch Publishing, London, 2000.

29 R. Moynihan, 'Taking The Soft Option', *Australian Financial Review*, 13 November 2000, p. 29.

30 J. Skatsoon, 'Drug companies provide money behind health support groups', *AAP*, 22 August 2003.

31 'Fed Court gives Viagra second chance for PBS—3', *AAP*, 2 July 2001.

32 In December 2000, the then Minister for Health, David Wooldridge, pushed through changes designed to dissolve the committee and prevent

long-standing members from being reappointed; *see* Mary-Anne Toy, 'Government to scrap drug watchdog', *The Age*, 1 December 2000. After the changes were pushed through, three committee members, including Professor David Henry, resigned. In January 2001, Wooldridge appointed Pat Clear, who until the September the year before had been Chief Executive Officer of the Australian Pharmaceutical Manufacturers Association (APMA)—APMA was later re-badged as Medicines Australia. Before that, Clear had worked for 15 years with Wellcome Australia, which is now wrapped into GlaxoSmithKline.

33   S. Stock, 'High price to get love life back on track', *The Australian*, 17 January 2002.

34   I. Henderson and J. Kerin, 'PM Backs veto on cheap Viagra', *The Australian*, 30 January 2002; 'Australia says it will not subsidize Viagra', *Associated Press*, 13 February 2002.

35   F. Hall and L. Harper, 'Using celebrities', *Pharmaceutical Marketing*, 1 July 2003, cited at <www.pmlive.com/on_the_job/inst_experts/ marketing.cfm?showArticle=1&ArticleID=2223>, accessed May 2006. Hall is managing director and Harper associate director at the PR company, Shire Health London.

36   'Sweet's potent drug', 'Media Watch', ABC Television, 22 March 2004, cited at <www.abc.net.au/mediawatch/transcripts/s1071337.htm>, accessed May 2006.

37   Medicines Australia, 'Levitra (753)', 2005 Code of Conduct Annual Report, pp. 14–15.

38   Consumer Health Forum and Medicines Australia, *Working Together: The Guide—A Guide to relationships between Health Consumer Organisations and Pharmaceutical Companies*, 2005, p. 4, cited at <www.chf.org.au/Docs/ Downloads/360_guide_for_relationships.pdf>, accessed March 2007.

39   H. Hopkins, Executive Director Consumers' Health Forum, letter to the Australian Competition and Consumer Commission, 19 December 2005.

40   H. Hopkins, interview with author, 21 August 2006.

41   D. Ball, K. Tisocki and A. Herxheimer, 'Advertising and disclosure of funding on patient organisation websites: a cross-sectional survey', *BMC Public Health*, 3 August 2006, cited at <www.biomedcentral.com/1471-2458/6/201>, accessed January 2007.

42   H. Hopkins, interview with author, 21 August 2006.

43   Nancy Turett, 'Thriving Amid Uncertainty: Relationships Reign', *Pharmaceutical Executive*, 1 September 2002, cited at <www.pharmexec.com/ pharmexec/article/articleDetail.jsp?id=29984&pageID=2>, accessed January 2007.

44   Edelman, 'Macular Degeneration Foundations and Novartis Ophthalmic', submission to the International Public Relations Association, 2000.

45   Macular Degeneration Foundation, 'Treatment options for Wet Macular Degeneration', undated, cited at <www.mdfoundation.com.au/ mdtreatments.aspx>, accessed November 2006.

46   Reed Weir Communications, 'Subutex—A New Heroin Treatment in Australia', IPRA Golden World Awards for Excellence in Public Relations, 28 March 2002.

47   Commonwealth Department of Health and Ageing, 'Expenditure and Prescriptions Twelve Months to 30 June 2005', Table 12b: Highest Volume PBS Drugs By Generic Name, cited at <www.health.gov.au/internet/

wcms/publishing.nsf/Content/pbs-stats-pbexp-jun05-index1>, accessed January 2007.

48 Pfizer Australia, 'Accolades: Prime Awards', media release, 30 June 2005, cited at <www.pfizer.com.au/Accolades/2005/PrimeAward.aspx>, accessed January 2007.

49 C. Regan, Pfizer's media spokesperson, email to author, 12 September 2006.

50 'What is the Lipitor Institute?', cited at <www.lipitorinstitute.com.au/default.htm>, accessed February 2006.

51 C. Regan, interview with author, 25 August 2006.

52 C. Regan, email to author, 7 September 2006.

53 A. Branthwaite and T. Downing, 'Marketing to Doctors—the human factor', *Scrip Magazine*, March 1995, pp 32–35.

54 P. Mansfield, interview with author, September 2006.

55 J. Hartzell, Novartis Pharmaceuticals Australia, Product Launch Winner, June 2005, cited at <http://link.viostream.com/?885BB720-1BC3-4EA8-BD76-70FF057639BD>, accessed December 2006.

56 'Eczema help mushrooms', *MX*, 16 April 2003, p. 11. The same story, which originated in London, was used is a slightly modified form: 'Cream comes up to scratch' in *The Sunday Times* (Perth), 20 April 2003.

57 Dr John D'Arcy, 'Easing eczema', 'Today Tonight', 8 October 2003, cited at <http://seven.com.au/todaytonight/story/?id=14547>, accessed August 2006.

58 New South Wales Public Relations Institute of Australia, State Awards of Excellence 2005, Entrants, p. 7.

59 *Australian Adverse Drug Reactions Bulletin*, vol. 24, no. 3, June 2005, cited at <www.tga.gov.au/adr/aadrb/aadr0506.htm>, accessed February 2006.

60 US Food and Drug Administration, 'FDA Approves Updated Labeling with Boxed Warning and Medication Guide for Two Eczema Drugs, Elidel and Protopic', media release, 19 January 2006, cited at <www.fda.gov/bbs/topics/news/2006/NEW01299.html>, accessed February 2006.

61 Cavil + Co, 'Case Study: Pfizer Australia/Royal Life Saving Society Australia', undated, cited at <www.cavill.com.au/pages.asp?area=9&page=59>, accessed May 2006.

62 C. Regan, interview with author, 25 August 2006. RLSSA did not respond to a request for a comment.

63 Pfizer, 'Proxy Statement 2005: Executive Compensation', cited at <www.pfizer.com/sec_filings/2005/proxy/p2004px47.htm>, accessed January 2007.

64 'Pfizer's Ex-Chief to Get Full Retirement Package', *The New York Times*, 22 December 2006, cited at <www.nytimes.com/2006/12/22/business/22pfizer.html?>, accessed January 2007.

4 Killing them softly

1 'What is CSR?', *CSRWire.com*, cited at <www.csrwire.com/page.cgi/intro.html>, accessed 27 July 2005.

2 The STW Communications Group surveyed 2000 Australians and found 78 per cent believed that large companies in Australia are 'probably committing human rights abuses', 74 per cent think that the larger a company is the more likely it is to abuse its power, and 45 per cent consider big business is a risk to their health and wellbeing. N. Shoebridge,

'We use them, but we love to abuse them', *Australian Financial Review*, 9 October 2006, p. 56.

3   L. McCoy, 'Cynicism in the Ranks—Are PR Practitioners Fighting an Uphill Battle in a Hostile Communications Environment?', Presentation to the PRISM Summit, June 2004.

4   A. Ray, 'CSR: The live debate', *PR Week*, 5 December 2003, cited at <www.prweek.com/uk/search/article/197492//>, accessed November 2006.

5   M. Prideaux, 'Meeting Reasonable Public Expectations of a Responsible Tobacco Company', Bates No. 325049576, 21 June 2004, cited at <http://bat.library.ucsf.edu/tid/hwg61a99>, accessed January 2007.

6   *Re Mowbray Brambles Australia Ltd v British American Tobacco Australia Services Ltd [2006] NSWDDT 15*, 30 May 2006, cited at <www.lawlink.nsw. gov.au/ddtjudgments/2006nswddt.nsf/c45212a2bef99be4ca256736001f37bd/ d32ba040dbae5550ca25717e00000739?OpenDocument>, May 2007.

7   K. Hogben, 'British American Tobacco—Corporate Responsibility in a controversial business', Proceedings of Stakeholder Communication Conference, Sydney, May 2003.

8   British American Tobacco, Proposed WHO Tobacco Free Initiative Strategy, undated, p. 1.

9   British American Tobacco, Strategy for launching 'sensible regulation', undated, Bates No. 325047787, cited at <http://bat.library.ucsf.edu/ tid/aro14a99>, accessed November 2006.

10 British American Tobacco, 'KPMG meeting 27 July 99—Results and Action Points', Bates No. 321310106, 18 January 1999, cited at <http://bat.library. ucsf.edu/tid/eqk23a99>, accessed March 2007.

11 Centre for Stakeholder Research, 'Statement of Charter', unpublished, 2001.

12 British American Tobacco Australia, *A Social Report 2001–2002*, March 2003, p. 11.

13 British American Tobacco, *Social Report 2001/2002*, cited at <www.bat.com>, accessed 27 February 2003.

14 Ceylon Tobacco Company, *Looking Beyond: Social Report 2001*, cited at <www.bat.com>, p. 23.

15 *See* British American Tobacco, 'Engaging stakeholder dialogue: our dialogue structure', *Social Report 2001/2002*, cited at <www.bat.com>, July 2002, p. 12.

16 Ceylon Tobacco Company, *Looking Beyond: Social Report 2001*, cited at <www.bat.com>, p. 78.

17 M. Broughton, speech introducing British American Tobacco, *Social Report 2001/2002*, London, 3 July 2002.

18 Action on Smoking and Health UK, *British American Tobacco—The Other Report to Society*, June 2002.

19 N. Greiner, 'Foreword', *A Social Report 2001-2002*, British American Tobacco Australia Limited, p. 3.

20 British American Tobacco Australia Limited, *A Social Report 2001-2002*, p. 139.

21 *ibid.*, p. 140.

22 M. Broughton (BAT CEO), letter to M. Moore, Bates No. 321309011, 9 September 1999, cited at <http://bat.library.ucsf.edu/tid/jkk23a99>, accessed November 2006.

23 N. Shears (BAT), memo to M. Broughton, Bates No. 321309012, 8 September 1999, cited at <http://bat.library.ucsf.edu/tid/kkk23a99>, accessed November 2006.

24 M. Moore (WTO Director-General), letter to M. Broughton, Bates No. 32530149, 5 October 2000, cited at <http://bat.library.ucsf.edu/tid/ora14a99>, accessed November 2006.

25 Credit Suisse First Boston Equity Research, 'International Tobacco Marketing Standards New Standards Create Consistent, Responsible International Marketing Practices', *Sector Review*, 25 September 2001.

26 I. Cobain and D. Leigh, 'Tobacco firm has secret North Korea plant: Firm with Tories' Ken Clarke on payroll runs factory in country with grim human rights record', *The Guardian*, 17 October 2005, cited at <http://www.guardian.co.uk/frontpage/story/0,16518,1593914,00.html>, accessed April 2007.

27 A. Day, 'Tobacco lobby splits', *Australian Financial Review*, 12 March 2004.

28 D. Simpson, 'Australia: BAT corporate social irresponsibility', *Tobacco Control*, vol. 15, August 2006, p. 275, cited at <http://tc.bmj.com/cgi/content/extract/15/4/275>, accessed November 2006.

29 British American Tobacco Australia Limited, *Progress Report: 2005*, p. 76.

30 S. Chapman, 'Flaws in the glass as business world looks in the mirror', Letters to the Editor, *Sydney Morning Herald*, 4 April 2005, cited at <http://www.smh.com.au/text/articles/2005/04/04/1112489420659.html>, accessed 27 July 2005.

31 D. Rogers, 'BAT fires warning over food issues', *PR Week*, 27 October 2005, cited at <http://testing.prweek.hbpl.co.uk/uk/search/article/524521/bat-fires-warning-food-issues/>, accessed April 2007.

32 P. Crush, 'CSR: From the inside out', *PR Week*, 5 January 2006, cited at <www.prweek.com/uk/news/article/534088/csr-inside-out/>, accessed April 2007.

33 'Meet Fran Morrison, Head of Corporate Communications (Globe House)', *Where Women Want to Work*, undated, cited at <www.www2wk.com/evidence/evidence2.asp?id=50&qid=12&eid=626>, accessed November 2006.

34 'The Perspective of PM International on Smoking and Health Issues (text of the discussion document used at the meeting of top management)', 29 March 1985, Bates No. 2023268329, cited at <http://legacy.library.ucsf.edu/tid/nky74e00>, accessed January 2007.

35 'The Issues Raised in HM's Memo', c. March 1985, Bates No. 2023268384, cited at <http://legacy.library.ucsf.edu/tid/pus98e00>, accessed January 2007.

36 Cited in P.A. McDaniel, E.A. Smith and R.E. Malone, 'Philip Morris's Project Sunrise: Weakening tobacco control by working for it', *Tobacco Control*, vol. 15, 2006, p. 218.

37 J. Spector, 'Direction for Altria', Bates No. 2085246857, 30 November 2001, cited at <http://tobaccodocuments.org/landman/2085246857.html>, accessed November 2006.

38 J. Slavitt, Public Policy Plan, Bates No. 2070437588, 15 January 1996, cited at <http://legacy.library.ucsf.edu/tid/uuh37c00>, accessed January 2007.

39 S. Chapman, 'Cigarette companies buying credibility', *Crikey*, 7 February 2003.

40 Senate Finance and Public Administration Legislation Committee, *Hansard*, 11 February 2003, pp. 300–01.

41 *ibid.*, pp. 317–19.

42 Rio Tinto, 'Rio Tinto and the Corporate Citizenship Research Unit', Deakin University, undated, cited at <www.riotinto.com/library/reports/PDFs/parship_DeakinUni.pdf>, accessed November 2006.

43 Rio Tinto, *1999 Social and Environmental Report*, p. 20. The report was finalised in February 2000.
44 S. Hilton and G. Gibbons, *Good Business: Your world needs you*, Texere, New York and London, 2002, pp. 122–23.
45 T. Dodd, 'Rio Tinto miners face sex claims in Borneo', *Australian Financial Review*, 30 June 200, pp. 1, 42.
46 Freeport-McMoRan Copper and Gold Inc, *Annual Report 2002*, US Securities and Exchange Commission, p. 20.
47 R. Bonner and J. Perlez, 'New York Urges U.S. Inquiry in Mining Company's Indonesia Payment', *The New York Times*, 28 January 2006, cited at <www.nytimes.com/2006/01/28/international/asia/28indo.html>, accessed January 2006.
48 J. Perlez and R. Bonner, 'Below a Mountain of Wealth, a River of Waste', *The New York Times*, 27 December 2005, cited at <www.nytimes.com/2005/12/27/international/asia/27gold.html?pagewanted=print>, accessed March 2007; J. Freed, 'Rio Tinto tarred with Freeport brush', *Sydney Morning Herald*, 29 December 2005, cited at <www.smh.com.au/news/business/rio-tinto-tarred-with-freeport-brush/2005/12/28/1135732641785.html>, accessed March 2007. Representatives from the Perth-based Aurora Gold met with Australian Embassy officials on several occasions, urging Indonesian security forces deal with small-scale miners at the Mt Muro gold mine in Indonesia. Between February and October 2001, Rio Tinto was a 35 per cent shareholder with a director on the board of Aurora. In June and August 2001, there were two shootings by security forces at the mine, resulting in two deaths. Neither were included in Rio Tinto's social report. B. Burton, 'Embassy ignored killings at Indonesian mine', *Mining Monitor*, vol. 7, no. 2, June 2002, pp. 1–3.
49 A. Fowler, 'Leaked documents reveal fossil fuel influence in White Paper', 'PM', ABC Radio National, 7 September 2004.
50 'Cole Inquiry: Statement: A. Lindberg, Managing Director, AWB Limited: Version Nine', 8.15 p.m., 10 January 2006.
51 G. Allen, 'The Future of Public Affairs', 2005 National Public Affairs Convention 7 September 2005.

5 Battle tanks

1 M. Nahan, interview with author, August 2003.
2 In a 2005 interview, IPA Executive Director, John Roskam, said: 'what think tanks can do is push policies and ideas which make them safe for political parties to adopt.' M. Cebon, 'Intellectual Armaments in the War of Ideas: The Roles and Influence of Independent Think Tanks on Australian Public Policy Making', Honours Thesis, University of Melbourne, October 2005, p. 21.
3 L. Hatfield and D. Waugh, 'Right Wing's Smart Bombs', *San Francisco Examiner*, 24 May 1992, cited in *People For the American Way*, 'Buying a Movement: Right-Wing Foundations and American politics', 1996, p. 6, cited at <www.pfaw.org/pfaw/dfiles/file_33.pdf>, accessed May 2007.
4 *See* <www.ipa.org.au/news/newsbydate.asp>, accessed December 2006.
5 J. Roskam, IPA Executive Director, interview with author, 10 May 2006.
6 Institute of Public Affairs, 'Profile: Ron Brunton', *In Touch*, July/August 1996, p. 3. One of Brunton's papers for the IPA was 'Environmentalism and Sorcery'

on the 'revealing similarities between the beliefs of the greens and beliefs in sorcery and witchcraft'. *See* R. Brunton, 'Environmentalism and Sorcery', *Environmental Backgrounder*, Institute of Public Affairs, 31 January 1992, p. 1.

7   'The Director's Report to the 1992 Annual General Meeting', *IPA Review*, vol. 45, no. 4, 1992, p. 61.

8   Philip Morris, 'Core Objectives', 1994. Bates No. 2044333554, cited at <http://legacy.library.ucsf.edu/tid/opf77e00>, accessed January 2007.

9   J. Shear, 'GOP Catch Phrase for the '90s: "Defunding the Left"', *The Sun* (Baltimore), 23 April 1995.

10 P.A. McDaniel (University of California, San Francisco), E.A. Smith (University of California, San Francisco) and R.E. Malone (University of California, San Francisco), 'Philip Morris's Project Sunrise: Weakening tobacco control by working with it', *Tobacco Control*, 2006, vol. 15, pp. 215–23, cited at <http://tc.bmj.com/cgi/content/abstract/15/3/215?etoc>, accessed March 2007.

11 Philip Morris, 'Tipping The Scales of Justice', August 1996, Bates No. 2071044284/4293, p. 12.

12 J. Slavitt, 'Public Policy Plan—Draft', Philip Morris, 30 January 1997, Bates No. 2063393720/3726, p. 5.

13 A. Adair, interview with author, 20 September 2006.

14 Tim Duncan was subsequently a policy officer with the Business Council of Australia before joining mining company Rio Tinto's PR section as Head of External Affairs in Australia. In 2003, he joined the financial PR firm, Hinton & Associates, and is a board member of the Institute of Public Affairs.

15 A. Adair, interview with author, 20 September 2006.

16 A. Adair, *A Code of Conduct for NGOs—A Necessary Reform*, Institute for Economic Affairs, 1 October 1999, cited at <www.iea.org.uk/record.jsp?type=book&ID=3747>. An earlier version identified Adair as a Senior Associate of the CIS at the time.

17 *ibid.*

18 'Corporate Affairs Forum', *In Touch*, September 2000, p. 5, cited at <www.ipa.org.au/files/InTouchSep2000.pdf>, accessed November 2006.

19 G. Johns, interview with author, April 2004.

20 In 2005, the Australian Taxation Office issued two draft rulings which replicate elements of Costello's failed Charities Bill. In particular, one states that 'a purpose contrary to public policy is not charitable' and 'political and lobbying purposes are not charitable. While such purposes may use educational means, this is not sufficient to show a charitable purpose', though with the qualifier that it is permissible as long as they are 'incidental' to a charitable purpose. Australian Taxation Office, 'TR 2005/21 Income tax and fringe benefits tax: charities', undated, cited at <http://law.ato.gov.au/atolaw/view.htm?locid='TXR/TR200521/NAT/ATO/ft 7'&PiT=99991231235958>, accessed December 2006. *See also* J. Staples, 'Public Interest Group or Special Interest Groups: An Investigation of the Extent of Attacks on Non-Government Organisations in Australia 1996-2005', unpublished thesis, 2005.

21 Institute of Public Affairs, 'About the IPA...', 28 November 2004. The file is now only available in an Internet archive at <http://66.102.7.104/search?q=cache:cxGNhITcq8MJ:www.ipa.org.au/about.htm>.

22   S. Rosenberg, Assistant Secretary (Community Branch), letter to
     M. Spence, September 2003.
23   Institute of Public Affairs, *The Protocol: Managing Relations with NGOs:
     Proposed by the Institute of Public Affairs to the Commonwealth Government*,
     30 January 2003, p. 2.
24   Department of Family and Community Services, 'Prime Minister's
     Community Business Partnership—Meeting 28 April 2003', unpublished.
25   Department of Family and Community Services, 'Table 86 FaCS—New
     consultancies let during 2002–03 to the value of $10 000', Department of
     Family and Community Services 2002–2003 Annual Report, p. 284.
26   FACs requested Johns assistance with a question which asked whether 'the
     IPA produces a register of donations and if this is publicly available'. (It
     doesn't.) *See* G. Purcell (Director, Secretariat to the Prime Minister's
     Community Business Partnership), email to G. Johns, 24 October 2003.
27   'DFAT Engagement With NGOs: Meeting with Gary Johns: Background
     Information', undated. (This document was released to The Wilderness
     Society in 2005 under the Freedom of Information Act.)
28   AusAid, 'IPA Report: The Protocol: Managing Relations with NGOs', memo,
     undated. (The cover note from Ausaid's C. Ballard was dated 27 July 2004.)
29   G. Purcell (Director, Secretariat to the Prime Minister's Community
     Business Partnership), email to G. Dunn (FACS), 17 June 2004.
30   Senator B. Mason, 'Charitable Organisations', Senate *Hansard*, 9 August
     2006, pp. 48–51.
31   N. Khadem, 'Bid to strip green groups' tax status', *The Age*, 9 August 2006,
     cited at <www.theage.com.au/news/national/bid-to-strip-green-groups-tax-
     status/2006/08/08/1154802891527.html>, accessed December 2006.
32   Matt Wade, 'Canberra's gagging us, say charities', *Sydney Morning Herald*,
     30 May 2007, cited at <www.smh.com.au/news/national/canberras-gagging-
     us-say-charities/2007/05/29/1180205251558.html>, accessed May 2007.
33   AID/WATCH, 'ATO decision has implications for all charities',
     Backgrounder, 30 May 2007, cited at <www.aidwatch.org.au/index.php?
     current=1&display=aw01071&display_item=2>, accessed May 2007.
34   M. Nahan, 'The IPA sings its own song', *The Australian*, 10 April 2000.
35   Institute of Public Affairs, 'About the IPA . . .', 28 November 2004. The file is
     now only available in an Internet archive at <http://66.102.7.104/search?q=
     cache:cxGNhITcq8MJ:www.ipa.org.au/about.htm>.
36   M. Nathan, interview with author, August 2003. Nahan made the same
     pledge to *Sydney Morning Herald* journalist Brad Norington; *see*
     B. Norington, 'Deep pockets behind deep thought', *Sydney Morning Herald*,
     12 August, 2003.
37   'Thinkers of influence', *The Age*, 10 December, 2005, cited at
     <www.theage.com.au/news/national/thinkers-of-influence/2005/12/09/
     1134086810518.html?page=fullpage#contentSwap2>.
38   Past and present funders have included British American Tobacco, Philip
     Morris, Exxon, Shell, Rio Tinto, the contracting company Clough
     Engineering and BHP-Billiton.
39   J. Roskam, interview with author, May 2006.
40   J. Gay, interview with author, December 2006.
41   In September 2003, a US group called Public Interest Watch (PIW) lobbied
     to have the Internal Revenue Service (IRS) strip Greenpeace USA of its

tax-deductible status. In September 2005, the IRS commenced a three-month-long audit. Six months later, the IRS wrote to Greenpeace notifying it that it retained its tax-exempt status. PIW spokesmen refused to disclose their sources of funding when asked. However, in March 2006 a whistleblower leaked internal documents to both *Businessweek* magazine and the *Wall Street Journal*. They revealed that in the 2003–04 financial year, $120 000 of the group's budget of $124 094 had come from the oil company, ExxonMobil. S. Stecklow, 'Did a Group Financed by Exxon Prompt IRS to Audit Greenpeace?', *Wall Street Journal*, 21 March 2006, p. A1, cited at <http://online.wsj.com/article/SB191044305003774.html?mod=todays_us_page_one>. *See also* Public Interest Watch's annual report to the Internal Revenue Service, cited at <www.guidestar.org/FinDocuments/2004/134/212/2004-134212779-01952a06-9.pdf–2003>, accessed March 2006.

42 G. Johns, interview with author, 14 December 2006.

43 D'Cruz wrote: 'The question is: why do corporations (and the World Bank for that matter) hand over such large sums to WWF? In a word "protection".' He then went on to extrapolate the point to other environmental groups. *See* D. D'Cruz, 'NGOs: Chasing the Corporate Dollar', *Review*, Institute of Public Affairs, September 2003, p. 28.

44 J. Roskam, interview with author, May 2006.

45 Institute of Public Affairs, 'Position Specification for the Executive Director of the Institute of Public Affairs (IPA)', 23 February 2005.

46 G. Johns, *Protocols with NGOs: The Need To Know*, Backgrounder, November 2001, p. 15.

47 *ibid.*, p. 8.

48 J. Roskam, interview with author, May 2006.

49 G. Johns, *Government and Civil Society: Which is More Virtuous*, Senate Occasional Lecture, Parliament House, 23 August 2002, p. 15.

50 J. Roskam, interview with author, May 2006.

51 T. Warren, 'Telecommunications in Regional and Remote Australia', *IPA Backgrounder*, November 2000, vol. 12, no. 2. Warren noted that just prior to writing this backgrounder he had undertaken consultancy work for Telstra. The IPA as publisher, however, did not disclose its financial ties to Telstra.

52 M. Nahan, 'There is still time to get it right', *Australian Financial Review*, 23 February 2001, cited at <www.ipa.org.au/files/news_511.html>, accessed January 2006.

53 J. Hoggett, 'Labor Launches Telstra Into the Past', *The Australian*, 1 November 2001, cited at <www.ipa.org.au/files/news_440.html>, accessed January 2006. *See also* J. Hoggett, 'Regulating Telecommunications: Trade Practices Overkill', *Review*, June 2002, pp. 15–17.

54 G. Johns, 'Stop Strangling Telstra', *Forum*, 1 May 2002, cited at <www.ipa.org.au/files/news_282.html>, accessed January 2006.

55 A. McIntyre, 'Outback Isolation is a Myth', *The Australian*, 11 October 2002, cited at <www.ipa.org.au/files/news_315.html>, accessed January 2006.

56 M. Nahan, 'The New Protectionism', *The Australian*, 16 January 2004, cited at <www.ipa.org.au/files/news_406.html>, accessed January 2006.

57 C. Berg, 'Telstra's regulatory waltz', *Australian Financial Review*, Letter to the Editor, 18 October 2004, cited at <www.ipa.org.au/files/news_936.html>, accessed January 2006; C. Berg, 'Splitting Telstra is not the right move', *Australian Financial Review*, 22 August 2005, cited at <www.ipa.org.au/

files/news_1015.html>, accessed January 2006; C. Berg, 'ACCC should be good sports', *Australian Financial Review*, 8 February 2005, cited at <www.ipa.org.au/files/news_906.html>, accessed January 2006.

58 A. Moran, C. Berg, J. Hoggett and K. Phillips, Submission to the Productivity Commission's Review of National Competition Policy Reforms, Institute of Public Affairs, December 2004.

59 C. Berg, 'Can we remove the ban on mobiles in planes without killing each other?', *IPA Review*, September 2005, pp. 22–23.

60 R. Kemp, Senate *Hansard*, 14 September 1990, cited at <www.aph.gov.au/senate/senators/homepages/first_speech/sfs-WW4.htm>, accessed April 2007. Kemp's father had been one of the founders of the Institute of Public Affairs.

61 Senator R. Kemp to Senator K. O'Brien, 'Communications, Information, Technology and Arts: Institute of Public Affairs', *Senate Hansard*, 10 February 2004, p. 19750–51, cited at <www.aph.gov.au/Hansard/senate/dailys/ds100204.pdf>, accessed January 2006. The total figure is unadjusted for the effects of inflation. The figures for each financial year that records were available for were 1999–2000: $50 000; 2000–01: $55 000; 2001–02: $30 000; 2002–03: $20 000; and 2003–04: $10 000.

62 'Unlike some other institutions, we do not accept government funding, nor are we beholden to, or the mouthpiece for, any particular section of the community or any particular economic activity or group.' This policy statement was last on the IPA's website in 2005 and is in an Internet archive at <http://66.102.7.104/search?q=cache:cxGNhITcq8MJ:www.ipa.org.au/about.htm>.

63 R. Breum, phone conversation with author, December 2004; R. Breum, email to author, 24 December 2004.

64 M. Nahan, letter to B. Scales, Managing Director of Corporate and Human Relations, Telstra, 8 September 2004.

65 *ibid.*

66 M. Nahan, email to J. Foley, Telstra, 9 September 2004.

67 J. Foley, Group Manager Regulatory Public Affairs Telstra, email to E. Corcoras, IPA, 12 November 2004.

68 J. Roskam, attachment to email to J. Foley, 24 August 2005.

69 *ibid.*, p. 3.

70 A. Maiden, Telstra's Group Manager of Public Affairs, letter to M. Nahan, 28 September 2001.

71 *ibid.*

72 R. Bruem, interview with author, September 2006.

73 House of Representative Standing Committee on Agriculture, Fisheries and Forestry, *Inquiry into future water supplies for Australia's rural industries and communities—Interim report*, Parliament of Australia, March 2004, cited at <www.aph.gov.au/house/committee/primind/waterinq/interimrpt/wireport.pdf>, accessed April 2007

74 A. Day, 'Queries on $40,000 IPA gift', *Australian Financial Review*, 4 June 2004.

75 In mid-2006, the former Chairman of Murray Irrigation Ltd, Bill Hetherington, joined the board of the IPA. See 'New Board Member', *In Touch*, Institute of Public Affairs, June 2006, p. 2, cited at <www.ipa.org.au/publications/publisting_detail.asp?pubid=547>, accessed April 2007.

76 J. Roskam, interview with author, May 2006.

77 J. Marohasy, 'Does the Murray River Still Need Saving?', 'Counterpoint', ABC Radio National, 22 May 2006, cited at <www.abc.net.au/rn/counterpoint/stories/2006/1640480.htm#>, accessed April 2007.
78 G. Warne, interview with author, September 2006.
79 Murray Irrigation Limited, 'Scientists speak on controversial Murray findings', media release, 6 January 2004. The original release is now only available in an Internet archive at <http://web.archive.org/web/20060113131722/http://www.murrayirrigation.com.au/mil/media_d.php?i=88>, accessed November 2006.
80 'Irrigator groups oppose Snowy Hydro sale', 'Rural', ABC, 19 May 2006, cited at <www.abc.net.au/rural/news/content/2006/s1642664.htm>, accessed June 2006.
81 M. Nahan, 'Spin versus substance in public affairs', speech to Public Affairs in Minerals and Energy, 18–20 March 1996, Hyatt Kingsgate, Sydney.
82 J. Marohasy, 'Environmental Fundamentalism', speech at the Centre for Independent Studies, 12 May 2004. An edited version of the speech appeared in the CIS magazine, *Policy*, vol. 20, no. 3, Spring 2004.
83 T. Lee, interview with author, December 2004.
84 M. Fyfe, 'Cool reception for new green group', *The Age*, 8 June 2005, cited at <www.theage.com.au/news/National/New-green-group-makes-conservationists-see-red/2005/06/07/1118123837470.html>, accessed April 2007.
85 J. Roskum, interview with author, May 2006.
86 J. Shoebridge, 'Burke ready to bloom in new role', 'Landline', ABC TV, 14 August 2005.
87 M. Duffy, speech to the Australian Environment Foundation conference, Brisbane, 24 September 2006.
88 P. Staines, 'You want policy? In cash?', *The Times* (London), 20 December 2005, p. 19, cited at <www.spinwatch.org/content/view/2267/9/>, accessed April 2007.

6 Toxic PR

1 P. Harris, 'Fire Investigation Report: Terminals Plant A 28-30 Mackenzie Rd, Footscray Wednesday 21st and Thursday 22nd August 1991', p. 14.
2 B. West, 'Crisis Management and the role of marketing', lunchtime presentation to the Australian Marketing Institute, 13 September 1995.
3 A. Awramenko, 'Explosion at Coode Island', 21 August 1991, 5.30 p.m.
4 B. West, 'Crisis Management and the role of marketing', lunchtime presentation to the Australian Marketing Institute, 13 September 1995.
5 Hill & Knowlton, 'Update report 8pm Wed 21.8.91'.
6 Terminals Ltd, News Information, 12.05 a.m., 22nd August 1991.
7 Senior Sergeant Alexander Robertson, brief submitted to the Coroner's Office, 1994, p. 21.
8 E. Olufson, media statement, 22 August 1991.
9 Victoria Police, 'Inquiry into Coode Island fire', media release, 23 August 1991.
10 A. Messina and D. Bruce, 'State faces "awesome" task on Coode Island', *The Age*, 28 August 1991.
11 Terminals Ltd, Coode Island, media statement, 26 August 1991, p. 1.
12 M. Clark, letter to G. McLean, Burns Philp, 'Monday', undated.

13 Hill & Knowlton, 'Terminals and Coode Island—Update Report',
    27 August 1991.
14 J. Connolly, Hill & Knowlton, 'Terminals Update—Thursday 5 September'.
15 Hill & Knowlton, 'Highly confidential: Terminals and Coode Island—
    update report', 27 August 1991, p. 3.
16 M. Clark, memo, 28 August 1991, p. 4
17 Terminals Ltd, 'Coode Island', media statement, 26 August 1991.
18 Hill & Knowlton, 'Highly confidential: Terminals and Coode Island—
    update report', 27 August 1991, p. 5.
19 Hill & Knowlton, 'Terminals update 3 and 4 September 1991', p. 2.
20 'Nothing ruled out', The Age, 7 September 1991, p. 5.
21 J. Silvester and C. Dixon, 'Coode Raid Bunglers', Herald Sun, 18 October
    1991, pp. 1, 2.
22 Victoria Police, 'Coode Island—Sabotage Suspected', media release,
    16 October 1991.
23 B. Tobin, 'Oxy-gear used to cut pipes: police', The Age, 18 October 1991.
24 Administrative Appeals Tribunal, 'Statement of Robert Masters',
    December 1996.
25 Administrative Appeals Tribunal, 'Statement of Mary Clark', December 1996.
26 Terminals, 'Re: Coode Island Fire', letter to Minister for Police and
    Emergency Services M. Sandon, 17 October 1991.
27 ibid.
28 Terminals Limited, statement, 16 October 1991.
29 M. Clark, 'Statement of Mary Clark (amended)', February 1998.
30 M. Clark, memo to H. Rimington, 17 October 1991.
31 L. Young, 'Police hunt saboteur', The Age, 17 October 1991, pp. 1–2
32 J. Silvester and C. Dixon, 'Coode raid bunglers', Herald Sun, 18 October
    1991, p. 2.
33 B. Tobin, 'Coode fire was an accident police find', The Age, 11 June 1992.
34 ibid.
35 Brief submitted by A. Robertson to the Coroners Office, Appendix 1, 1994,
    pp. 38–39.
36 Coroner's inquiry transcript, Appendix 3, pp. 257–58.
37 ibid., Appendix 2, p. 528.
38 J. Heffey, Record of investigation into fire, State Coroner's Office, 17 June
    1994, p. 37.
39 Coroner's inquiry transcript, p. 1199.
40 B. Pratt, Uniquest Ltd, 'Fires at Terminal "A" storage depot, McKenzie Rd,
    Coode Island, 21 & 22 August 1991', Technical Report, Victorian
    Occupational Health and Safety Authority, May 1992, p. 17.
41 ibid.
42 D. Wadeson, Transcript of Proceedings, Coroner's Court, Appendix 6,
    3 May 1994, pp. 579–80.
43 R. Bennett, Transcript of Proceedings, Coroner's Court, 3 May 1994,
    Appendix 4, pp. 690–91.
44 J. Heffey, Record of investigation into fire, State Coroner's Office, 17 June
    1994, p. 37.
45 G.E. Fitzgerald, Report of a Commission of Inquiry Pursuant to Orders In
    Council, 3 July 1989, p. 141, cited at <www.cmc.qld.gov.au/data/portal/
    00000005/content/81350001131406907822.pdf>, accessed January 2007.

46   J. Smith, 'Effectiveness in the face of hostility—lessons learnt from the
     Forest Industries public awareness campaign', Proceedings of 1994 National
     Conference Key Innovative Strategies for Effective Advertising, Sydney,
     October 1994, p. 132.
47   S. Murrihy, North Forest Products and the Hampshire woodchip mill—
     Winning case studies workshop, Proceedings of Public Relations Industry of
     Australia and New Zealand Vox Pop Conference, Sydney, 10 November 1995.
48   In its initial newsletter, the Forest Protection Society described itself as a
     'grass roots community organisation'. See Forest Protection Society News,
     vol. 1, no. 1, January 1987, p. 1.
49   M. Attard, 'Col Dorber apologies for publicly supporting violence against
     environmentalists', 'PM', ABC Radio National, 14 February 1995.
50   M. Devine, Telegraph-Mirror, 16 February 1995, p. 10.
51   G. Hillier, 'NSW election', 'Background Briefing', ABC Radio National,
     19 March 1995.
52   'Forest Protection Society State Coordinator', The Mercury, 17 April 1993, p. 78.
53   B. Prismall, 'Forest War Twist', The Mercury, 27 November 1987.
54   'A force to be reckoned with', The Sunday Tasmanian, 17 November 1996, p. 9.
55   Leaked minutes of Forest Protection Society 'Strategy meeting', 19 August
     1988. See also 'Leaked strategy of disruption', The Mercury, 7 February
     1989; 'Infiltration of greenies admitted', The Examiner, 7 February 1989;
     '"Logger Moles" Uncovered', Sydney Morning Herald, 8 February 1989, p. 1.
56   P. Lazar, interview with author, July 1998.
57   T. Harrison, interview with author, March 1997.
58   P. Collenette, 'Police briefed on forest terror', The Examiner, 19 January 1993.
59   R. Groom, media statement, 11 March 1993.
60   M. Addis, ABC TV News, 11 March 1993. 'That action is entirely
     consistent with what the Earth First! people have indicated they are
     prepared to do', he stated.
61   'Tasmania Police, Explosive Incident—Black River', 11 March 1993.
     'Innuendo in the Smithton community espoused the view that the incident
     was the work of the pro-logging community, the aim of which was to
     discredit the conservation movement's program during the summer
     months. Available direct evidence does not support this argument', the
     memo stated. (Emphasis added.)
62   Victoria Police, Counter Terrorist Intelligence Section, 'Intelligence
     Investigator Report: Earth First Bomb Tasmania', 12 July 1993.
63   Detective Senior Sergeant T. Walsh, speech to 'Media Seminar on Eco-
     Terrorism', 20 October 1994.
64   R. Bain, National Forest Policy: Implications of a National Reserve System,
     Public Affairs in Minerals and Energy, Hyatt Kingsgate Sydney, 20 March 1996.
65   Superintendent Haldane, 'Forest Protection Society', email, 14 March 1995.
66   Superintendent Haldane, 'Damage to Logging Equipment', email, 16 March
     1995.
67   Victorian Administrative Appeals Tribunal, Freedom of Information appeal,
     November 1997.
68   Victoria Police Counter Intelligence Section, 'Environmental Activist',
     4 November 1991.

69 M. Warren, 'Ferguson stands up for forestry tactics', *The Australian*, 3 October 2006, cited at <www.theaustralian.news.com.au/story /0,20867,20514904-2702,00.html>, accessed January 2007.
70 Otway Forest Industries Information Group, press release, 19 January 1999.
71 J. Robinson, diary entry, 21 January 1999.
72 J. Robinson, 'Forest Industry meeting at Colac on 21/1/99', memo, 25 January 1999.
73 B. Gross and others, signed statement witnessed by Police Senior Constable Gurrie, 28 January 1999.
74 K.J. Merry, Victoria Police, 'Logging Protest in the Otways', undated c. 28 January 1999.
75 M. O'Connor, interview with author, April 2007.
76 J. Gay, interview with author, April 2007.
77 K. Carnell, interview with author, April 2007.

7 When corporations want to cuddle

1 P. Sandman, interview with author, December 2005.
2 P. Sandman, 'Goals for Dealing with Activist Groups', 1998, cited at <www.petersandman.com/handouts/sand21.pdf>, accessed January 2007.
3 P. Sandman, interview with author, October 1998.
4 P. Sandman, *OUTRAGE Prediction & Management: Reference Manual*, Qest Consulting Engineers, 1998, p. 23.
5 P. Sandman, interview with author, October 1998.
6 H. Burson, *The Next Steps in Going Global: Offices in Asia and Australia*, August 2003, cited at <www.burson-marsteller.com/pages/about/ history/memos/6>, accessed November 2006.
7 G. David and P. Beresford, 'BR gives sell-off signals; Government plans to privatise British Rail', *The Sunday Times* (UK), 22 May 1988.
8 G. Bourne, 'Demonstrate Net Social, Environmental and Economic Benefits or Lose the Social Licence to Operate', Presentation to Minerals Council of Australia's Sustainable Development Conference, Alice Springs, 1 November 2005.
9 WWF Australia, 'How we work', undated, cited at <wwf.org.au/about/ howwework/>, accessed June 2006.
10 B. May, D. Leadbitter, M. Sutton and M. Weber, 'The Marine Stewardship Council (MSC): Background, Rationale and Challenges' in B. Phillips, T. Ward and C. Chaffee (eds), *Eco-labelling in Fisheries: What is it all about?*, Blackwell Publishing, 2003, p. 17.
11 S. Heap, *NGOs Engaging with Business: A World of Difference and Difference to the World*, Intrac, Oxford, 2000, p. 133.
12 B. May, D. Leadbitter, M. Sutton and M. Weber, 'The Marine Stewardship Council (MSC)', p. 32.
13 WWF Australia, *Annual Report 2000*, p. 14.
14 J. Breese, email to C. Martin, 5 February 2001.
15 Marine Stewardship Council, 'New Zealand Hoki Fishery Certified to Marine Stewardship Council Standard', media release, 15 March 2001, cited at <www.msc.org/html/ni_42.htm>, accessed June 2006.
16 *ibid.*

17 WWF New Zealand, 'WWF Responds To Global Eco-Label Approval Of New Zealand Hoki Fishery', media release, 15 March 2001.

18 Unilever, *Listening, Learning, Making Progress: 2002 Social Review of 2001 Data*, p. 25.

19 Sandford Limited, 'Environmental Sustainability', Triple Bottom Line Report 2001/2002, p. 6.

20 P. Manning and S. Keen, 'Green fair', *Ethical Investor*, September 2002, p. 15.

21 Marine Stewardship Council, New Zealand Hoki Fishery—independent panel decision, 16 December 2002, p. 6.

22 K. Short, 'The WWF Perspective' in B. Phillips, T. Ward and C. Chaffee (eds), *Eco-labelling in Fisheries: What is it all about?*, Blackwell Publishing, 2003, p. 160.

23 C. Howe, interview with author, September 2006.

24 Australian Competition and Consumer Commission, 'News for Business: Self-declared environmental marketing claims', 30 April 1999, cited at <www.accc.gov.au/content/index.phtml/itemId/303223>, accessed July 2006.

25 J. Breese, letter to A. Hilbrands, SGS Product & Process Certification, 8 February 2006, cited at <www.msc.org/assets/docs/New_Zealand_Hoki/Final_RepApri2006.pdf>, accessed June 2006.

26 WWF Australia, *Annual Report 2006*, p. 9, cited at <wwf.org.au/publications/annual-report-2006/>, accessed April 2007.

27 S. Highleyman, A. Mathews Amos and H. Cauley, 'An Independent Assessment of the Marine Stewardship Council: Draft Report' (unpublished), Wildhavens, 15 January 2004.

28 WWF, *An assessment of Kikori Pacific Limited's financial position*, internal report, p. 5.

29 'WWF linked to illegal logging', Channel 4 News (UK), 22 February 2001.

30 A. Neville (Head of Press & Campaigns), 'WWF Position Statement on Channel Four's piece regarding Kikori Pacific Limited', March 2000.

31 A. Rowell, 'No way to save trees', *Sydney Morning Herald*, 2 March 2001.

32 R. Purves, 'Eco-forestry the only real alternative', *Sydney Morning Herald*, 5 March 2001.

33 B. Carbarle, 'Illegal Logging, WWF, The World Bank and PNG', email, 13 March 2001.

34 *ibid*.

35 British Environment and Media Awards, 25 October 2001, cited at <www.wwf.org.uk/news/n_0000000460.asp>, accessed July 2006.

36 R. Blakers, interview with author, December 2006. Groups such as WWF have also been dubbed BINGOS: 'Big International Non-Government Organisations'; *see* 'Bingos', *New Internationalist*, October 2005, cited at <www.newint.org/issue383/index.htm>, accessed January 2007.

37 R. Purves, President WWF, 'Where do the Environmental NGOs stand as the environment goes mainstream?', speech to the Environment Business Australia Sustainability Summit, 19 November 2004, cited at <www.environmentbusiness.com.au/conference_papers/Purves.pdf>, accessed November 2006.

38 R. Ashton (ed.) and WWF, *Tarkine*, Allen & Unwin, October 2004.

39 'WWF accused of pandering to Government', ABC News, 3 August 2004, cited at <www.abc.net.au/news/newsitems/200408/s1167422.htm>, accessed January 2007.

40 Wilderness Photographers for Conservation, 'Letter from Major
    Photographic Contributors to WWF's Book on the Tarkine Wilderness'
    (unpublished), August 2004; A. Darby, 'Photographers oppose green group
    forest plan', *The Age*, 9 September 2004, cited at <www.theage.com.au/
    articles/2004/09/08/1094530691578.html?from=storylhs>, accessed
    November 2006.

41 WWF Australia, 'Third Party Return of Electoral Expenditure for the
    election held on 9 October 2004', 24 January 2005, cited at <http://fader.
    aec.gov.au/erThirdParty.asp?EventID=12246&ThirdPartyCo=T1027&Return
    TyCo=FAD06>, accessed January 2007; WWF Australia, 'Third Party
    Return of Donations received for the election held on 9 October 2004',
    24 January 2005, cited at <http://fader.aec.gov.au/erThirdParty.asp?
    EventID=12246&ThirdPartyCo=T1027&ReturnTyCo=FAD05>, accessed
    January 2007.

42 *The Age*, 6 October 2004, cited at <www.theage.com.au/news/Election-
    2004/Timber-jobs-wont-be-risked-PM/2004/10/06/1096949573022.html>;
    'I'll protect forests but jobs come first: PM', *Sydney Morning Herald*,
    6 October 2004, cited at <www.smh.com.au/articles/2004/10/06/
    1096949549192.html>, accessed March 2007.

43 R. Purves, 'Where do the Environmental NGOs stand as the environment
    goes mainstream?', speech to the Environment Business Australia
    Sustainability Summit, 19 November 2004, cited at
    <www.environmentbusiness.com.au/conference_papers/Purves.pdf>,
    accessed March 2007.

44 B. Burton, 'WWF Signs $1.2M Partnership with Rio Tinto', *Mining
    Monitor*, March 2000, pp. 9–10.

45 G. Espiner, 'Fears over business links', *Sunday Star Times*, 8 October 2000, p. 6.

46 G. Espiner, 'WWF has links with oil company', *Sunday Star Times*,
    8 October 2000, p.1.

47 World Wide Fund for Nature/Placer Dome Asia Pacific, *Mining
    Certification Evaluation Project: Independent Certification of Environmental
    and Social Performance in the Mining Sector*, WWF Australia Resource
    Conservation Program Mineral Resources Unit, January 2001.

48 United Nations Environment Programme, *Accident Prevention in Mining:
    Environmental regulation for accident prevention: Tailings and chemicals
    management; Summary report*, Perth, 26–27 October 2000, p. 20.

49 Cyanide Code Steering Committee, 'Minutes of 4th meeting, 23 July 2001,
    held in Vancouver BC', p. 5.

50 A. Bravos et al., letter to F. Balkau (unpublished), 3 December 2001.

51 H. Barnes et al., letter to F. Balkau (unpublished), 10 January 2002.

52 B. Burton, 'Industry enlists WWF to back cyanide code', *Mining Monitor*,
    April 2002, pp. 910.

53 'Michael Rae: Chief Executive Officer', Council for Responsible Jewellery
    Practices, cited at <www.responsiblejewellery.com/staff.htm>, accessed
    January 2007.

54 A. Parker, Presentation to 'The Future of Public Affairs', 2005 National
    Public Affairs Convention, 7 September 2005.

55 A. Parker, interview with author, April 2007.

56   G. Bourne, '2005 Annual Hawke Lecture', The Bob Hawke Prime
     Ministerial Centre, 9 November 2005, cited at <www.unisa.edu.au/hawke/
     events/ahl/2005_ahl_bourne.asp>, accessed January 2007.
57   A. Hodge, 'Green group accepts uranium mines', The Australian, 4 May 2006.
58   A. Hodge, 'WWF boss to push N-power at meeting', The Australian, 9 May
     2006.
59   T. Flannery, The Weather Makers, Text, Melbourne, 2005, p. 273.
60   T. Flannery, interview with author, October 2006.
61   C. McGrath, 'Howard faces stiff opposition in nuclear debate', 'PM', ABC
     Radio National, 7 June 2006, cited at <www.abc.net.au/worldtoday/
     content/2006/s1657445.htm>, accessed November 2006.
62   J. Lovelock, 'We need nuclear power, says the man who inspired the
     Greens', Daily Telegraph (London), 15 August 2001, cited at
     <www.telegraph.co.uk/connected/main.jhtml?xml=/connected/2001/
     08/16/ecfsci16.xml>, accessed April 2007.
63   In a 1973 article in Nature magazine, Lovelock claimed, much to his later
     regret, that 'the presence of these compounds [CFCs] constitutes no
     conceivable hazard'. See J. Gribbin, The Hole in the Sky—Man's Threat to
     the Ozone Layer, Corgi, 1988, pp. 40–41. Not surprisingly, Lovelock was a
     darling of the chemical industry, which was trying to fend off a mandatory
     phase out of CFCs. Lovelock appeared before a US Congressional
     committee hearing as, he later wrote, 'the principal witness for the
     industry's defence'. See J. Lovelock, Homage to Gaia, Oxford University
     Press, 2000 p. 220. The above material is cited in 'James Lovelock',
     NuclearSpin, cited at <www.nuclearspin.org/index.php/James_Lovelock>,
     accessed January 2007.
64   T. Flannery, 'Nukes', Good Weekend, 5 August 2006, p. 22.
65   T. Flannery, interview with author, October 2006.
66   K. O'Brien, 'Campaigner attacks nuclear inquiry's credibility', '7.30 Report',
     ABC TV, 3 July 2006, cited at <www.abc.net.au/7.30/content/2006/
     s1677668.htm>, accessed May 2007.
67   T. Flannery, 'Nukes', Good Weekend, 5 August 2006, p. 23.
68   K. O'Brien, 'Tim Flannery announced Australian of the Year', '7.30 Report',
     ABC TV, 25 January 2007, cited at <www.abc.net.au/7.30/
     content/2007/s1833950.htm>, accessed June 2007.
69   J. Scruggs, 'The "Echo Chamber" Approach to Advocacy', Philip Morris,
     Bates No. 2078707451/7452, 18 December 1998.
70   R. Purves, President WWF, 'Where do the Environmental NGOs stand as
     the environment goes mainstream?', Speech to the Environment Business
     Australia Sustainability Summit, 19 November 2004, cited at
     <www.environmentbusiness.com.au/conference_papers/Purves.pdf>,
     accessed January 2007.

8   Governing with spin

1   G.E. Fitzgerald, Report of a Commission of Inquiry Pursuant to Orders In
     Council, 3 July 1989, p. 42, cited at <www.cmc.qld.gov.au/data/portal/
     00000005/content/81350001131406907822.pdf>, accessed April 2007.

2 Parliamentary Committee for Electoral and Administrative Review, *Review of Government Media and Information Services*, Report No. 22, April 1994, pp. 26–43.

3 E. White, letter to R.G. Menzies, 27 July 1959, p. 2. This and subsequent documents were obtained from the National Archives of Australia.

4 W.A. McClaren, letter to Secretary, Prime Minister's Department, 3 September 1959.

5 J. McEwen, letter to R.G. Menzies, 17 September 1959.

6 *ibid.*

7 R. Menzies, letter to E. White, 30 November 1959.

8 R. Menzies letter to E. Harrison, 28 November 1959. Sir Eric Harrison was the Australian High Commissioner in London.

9 T.J. Dwyer, *The Australian Public Relations Handbook*, Ruskin Publishing, December 1961. H. Burson, 'The Next Steps in Going Global: Offices in Asia and Australia', Burson-Marstseller, August 2003, cited at <www.burson-marsteller.com/pages/about/history/memos/6>, accessed April 2007.

10 Eric White Associates, 'Australia' in *Handbook on International Public Relations: Prepared by Executives and Associates of Hill & Knowlton International*, vol. II, Frederick A. Praeger, New York, Washington, London, 1968, p. 4.

11 M. Byrnes, 'Our Own Less Than Perfect Spies', *Sydney Morning Herald*, 31 August 1989.

12 R. Haupt, 'How a PR Chief Provided Cover for Australian Spies', *Sydney Morning Herald*, 24 July 1989.

13 B. Toohey and W. Pinwell, *Oyster: The Story of the Australian Secret Intelligence Service*, William Heinemann Australia, 1989, p. 164.

14 Australian Security Intelligence Organisation, 'Eric White Associates— Contact With Soviet Trade Office' (unpublished), 20 May 1966.

15 Australian Security Intelligence Organisation, 'Political Development—Nauru' (unpublished), 21 March 1967. The following year Eric White Associates published a book, *Republic of Nauru: Independence Day, January 31, 1968*.

16 Australian Security Intelligence Organisation, 'Arab/Jew Tension in Australia' (unpublished), June 1970.

17 M. Byrnes, 'Our Own Less Than Perfect Spies', *Sydney Morning Herald*, 31 August 1989.

18 J. Elder, 'Custom-made entertainment stems from fear', *The Age*, 9 July 2006, cited at <www.theage.com.au/news/tv—radio/custommade-entertainment-stems-from-fear/2006/07/08/1152240539906.html>, accessed January 2007.

19 S. Latimer and M. Wardell, 'Border Security…a look behind the scenes of a major TV "docudrama"…' Presentation to 15th Public Affairs in the Public Sector Conference, 17 March 2005.

20 *ibid.*

21 Australian Customs Service, 'Review by the CEO', *Annual Report 2004–2005*, Commonwealth of Australia, p. 3, cited at <www.customs. gov.au/webdata/miniSites/annualReport0405/overview/Overview_1.html>, accessed November 2006.

22 M.K. McIntosh and J. Prescott, Report to The Minister for Defence on the Collins Class Submarine and related Matters, June 1999, cited at <www.defence.gov.au/minister/1999/collins.html>, accessed November 2006; P. Kalina, 'In depth look at submariners', *The Age*, 15 December 2005.

23 K. Austin, Australian Pharma Marketing Congress, 17 May 2005. While Austin made the comment in the context of stories on the drug industry, she inferred the ratio was a general 'rule of thumb'.

24 'Toowoomba Preparatory School: Statement by the Governor-General, Dr. Peter Hollingworth', media release, 19 December 2001, cited at <www.australianpolitics.com/news/2001/01-12-19.shtml>, accessed November 2006.

25 Finance and Public Administration Legislation Committee, Consideration of Additional Estimates, 18 February 2002, p. 27.

26 H. Grasswill, 'The Gilded Cage', 'Australian Story', ABC TV, 18 February 2002, cited at <www.abc.net.au/austory/transcripts/s479623.htm>, accessed March 2006.

27 Finance and Public Administration Legislation Committee, Consideration of Additional Estimates, 18 February 2002, p. 27.

28 M. Smith, Speech to 4th National Public Affairs Convention, Media Entertainment Arts Alliance, Canberra, 22–24 October 2003.

29 Senate Finance and Public Administration Estimates Committee of 27 May 2002, *Hansard*, 27 May 2002, pp. 66–74.

30 Inside Public Relations, 'Governor-General: Crisis Management', cited at <www.insidepr.com.au/case_studies.html#gg>, accessed March 2006.

31 N. Strahan, 'PR doctor called in to cure G-G's ills', *The Australian*, 21 February 2002.

32 M. Smith, Speech to 4th National Public Affairs Convention, Media, Entertainment and Arts Alliance, Canberra, 22–24 October 2003.

33 Senate Finance and Public Administration Estimates Committee, *Hansard*, 27 May 2002, p. 70.

34 *ibid.*

35 Office of the Official Secretary to the Governor-General, 'Answers to Questions on Notice—Budget Estimates Hearings 2002–2003, 27 May 2002: Question PM02' (unpublished).

36 Office of the Governor-General's 2001–2002 annual report, Appendix G: Consultancy Contracts awarded in 2001–2002, cited at <www.gg.gov.au/reports/ar2001-02/appendices_g.htm>, accessed March 2006.

37 Commonwealth Department of Education, Science and Training, Public Relations Brief for the Provision of Public Relations Services Surrounding the Announcement of the Decision of Where to Establish the National Repository for the Disposal of Australia's Low Level Radioactive Waste, October 2002, p. 4.

38 Hill & Knowlton, National Repository for the Disposal of Australia's Low Level Radioactive Waste (unpublished), October 2002, p. 2.

39 *ibid.*, p. 6.

40 *ibid.*, p. 11.

41 *ibid.*, p. 16.

42 *ibid.*, p. 18.

43 Hill & Knowlton, Proposed Protocol for Approaching and Recruiting Expert Panel Members (unpublished), 3 February 2003.

44 R. Nockles, email to C. Perkins, 28 January 2003.

45 C. Perkins, email to B. Royce, 5 February 2003

46 Commonwealth Department of Education, Science and Training, Listing of Departmental Files—Science Group, cited at <www.dest.gov.au/library/senate_report/2002/science2.htm>, accessed November 2006.

47   B. Royce, email to C. Perkins, 24 February 2003.

48   G. Cook, letter to B. Royce, 26 February 2003.

49   B. Royce, letter to G. Cook, 27 February 2003.

50   H. Ratcliffe, Assistant Manager Communications & Public Awareness,
     Biotechnology Australia, 'Ministerial Committee on Government
     Communications Meeting Wednesday 15 December 1999: Note for File',
     memo, 21 December 1999.

51   C. Cormack, 'Concerns over TPN contract', email, 11 August 2000.

52   *ibid.*

53   P. Kelly, Head of Division, Services & Emerging Industries Division,
     'Biotechnology Australia: Approval to amend public awareness consultancy
     contract', 27 September 2000.

54   W. Birnbauer, 'CSIRO job for tobacco defender', *The Age*, 25 April 2004,
     cited at <www.theage.com.au/articles/2004/04/24/1082719674276.html>,
     accessed January 2007.

55   P. Roberts, 'Staff Slap CSIRO's Public Face', *Australian Financial Review*,
     7–8 January 2006.

56   R. Beeby, ' "Damaging" public comment policy scrapped', *Canberra Times*,
     14 July 2006. cited at <http://canberra.yourguide.com.au/detail.asp?
     class=news&subclass=environment&story_id=494598&category=
     Environment&m=7&y=2006>, accessed October 2006.

57   In August 2003, Manning was set to appear before a public hearing of the
     committee in Launceston, but Tasmanian Labor Senator Kerry O'Brien
     successfully moved a motion that Manning's evidence be heard in confidence
     and that members of the public and media be expelled. However, Manning
     refused to agree to give evidence in secret, forcing the committee to cancel
     the hearing. *See* Senator Bob Brown, Minority report: Australian Forest
     Plantations: A review of Plantations for Australia: The 2020 Vision, Senate
     Rural and Regional Affairs and Transport References Committee, p. 161.

58   W.J. Manning, Evidence to the Rural and Regional Affairs and Transport
     References Committee, Committee *Hansard*, 8 October 2003, p. 501.

59   Futureye, 'Forest Practices Authority, Tasmania (formerly the Forest Practices
     Board) "Re-visioning their organisation through the eyes of stakeholders"',
     undated, cited at <www.futureye.com/work2.html>, accessed June 2006.

60   V. Birkinshaw, 'Futureye Proposal: Forest Practices Board, Tasmania:
     Communications Plan', September 2004.

61   B. Montgomery, interview with author, October 2005.

62   G. Law, interview with author, September 2006.

63   A. Graham, interview with author, September 2006.

64   A. Ramsay, 'Titanic spending is first-class hypocrisy', *Sydney Morning
     Herald*, 27 May 2007, cited at <www.smh.com.au/news/opinion/titanic-
     spending-is-firstclass-hypocrisy/2007/05/25/1179601668734.html>, accessed
     May 2007.

65   Finance and Public Administration References Committee, Government
     Advertising and Accountability, Commonwealth of Australia, December
     2005, cited at <www.aph.gov.au/senate/committee/fapa_ctte/
     govtadvertising/report/index.htm>, accessed April 2007.

66   'Work Choices a bonanza for Jackson Wells Morris, Colmar Brunton',
     WorkPlace Express, 12 July 2006, cited at <www.contracts.gov.au/
     OutputContract.asp?ContractID=1588202> and <www.contracts.gov.au/

OutputContract.asp?ContractID=1588426>; 'AIRC joins Federal
Government as Jackson Wells Morris client', *Workplace Express*, 31 March
2006, cited at <www.contracts.gov.au/OutputContract.asp?
ContractID=1588992>, accessed October 2006.

67   J. Andreoli, (no article title available) *Le Figaro*, 8 April 2003, cited at
<www.tasmaniantimes.com/jurassic/figaro.html>, accessed November
2006); Lindsay Tuffin, 'Legal Threat', *Tasmanian Times*, 17 April 2003, cited
at <www.tasmaniantimes.com/jurassic/ken.html>, accessed November
2006; C. Altman, 'Internet papers allow media mice to roar', *The Australian*,
Media, 22 May 2003, p. B07.

9 It takes two to tango

1   B. Rowlings, 'Spinners and the Spinned', The Third Canberra Weekend of
Ideas, 6 March 2004.

2   J.McNamara, interview with author, November 2002.

3   J. McNamara, Public Relations & the Media: A new Influence in 'Agenda-
Setting' and Content, thesis submitted for a Masters of Arts by research,
School of Literature and Journalism, Faculty of Arts, Deakin University,
March 1993. J. McNamara, The Impact of PR on the Media, Mass
Communication, June 2001, cited at <www.carma.com%2Fresearch%
2FImpact(A4).pdf>, accessed November 2006.

4   *See* C. Zawawi, 'Sources of news—who feeds the watchdogs?', *Australian
Journalism Review*, vol. 16, no. 1, pp. 67–71. The exact percentages were 64
per cent for *The Australian*, 65 per cent for the *Sydney Morning Herald* and
53 per cent for the *Gold Coast Bulletin*. It is arguable that the breadth of
the definition used—stories derived from media releases, press conferences,
the release of reports and government announcements—overstates the role
of PR. For example, government reports are not all flattering or released at
a time to gain prominence, and corporate announcements, such as
financial results, are often mandatory and newsworthy. That quibble aside,
however, the broad point remains valid.

5   G. Hughes, '"Just the facts please"—Investigative reporting for freelancers',
Presentation to the Media, Entertainment and Arts Alliance Convention,
5–7 May 2000.

6   J. Raymond, interview with author, May 2006.

7   *ibid.*

8   *ibid.*

9   J. Wilson, 'Testimonials', cited at <www.vnr.com.au/testimonials/>, accessed
January 2006.

10 Medialink Productions, 'Metabolic—Obesity Drug—7.6 million viewers',
Media Matters, no. 27, June 2005, p. 2.

11 L. LaMotta, 'Consumer media's relevance, bolstering a VNR, and more', *PR
Week*, 13 March 2006, cited at <www.prweek.com/us/search/article/544824/>,
accessed November 2006.

12 Palin Communications, 'Ten Tips for Healthy Video News Releases',
PRescribe, August 2002, cited at <http://i-works.comstrategies.com.au/news/
2023/palin_10_tips.asp?id=114080>, accessed February 2006.

13 Medialink Productions, 'Audio News Release—ANR', cited at
<www.medialinkproductions.com/ANR.htm>, accessed December 2006.

14 J. Raymond, interview with author, May 2006.

15 Medialink Worldwide, Annual Report 2005, p. 3, cited at <http://library. corporate-ir.net/library/82/829/82939/items/201915/2005AnnualReport on10K.pdf>, accessed October 2006.

16 Medialink Worldwide, Annual Report to December 2003, United States Securities and Exchange Commission Form 10-K.

17 J. Raymond, interview with author, May 2006.

18 M. Palin, interview with author, June 2006.

19 N. Goldie, 'Walking the talk: Speech writing', National Science Writers Festival, 12 August 2003, cited at <http://web.archive.org/web.20060820172416/ http://swfaus.org/Workship.htm#Walk>, accessed January 2006.

20 Australian Greenhouse Office, 'Australia's Third National Communication on Climate Change: A report under the United National Framework Convention on Climate Change', Australian Greenhouse Office, 2002, p. 139, cited at <www.greenhouse.gov.au/international/third-comm/pubs/ third-comm.pdf>, accessed April 2007.

21 CSIRO, 'Australia Advances', cited at <www.csiro.au/promos/ozadvances/ index.html#series5>, accessed April 2007.

22 Senate Community Affairs Committee, *A cautionary tale: Fish don't lay tomatoes: A report on the Gene Technology Bill 2000*, Parliament of Australia, Senate, November 2000.

23 CSIRO, 'Rabbit calicivirus', 'Australia Advances', Series Five, cited at <www.csiro.au/promos/ozadvances/Series5Rabbit.html>, accessed January 2006.

24 R. Alston, 'Radio Industry Inquiry', media release, 8 September 2000. The inquiry was known as the Parliamentary Inquiry into the relationship between Regional Radio and Local Communities.

25 W. Frew, 'DMG Radio's baby wants to be king', *Sydney Morning Herald*, 3 May 2004.

26 DMG Radio Australia, Submission by DMG Radio to the House Committee on Communications, Transport and the Arts Radio Industry Inquiry, cited at <www.aph.gov.au/house/committee/cita/regional_radio/ Submissions/irsub106-a.pdf>, accessed January 2007.

27 A. Davies, 'Public relations, private interests', *Sydney Morning Herald*, 16 December 2000.

28 A. Davies, 'PR Director caught sending bogus letter', *Sydney Morning Herald*, 9 December 2000.

29 'Settlement of Litigation by Subsidiary', media release, 16 August 2001, cited at <www.dmgt.co.uk/mediacentre/newsreleases/20010816/2002/>, accessed June 2006.

30 N. Chenoweth, 'Bid mired in media war, court told', *Australian Financial Review*, 7 October 2005, p. 10.

31 *ibid.*

32 Countrywide Porter Novelli, 'On the Front Foot—cricket fights back', submission to the International Public Relations Association (unpublished), 2002, p. 1.

33 J. McNamara, interview with author, November 2002.

34 Countrywide Porter Novelli, 'International Cricket Council Anti Corruption Investigation', Submission to the International Public Relations Association, October 2003 (unpublished), p. 1.

35 *ibid.*, p. 2.
36 *ibid.*, p. 3.
37 *ibid.*
38 *ibid.*
39 B. Mongomery, interview with author, October 2005.
40 Walkley Foundation, 'The Walkley Awards—History', undated, cited at <www.walkleys.com/history.html>, accessed November 2006.
41 P. Cross, interview with author, 21 August 2006.
42 P. Mansfield, interview with author, September 2006.
43 M. Sweet, interview with author, August 2006.
44 M. Sweet, 'Sponsored journalism award shocks Australian media', *British Medical Journal*, 24 November 2001.
45 R. Moynihan, 'Good Medicine', *Walkley Magazine*, no. 17, Winter 2002, p. 34.
46 Citigroup Journalism Awards for Excellence, cited at <www.citigroup. com.au/Citigroup/Dyn/Content/about/community/awards.html>, accessed December 2006.
47 Minerals Council of Australia, 'Minerals Week 2006 Program', May 2004, p. 4. *See also* Minerals Council of Australia, 'Six Young Journalists Come to Canberra', media release, 29 May 2006, cited at <www.minerals.org.au/ __data/assets/pdf_file/11793/MCA_mr006_16JFP.pdf>, accessed December 2006.
48 Phillip Morris Asia Region, 'Corporate Affairs Review', Bates No. 2074188961-2074189005, cited at <http://legacy.library.ucsf.edu/tid/ojk45c00>, accessed August 2006.
49 C. Barrass, British American Tobacco Corporate Communications, 'South American Journalists—UK Visit', Bates No. 500820678, 3 November 1994, cited at <http://bat.library.ucsf.edu/tid/umv00a99>, accessed January 2007.
50 T. Davis, 'Perks of the job: a half-price car', *Sydney Morning Herald*, 21 June 2005, cited at <www.smh.com.au/news/national/perks-of-the-job-a-halfprice-car/2005/06/20/1119250928016.html>, accessed April 2007.
51 L. Wood, Senate Standing Committee on Foreign Affairs, Defence and Trade: Department of Foreign Affairs and Trade, *Hansard*, 15 February 2007, pp. 57–60, cited at <http://parlinfoweb.aph.gov.au/piweb/Repository/ Commttee/Estimate/Linked/5240-1.PDF>, accessed April 2007.

10 Spinbusters

1 'Masters of deception', *Der Spiegel*, August 2006. This translation of the article was posted to the Speak Up blog of Richard Edelman, cited at <www.edelman.com/documents/Der_Spiegel_article_7.31.2006.doc.>, accessed April 2007.
2 'Rough puffs', Intelligence, *Far Eastern Economic Review*, 22 April 1993.
3 Public Relations Institute of Australia, *Code of Ethics*, 1962.
4 A. Leyland, 'One in Four Pros Admits To Lying On Job', *PR Week*, 1 May 2000, cited at <www.prweek.com/uk/search/article/102766/one-in-four-pros-admits-to-lying-on-job/>, accessed December 2006.
5 The survey found that 21 per cent of PR consultants surveyed admitted they had 'knowingly told lies to the press about a client' as a result of pressure from their clients, and a further 8 per cent admitted that they had

lied of their own volition. 'Industry admits to lying to media', *Asia PR Week*, 10 August 2001.

6   Harris Interactive, *Executive, Congressional and Consumer Attitudes Toward Media, Marketing and the Public Relations Profession*, Public Relations Society of America, 9 November 2005.

7   J. McNamara, interview with author, November 2002.

8   Public Relations Society of America, *Member Code of Ethics*, October 2000, p. 1, cited at <www.prsa.org/_About/ethics/pdf/codeofethics.pdf? indent=eth10>, accessed August 2006.

9   'PRSA Ethics board is deeply frustrated', *O'Dwyers PR Services Report*, October 1999, pp. 76–79.

10 'PRSA Ethics board is deeply frustrated', *O'Dwyers PR Services Report*, October 1999, p. 78.

11 Public Relations Society of America, *Member Code of Ethics*, October 2000, cited at <http://prsa.org/aboutUs/ethics/preamble_en.html>, accessed January 2007.

12 T. Cook, 'PR bloggers urged to fight against astroturfing', *Corporate Engagement*, 16 July 2006, cited at <http://trevorcook.typepad.com/ weblog/2006/07/pr_bloggers_urg.html>, accessed November 2006.

13 Public Relations Institute of Australia, 'Where the grass is not greener', media release, 19th July 2006, cited at <www.pria.com.au/ prianews/id/111>, accessed April 2007.

14 S. O'Sullivan, interview with author, April 2007.

15 Piper Rudnick LLP, Lobbying Registration, 2 September 2004.

16 Department of the Special Minister of State, *Lobbyists and the Australian Government and Parliament: A Discussion Paper*, Australian Government Publishing Service, Canberra, September 1983.

17 K. Beazley, 'Registration of Lobbyists', media release, 6 December 1983.

18 D. Jull, 'Lobbyists', *Hansard*, 21 November 1996, p. 7275.

19 C. Lawrence, 'Buying the policy of your choice', *Sydney Morning Herald*, 4 March 2004.

20 L. Taylor, 'Latham has lobbyists in his sights', *Australian Financial Review*, 20–21 March 2004.

21 A. Parker, 'Lobbying is an essential component of our democracy', *The Australian*, 9 March 2007, cited at <www.theaustralian.news.com.au/ story/0,20867,21348557-7583,00.html>, accessed April 2007.

22 A. Parker, interview with author, April 2007.

23 M. Mangahas, 'Despite Hard Times, GMA Hires Pricy Foreign Consultants for Charter Change', Philippine Center for Investigative Journalism, 13 September 2005; 'Agreement between the Government of the Republic of the Philippines and Venable LLP', 25 July 2005, cited at <www.pcij.org/stories/2005/venable.pdf>, accessed September 2006.

24 M.V. De Leon and M.V. Cruz, 'Palace on Venable: It's closed, let's move on', *Manila Times*, 20 September 2005.

25 *See* D. Vogel, *The Market for Virtue: The Potential and Limits of Corporate Social Responsibility*, Brookings Institution Press, Washington D.C., 2005, for further discussion on this point.

26 R. Kendall, 'Don't promote CSR, just do it!—Hugh Mackay', *Ethical Investor*, 2 March 2006.

27 G. Lindsay, interview with author, 6 September 2006.

28 It is notable that when the IPA have disclosed a funder at the foot of an opinion column, the disclosure statement has been stripped off when reposted on the think tank's own website. For example, the 'Give smokers some respect' column by Don D'Cruz in *The Australian* on 15 April 2002 notes: 'The IPA receives support from tobacco companies'. On the IPA's website, the same column has no disclosure statement. *See* D. D'Cruz, 'Give smokers some respect', *The Australian*, 15 April 2002, cited at <www.ipa.org.au/files/news_279.html>, accessed November 2006. Two years earlier, *The Australian* had carried another IPA opinion column defending smoking but without any disclosure. *See* G. Johns, 'Smokers pay their silly way', *The Australian*, 3 April 2000.

29 ExxonMobil, 'Public Information and Policy Research: 2005 Worldwide Giving Report', cited at <www.exxonmobil.com/Corporate/Files/Corporate/giving05_policy.pdf>, accessed November 2006.

30 S. Miskin and G. Baker, *Political finance disclosure under current and proposed thresholds*, Parliament of Australia Parliamentary Library, Research Note no. 27 2005–06, 23 March 2006, cited at <www.aph.gov.au/library/pubs/rn/2005-06/06rn27.htm>, accessed November 2006.

31 P. Costello, 'Economic reform Directions and the Role of The Public Service', Speech for the Australian Public Service Commission Ministerial Conversations, Parliament House, 2 November 2005, cited at <www.treasurer.gov.au/tsr/content/speeches/2005/020.asp>, accessed December 2006.

32 *See* P. Malone, 'From Timber to Tax—Ken Henry', The Treasury, *Canberra Times*, 23 January 2006, cited at <http://epress.anu.edu.au/anzsog/dept_heads/mobile_devices/ch03.html>, accessed April 2007.

33 M. McKinnon, 'Mandarins told how to beat FOI', *The Australian*, 21 July 2006.

34 G. Tooth, 'High Court decides on FOI and conclusive certificates', 'Media Report', ABC Radio National, 7 September 2006, cited at <www.abc.net.au/rn/mediareport/stories/2006/1735361.htm#>, accessed April 2007.

35 N. Waters, *Print Media Use of Freedom of Information Laws in Australia*, Australian Centre for Independent Journalism, January 1999.

36 *ibid.*

37 *Australian Financial Review*, 'Subscribe and get better red', February 2005.

38 C. Mitchell, 'A word from our Editor-in-Chief', *The Australian*, undated, cited at <http://newsmedianet.com.au/home/titles/title/index.jsp?titleid=5>, accessed September 2006.

39 M. Pascoe, 'Swimming with Sharks', *The Walkley Magazine*, The Media, Entertainment and Arts Alliance, no. 18, Spring 2002, p. 14.

40 M. Sweet, interview with author, August 2006.

41 W. Picnus, 'Fighting Back Against the PR Presidency', *Nieman Reports*, Summer 2006, 13 July 2006, cited at <www.niemanwatchdog.org/index.cfm?fuseaction=background.view&backgroundid=00102>, accessed November 2006.

42 GolinHarris, *The Next Fifty Years*, undated, p. 11, cited at <www.gh-ipr.com/nextfiftyyears/GolinHarris_TheNextFiftyYears.pdf>, accessed September 2006.

43 *See* <www.publicintegrity.org/rx/>.

44 See <http://dida.library.ucsf.edu/abouttheproject.html>.

RECOMMENDED READING

William Dinan and David Miller (eds), *Thinker, Faker, Spinner, Spy: Corporate PR and the assault on democracy*, Pluto Press, June 2007.

Nicky Hager, *The Hollow Men: A study in the politics of deception*, Craig Potton Publishing, New Zealand, January 2007.

Nicky Hager and Bob Burton, *Secrets and Lies: The anatomy of an anti-environment PR campaign*, Craig Potton Publishing, New Zealand, August 1999. (There was also a US edition published by Common Courage Press in 2000.)

John Stauber and Sheldon Rampton, *Toxic Sludge is Good for You: Lies, damn lies and the public relations industry*, Common Courage Press, 1995.

Websites for Spinbusters

The US-based Center for Media and Democracy (CMD) publishes a weekly email bulletin, *Weekly Spin*, which you can sign up for at <www.prwatch.org>. CMD also hosts SourceWatch <www.sourcewatch.org>, a wiki-based website for tracking PR and politics where you can register and become a citizen editor, building profiles on PR companies and their campaigns that pique your interest. Blog postings on the site and other pages can also be accessed via an RSS reader.

The UK-based Spinwatch <www.spinwatch.org> is the main organisation tracking the PR industry in the United Kingdom and Europe. Blog postings on the site and other pages can also be accessed via an RSS reader.

INDEX

THE

IREMONGER AWARD

FOR WRITING ON PUBLIC ISSUES

Allen&Unwin is pleased to offer The Iremonger Award for Writing on Public Issues, an award given anually for non-fiction works of political, social and cultural commentary that deal with contemporary Australian issues and contribute to public debate. John Iremonger's outstanding 35-year publishing career helped shape Australia's perception of its past and spotlighted the challenges for its future. Previous winners of the award are:

Australian Heartland by **Brendan Gleeson** (published May 2006)
A provocative exploration of urbanised Australia and a passionate plea for the suburbs to be given their rightful place in Australia's consciousness.

Inside Spin by **Bob Burton** (published August 2007)
A blistering critique of the largely hidden role of the public relations industry in Australia.

The End of Charity by **Nic Frances** (to be published in 2008)
A timely look at how social enterprise can help address the problems of poverty, inequality and environmental sustainability.

For more information, please visit our website at:
<www.allenandunwin.com/awards/iremonger_award.asp>